Canyon Creek Lakes

HIKING CALIFORNIA'S TRINITY ALPS WILDERNESS

A GUIDE TO THE AREA'S GREATEST HIKING ADVENTURES

THIRD EDITION

Dennis Lewon

FALCONGUIDES

GUILFORD, CONNECTICUT

FALCONGUIDES®

An imprint of The Rowman & Littlefield Publishing Group, Inc.
4501 Forbes Blvd., Ste. 200
Lanham, MD 20706
www.rowman.com

Falcon and FalconGuides are registered trademarks and Make Adventure Your Story is a trademark of The Rowman & Littlefield Publishing Group, Inc.

Distributed by NATIONAL BOOK NETWORK

Photos by Dennis Lewon, Leon Nelson and Paul Imperia
Maps updated by Melissa Baker, © The Rowman & Littlefield Publishing Group, Inc.

British Library Cataloguing in Publication Information available

Library of Congress Cataloging-in-Publication Data

Names: Lewon, Dennis, author.
Title: Hiking California's Trinity Alps wilderness : a guide to the area's greatest hiking adventures / Dennis Lewon.
Description: Third edition. | Guilford, Connecticut : FalconGuides, [2021]| Includes index. | Summary: "Each trail in the Trinity Alps Wilderness is a gift of backcountry beauty and solitude. This guide covers everything you need to know to plan your outdoor adventure"— Provided by publisher.
Identifiers: LCCN 2021000261 (print) | LCCN 2021000262 (ebook) | ISBN 9781493043286 (trade paperback) | ISBN 9781493043293 (epub)
Subjects: LCSH: Hiking—California—Trinity Alps Wilderness—Guidebooks. | Trinity Alps Wilderness (Calif.)—Guidebooks.
Classification: LCC GV199.42.C22 T753 2021 (print) | LCC GV199.42.C22 (ebook) | DDC 796.5109794/3—dc23
LC record available at https://lccn.loc.gov/2021000261
LC ebook record available at https://lccn.loc.gov/2021000262

CONTENTS

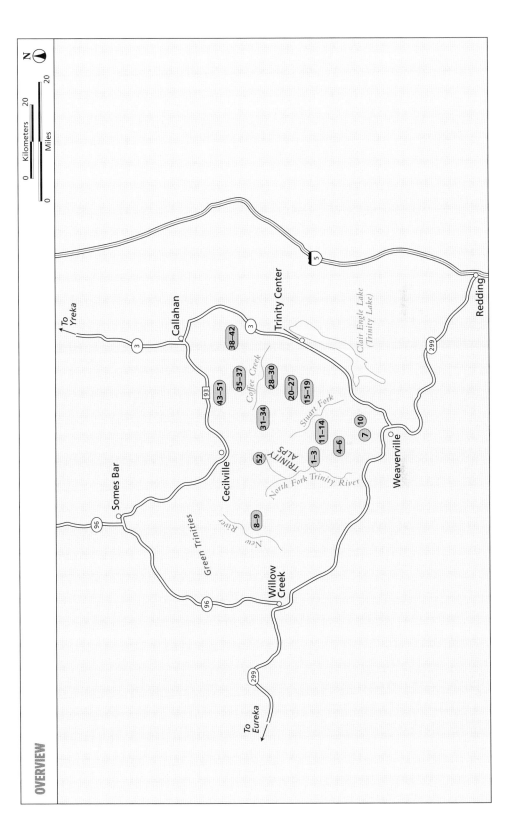

ACKNOWLEDGMENTS

I spent most of two seasons hiking trails in the Trinity Alps for this book. And while I kept seeing new sights, I also kept returning to familiar places I'd been visiting since childhood: lakes I had been to before I was old enough to carry a pack; the trail I hiked with my dad when I was 8; the hike I did the year I got my first real backpack; the campsite I slept at the first time I hiked in Trinity on my own, shortly after getting my driver's license. During this period I tried to remember the first time I ever went hiking in the area. I couldn't. As far back as I can remember, I've been hiking in the Trinity Alps. For that I am grateful to my parents, Bob and Elaine, for putting me on the right path when I was just learning to walk.

While hiking hundreds of miles of trails for this book, I discovered my childhood trips had barely scratched the surface of this vast wilderness. I got to rediscover the Trinity Alps all over again. Thanks to all the friends and strangers who made that possible. And thanks especially to my wife, Jen, who joined me even when there was no trail.

I still spend a couple of weeks a year in the Trinity Alps, and my own kids have hiked there while learning to walk and have backpacked to the lakes I enjoyed as a child. In the most important way—as a refuge of raw nature—Trinity hasn't changed in the decades since I first started hiking there. But of course, nothing stays the same forever, so I was glad to check in with rangers and local hikers and revisit some trails myself while updating hike information for this third edition. And thanks, of course, to the folks at Falcon, without whom this project wouldn't be possible.

INTRODUCTION

The hike to Horseshoe Lake is one of my favorite treks in the Trinity Alps Wilderness. The trail climbs gradually along Swift Creek, crossing numerous tributaries and passing through Mumford Meadow, an oasis of lush grass and wildflowers. The last mile ascends a steep, shadeless slope before arriving at the lake, where an inviting swim-and-picnic slab of granite awaits on the far side. I've been hiking to Horseshoe Lake—with family and friends, alone, and as a guide—for more than four decades.

For much of that time, Horseshoe Lake, like much of the Trinity Alps, remained largely unknown compared with California's more popular wilderness areas. I admit there were times I thought of Horseshoe as "my" lake and was surprised if I saw anyone else there. Not that I mind sharing the trails. As a guidebook writer, longtime editor of *Backpacker* magazine, and former wilderness guide for teens, I've devoted my entire career to encouraging and helping others to spend more time outdoors. But we all have places that we come to feel a special bond with, and Horseshoe is one of mine.

So I was surprised the last time I went there and the trailhead parking lot was absolutely packed. This was just a couple years ago, and I recalled the old adage "Be careful what you wish for." I was glad to see so many people had discovered this Trinity gem, but would the hike be overrun?

In a word, no. When we arrived at my favorite meadow-side campsite, there was no one around. At the lake the next day, we had that granite slab to ourselves. The Swift Creek Trail accesses a network of trails and lakes and river valleys, and what looked like a crowd at the trailhead had all but evaporated in the vast wilderness.

That's not to say you won't encounter other people. There's no doubt more people are making it to the Trinity Alps now than when I wrote the first edition of this book more than twenty years ago, and some of the more popular destinations are suffering from overuse (I've indicated these hot spots throughout). But some things haven't changed. The wilderness is still just a little bit farther from major population centers, the peaks just a little bit lower than the ones in the Sierra Nevada. Unlike in many of California's more accessible and popular wilderness areas, you can still go backpacking anywhere in the Trinity Alps without reservations. And when you leave the trailhead, there's plenty of room to spread out. Once you do, granite peaks, glacier-carved canyons, lush meadows, sparkling lakes and streams, and a chance for real wilderness solitude await.

Located in an isolated region at the southern end of the Klamath Mountains, along the headwaters of the Trinity and Salmon Rivers, the Trinity Alps Wilderness encompasses more than half a million acres—nearly 800 square miles—of rugged backcountry. The protected area constitutes one of the largest parcels of federally designated wilderness in California.

Elevations in the wilderness range from 2,000 to 9,000 feet. Within this zone you'll find a diverse environment that includes a multitude of jagged peaks, deep forested canyons, and gentle river valleys. More than 600 miles of trails crisscross the wilderness, making it easy to reach the heart of the backcountry in just a day or two of hiking. There are also numerous drainages where no paths—and few humans—have yet to intrude. Whether you want an easy day hike or a challenging weeklong trek, you'll find exactly what you're looking for within the boundaries of the Trinity Alps.

WHAT TO EXPECT

Trails in the Trinity Alps are generally well maintained and easy to follow. Most trails are signed, but don't expect to rely on signs alone—they disappear from time to time and may not be replaced for years. (The best resource for current conditions is the Weaverville Ranger Station. Call ahead as you may need to wait for a response: 530-623-2121.) Except for early-season stream crossings, there are few trail hazards to worry about in the Trinity Alps. Elevations are relatively low, so altitude sickness and summer snowstorms are not much of a concern.

With more than 600 miles of trails and upwards of one hundred lakes in the Trinity Alps, there's more than enough room for a large number of hikers to explore the backcountry and still enjoy the peace and solitude of the wilderness (however, some lakes are quite popular; see below). There's no quota or reservation system for backcountry camping (permits are still required), and land managers have yet to impose restrictions on where you can camp (except for those implied by standard Zero Impact practices; see appendix B). The vast wilderness of canyons, forests, and basins can absorb a lot of people without feeling crowded. The biggest problem here is that trailheads for the most popular destinations, like Canyon Creek, fill up on summer weekends. Even then, if you find a place to park and are flexible about where you camp, you'll find plenty of space to spread out.

That being said, you should avoid certain destinations or only visit them on weekends "out of season" or on weekdays in summer if solitude is what you're after. Renowned lakes like Canyon Creek, Emerald, Sapphire, Caribou, and Grizzly host a constant stream of human traffic all summer long, while less-publicized places like Bullards Basin may go weeks without a single visitor. But even the most popular spots have their moments of solitude: I've been to each of the lakes mentioned above without seeing another soul —in October. For experienced backcountry travelers, there are myriad off-trail destinations with guaranteed solitude. A small number of off-trail routes are included in this guidebook, but they constitute only the tip of the iceberg.

Backpackers far outnumber equestrians in the Trinity Alps, but each type of trail user is apt to encounter the other at some point. Consideration and good trail etiquette can go a long way toward helping everyone get along. Hikers should step off the trail and let horses or other pack animals (like llamas) have the right-of-way. It's much easier for hikers to make the accommodation. Likewise, stock users should observe good Zero Impact principles. Everyone should keep in mind that the wilderness is public land—ours to share.

GETTING THERE

The Trinity Alps Wilderness is located in northwest California in a remote slice of backcountry between Redding and Eureka. The wilderness is within the boundaries of the Shasta-Trinity, Klamath, and Six Rivers National Forests. The main access routes from points north and south are off I-5 and US 101. Depending on your destination, take either

CA 299 or CA 3 to reach the wilderness area and trailhead access roads. Weaverville, on CA 299 about 46 miles west of Redding, is the largest town on the outskirts of the Trinity Alps. Other settlements on the fringes of the forest include Trinity Center, Coffee Creek, Callahan, Cecilville, Willow Creek, and Junction City. The closest commercial airport (with rental cars available) is in Redding. Most trailheads are accessed via unpaved forest service roads. All roads included in this guidebook are passable to passenger cars.

SEASONS

The best hiking season in the Trinity Alps is the middle of June through the end of October. Keep in mind that snowfall changes dramatically year to year, so the early-season hiking sometimes varies by as much as a month. Even when streams are high and lakes are frozen, however, there are often good alternative destinations in the lower elevations. Check with rangers for specific snowpack information if you plan a trip before late June.

Summer days tend to be warm and clear (80°F–95°F) and nights cool (25°F–45°F). Summer rain is rare and sporadic, arriving chiefly in the form of brief and intense thundershowers. In fall the weather is generally dry and cooler, with October nights getting downright chilly. Autumn is a great time to hike if you want to avoid crowds. Some of my favorite trips have been in late October, after most people have gone and before the first snowfall. And with climate change affecting weather patterns, it pays to check conditions into November (in 2019 I went backpacking to Foster Lake just before Thanksgiving). Fall is also hunting season, so check current dates if you prefer not to see hunters. The forest service locks gates across some access roads from approximately October 31 to May 15.

For most people winter means the wilderness is out of season. And with more than a dozen feet of snow in many years, the Trinity Alps is no exception. But for those with appropriate experience, the area offers excellent opportunities for winter recreation and mountaineering. Just remember that you are truly on your own.

WATER

Water is readily available in streams and lakes throughout the Trinity Alps Wilderness. Unless otherwise noted, you can expect to encounter water sources frequently as you hike through the region. All water, however, should be treated before drinking. Many devices are now available to backpackers for this purpose. Boiling, filtering, chemical purification tablets, ultraviolet light, and ozone are all adequate treatments for preventing giardiasis and other water-borne illnesses.

BUGS

In general, mosquitoes and other biting bugs are not a major nuisance in the Trinity Alps, which is not to say the wilderness is bug-free. Some of the lower-elevation lakes and meadows host swarms of mosquitoes in early summer. But mosquito swarms, like everything else in Trinity, tend toward the smaller end of the spectrum. If you're used to Sierra- or Alaska-sized mosquito swarms, you may be pleasantly surprised by Trinity's gentler, kinder version—though you should still throw some insect repellent into your pack.

Ticks may pose a threat if they carry Lyme disease, but they are extremely rare above the lower elevations (at least I have yet to encounter any). The best prevention is a daily body check and prompt removal of any ticks you find. (Ticks must be embedded more than 24 hours to transmit Lyme disease.) To remove ticks, using tweezers, grasp the tick's head right next to your skin and pull gently until it releases. Tugging on the tick's body will make it act like a syringe, injecting tainted blood into your system.

FISHING

Some hikers can't tell a fly rod from a fly on the wall, while others spend every moment in the backcountry either fishing or thinking about fishing. If you're one of the latter, you'll find plenty to occupy your time in the Trinity Alps. Stocking programs have filled many backcountry lakes and streams with eastern brook, rainbow, and brown trout. Salmon and steelhead also persist in the Trinity River and some of its tributaries. A valid California fishing license is required for all angling in the Trinity Alps Wilderness. Because parts of the Trinity Alps watershed serve as spawning habitat for endangered salmon, it's vital that you check current California Fish and Game regulations before casting a line.

CATTLE

What's a cow doing in my camp? The Wilderness Act of 1964 allows livestock grazing to continue in forest service wilderness areas where it existed prior to the designation. In the Trinity Alps that means you might run into cattle in some drainages between July and October. Fortunately (if you oppose cows in camp), grazing in the wilderness is now the exception rather than the rule. Most grazing permits have been phased out of a large portion of the Trinity Alps. If you want to avoid cows, stay away from the drainages on the north side of the Scott Mountains and a few areas north of Coffee Creek. Grazing is mentioned in hike descriptions where applicable.

WILDERNESS PERMITS

All overnight visitors to the Trinity Alps Wilderness must obtain wilderness permits before entering the backcountry. Permits are free and are available without reservation. Simply stop by one of the ranger stations or self-serve kiosks (see Appendix A: Contact Information) on the way to the trailhead and pick one up. (The Weaverville Ranger Station is the most convenient place to stop for most visitors; along CA 3 the Mule Creek and Coffee Creek fire stations have self-serve kiosks.) If you arrive at the Weaverville Ranger Station after hours, you can fill out a permit form at a self-registration box located outside. Free campfire/stove permits are also required (and available at the same locations as wilderness permits), and you should always check to see if any special fire hazards or restrictions are in effect. (See appendix A.)

EMERGENCY MEDICAL SERVICES

In case of emergency, 9-1-1 works in the Trinity Alps area. Cell phone coverage is sparse at best, so don't plan on calling for help when in the backcountry. The nearest major hospitals are in Redding, and limited medical services are available in Weaverville.

USING THIS GUIDE

TYPE OF TRAIL
Suggested hikes have been split into the following categories:

Day hike: Best for a short excursion only due to lack of water or suitable camping sites.

Backpack: Best for backpacking with at least one night in the backcountry. Many of the overnight hikes can be done as day hikes if you have the time and stamina.

Loop: Starts and finishes at the same trailhead with no (or very little) retracing of your steps. Sometimes the definition of a "loop" includes creative shapes (like a figure eight or lollipop), and some loops require a short walk on a dirt road to get back to the trailhead.

Out-and-back: Traveling the same route coming and going.

Hike-in: Backcountry trails that are accessible only by foot. A few of these are included because they serve as useful connectors that can be used to create multiple routes.

RATINGS
Difficulty ratings are inherently flawed: What's easy for you might be difficult for me and vice versa. Still, such ratings serve as a general guide and provide a useful approximation of a hike's challenge. Remember that ratings are not the final word; the most important factor is to be honest about your own fitness level when planning your trip, and pay attention to details like mileage and elevation gain. In this guidebook, difficulty ratings consider both how long and strenuous a hike is. Here are general guidelines for ratings:

Easy: Suitable for any hiker—young or old. Expect no serious elevation gain, hazards, or navigation problems.

Moderate: Suitable for hikers who have at least some experience and average fitness level. Likely includes some elevation change and may have places where the trail is faint.

Strenuous: Suitable only for experienced hikers with above-average fitness level. Possible hazardous trail sections, navigation difficulties, and serious elevation change.

DISTANCE
Measuring trail distances is an inexact science at best. Most distances in this guidebook have been taken from map measurements and from in-the-field estimates. Most trail signs in the Trinity Alps do not include distances, and when they do you can bet they are just somebody else's best guess. Keep in mind that distance is often less important than difficulty of terrain and grade. A steep 2-mile climb on rocky tread can take longer than a 4-mile stroll through a gentle river valley. When planning trips remember that most hikers average about 2 miles per hour over level terrain.

MAPS

The maps in this book serve as a general guide only. Don't hit the trail without a detailed topographic map. There are a few choices when it comes to maps for the Trinity Alps. The USDA Forest Service Trinity Alps Wilderness map (2017 ; 1:63,360) is a comprehensive topographic map that covers the entire wilderness. It will serve most visitors who don't plan on doing extensive off-trail hiking. For those who do—or for anyone who wants a scale with more detail—get the US Geological Survey (USGS) quads. The USDAFS map is available from the ranger stations listed in appendix A. USGS quads can often be obtained through your local sports store, or you can download or purchase them at usgs.gov. Digital maps are also available through a number of online sources and apps.

ELEVATION CHARTS

As in all mountain areas, hikes in Trinity generally start low and go high. Expect to climb 2,000 to 4,000 feet (some of the shorter routes are much less). But lakes are relatively low (below 7,500 feet), and the highest peak is 9,002 feet. That means elevation gains are on the moderate side, and altitude sickness is not an issue for most hikers.

BACKCOUNTRY REGULATIONS

The Trinity Alps Wilderness is a federally designated wilderness area. As such, it's been given the highest level of protection public lands receive. The underlying principle behind all wilderness regulations was best summed up by President Theodore Roosevelt in 1903. He was talking about the Grand Canyon at the time, but he might as well have been talking about all wilderness areas. "Keep this great wonder of nature as it now is," proclaimed Roosevelt. "Leave it as it is. You cannot improve on it; not a bit. The ages have been at work on it, and man can only mar it."

The following backcountry regulations are intended to help Trinity Alps visitors leave well enough alone.

- Get a wilderness permit for all overnight use (see appendix A).
- Camp only in appropriate places.
- Stay on trails (where possible) and don't create shortcuts.
- Dispose of human waste in a cat hole at least 200 feet from all water sources and campsites (pack out toilet paper). Dishwater and water used for bathing also should be disposed of well away from water sources.
- Use camp stoves rather than cooking fires whenever possible.
- Carry out all trash. If you can pack it in, you can pack it out.
- Limit group size to ten or fewer.
- Suspend food out of reach of bears.
- Do not feed or in any way disturb wildlife. Do not leave behind food scraps.
- Do not operate any motorized vehicle in the wilderness.
- Do not destroy, deface, disturb, or remove from its natural setting any plant, rock, animal, or archaeological resource.
- Please read "Zero Impact" (appendix B) for more details on minimizing impact.

NATURAL AND CULTURAL HISTORY

PEOPLE

This book is intended to support your exploration. Readers will come away with a deeper knowledge of the area, and the opportunity to connect more closely and experience more fully the wonders these lands offer. We respectfully acknowledge that this book covers the traditional land of Native peoples. The story of human settlement in the Trinity Alps is a familiar one in the West: Native Americans were displaced by miners, who gave way to loggers and ranchers, who in turn have been largely replaced by outdoor recreationists.

In this case it was the Wintu who were here first. The relatively small Native American tribe met a fate similar to many other California tribes: They were nearly wiped out by the influx of European settlers. Starting in the early 1800s, disease, violence, and loss of their native lands decimated the Wintu population. In the newcomers' mad rush for gold and good land, the Wintu were never awarded a reservation. There's little archaeological record of their presence in the wilderness. Arrowheads and other small items turn up now and then, small reminders that this remote slice of mountain country has a human history we can barely surmise. Be sure to leave what you find if you encounter any of these artifacts on your travels. Interested in learning more about the Wintu and their descendents? Visit the Wintu Cultural Resource Center and Museum in the town of Shasta Lake (https://wintutribe.org).

Recorded history in the Trinity Alps region began in the early 1830s, when explorers and fur trappers first made forays through the area. These early visitors followed Native American trails to the Trinity River valley and headwaters. Jedediah Smith passed through, as did Major Pierson Reading, who named the Trinity River because he assumed (wrongly) that the river ran all the way to Trinidad Bay on the Pacific coast. In fact, the Trinity River flows into the Klamath River.

The discovery of gold near Douglas City in 1848 put the Trinity River region on the map. Miners with gold in their eyes arrived in hordes. Weaverville was established in 1850, and four years later the boomtown boasted twenty-two stores, two banks, two drugstores, six hotels, four restaurants, six saloons, three bakeries, three blacksmith and carpenter shops, seven lawyers, and a population well over 1,000. Mining claims by the hundreds sprang up overnight in the rugged country, and soon a number of satellite towns appeared in the mountains: Places like Saloon City, Lake City, and Old Denny housed hundreds of miners deep in the wilderness. As you hike through the backcountry, don't be surprised to come across a few nineteenth-century relics from the heyday of gold fever. Miners built cabins, roads, stamp mills, and flumes in what today appears to be the most remote of backcountry backwaters. A substantial Chinese population—some 2,000-strong—lived and worked in Weaverville during this era. The Joss House, a Taoist

Temple built in Weaverville in 1874, has been preserved and today is a state historic park that is well worth a visit. It's the oldest continuously used Chinese temple in California.

The tide of mining rose and fell over the next seventy-five years or so as first the placer mines played out and then the more efficient hydraulic and dredge mining had their turn. The many tailing piles scattered around the region indicate just how extensive these operations were. Falling gold prices and the high price of corporate mining made prospecting in the Trinity Alps unprofitable by the 1930s. In recent years, however, the high price of gold has lured a few treasure seekers back to the area. Miners have returned to the Trinity Alps, often with wetsuits and high-tech dredges, to gather gold the old-timers missed. Any claims being worked today predate the area's wilderness designation; no new claims may be filed in the wilderness.

During the heyday of mining and settlement, the Trinity Alps region became the main thoroughfare between the Sacramento Valley and Oregon. The California–Oregon Stage Road, opened in 1860, closely followed the route of present-day CA 3, with numerous stops along the upper Trinity River and even a hotel up on Scott Mountain.

Industrial logging in the Trinity Alps region didn't start until the late 1800s and the coming of the railroads. Though you'll see evidence of clear-cuts surrounding the wilderness, the heart of the Alps escaped the ax and saw. As early as 1926, a portion of the Alps had been set aside for its outstanding scenic and recreation value (in 1932 the forest service officially designated the Salmon–Trinity Alps Primitive Area). Even where logging occurred within the modern-day wilderness, enough time has passed that most visitors will be hard-pressed to identify it. Logging still occurs on private and national forest land outside the wilderness boundary.

Recreation in the region started as early as the 1920s, when a local couple, the Webers, established the Trinity Alps Resort on Stuart Fork. Legend has it, this enterprising couple coined the term "Trinity Alps" after returning from a trip to Europe and the Austrian Alps. The Trinity Alps Resort, as well as other area lodges, is still in operation today. Lodges, horse packers, hiking guides, hunting and fishing guides, and rafting companies are now an important part of the local economy. Consult the Trinity County Chamber of Commerce for a list of local services (see appendix A).

GEOLOGY

The Trinity Alps Wilderness stands alone—an island of alpine splendor cut adrift from California's better-known ranges. Geologically speaking, the Alps are distinct from most of their neighbors. The mountains are unrelated to both the nearby Coast Range and the volcanic Cascades, which include Mount Shasta and Lassen Peak to the north and east. In fact, the Trinity Alps form the southern end of the Klamath Mountains.

Some 2.5 million years ago, the region was much gentler in nature than today. But a general uplift caused valleys to deepen; granitic magmas welled up at various times and pushed through the overlying rock (made up of various metamorphic and sedimentary rocks) to create many of the area's most spectacular peaks. The high iron content in some of the Alps' igneous rocks accounts for the rust-colored appearance of peaks like Red Rock Mountain and Seven Up Peak (this area is sometimes called the Red Trinities, while the granite epicenter is the White Trinities, and the forested western region the Green Trinities).

Glaciers delivered the finishing touches on the awesome scenery. In four separate glaciation periods over the last 1.5 million years, deep ice accumulated in the high mountains and slowly slid down the valleys, carving and slicing the terrain into the spectacular landscape you see today. The glaciers left behind dramatic cirques with exquisite lakes and classic U-shaped valleys with polished sides and knife-edge ridges. Terminal moraines dammed low-lying valleys and created large lakes that eventually became the lush, sprawling meadows you see today. The most recent glaciers receded some 10,000 years ago. Grizzly Glacier, a remnant "glacieret" from this last mini–ice age, still persists on the high north-facing slopes of Thompson Peak, though it has shrunk to only about 4 acres and will likely disappear entirely in the next few decades.

PLANTS

The Trinity Alps are home to an incredible variety of trees, flowers, and shrubs. From giant ponderosa and sugar pines towering overhead to tiny and fleeting wildflowers like blue gentians, the plant communities in the Trinity Alps represent one of the most diverse ecosystems in the United States. What follows is a brief description of a few of the more common or noteworthy plants you can expect to see in the Trinity Alps.

The lower elevations (below 4,000 feet) are dominated by mixed forests of Douglas fir, ponderosa and digger pines, as well as a healthy smattering of oaks (several varieties), madrones, bigleaf maples, and dogwoods. Ferns, berries, alders, and poison oak thrive in streamside riparian zones at this level. (Poison oak is uncommon on most hikes described in this guidebook, but it is prevalent on trails in the western, or "Green," Trinities.) Chaparral, consisting mostly of ceanothus and manzanita bushes, covers the dry, exposed hillsides at this elevation.

Between 4,000 and 6,000 feet, you find Trinity's forest giants: Douglas fir, ponderosa and sugar pine, and incense cedar. Smaller conifers, including white fir, Jeffrey pine, lodgepole pine, and western white pine, also thrive at these elevations. The understory is dominated by azaleas (beautiful and fragrant in early summer), mountain ash, several kinds of berries, and manzanita. Scrub and black oak also appear on dry slopes. Lush mountain meadows of thick grasses and corn lilies and other wildflowers exist at this and higher elevations. You can even see a few aspen stands, rare in the Trinity Alps.

Above 5,000 feet red fir starts to replace white fir (though they often overlap) and western white and Jeffrey pines outnumber their larger cousins. Cottonwoods and mountain ash appear in a few scattered riparian environments at this elevation. Alders and willows grow shrub-like along the creeks and on the fringes of wet meadows. Sunny slopes at this elevation may be covered with manzanita, ceanothus, and other hardy shrubs. Do not take a shortcut across one of these slopes if you value your skin.

The subalpine environment above 6,500 feet is dominated by stunted versions of some of the lower-elevation trees, plus a number of new species like foxtail pine, mountain hemlock, and weeping spruce. Trees that grow along the rocky ridgelines and inhospitable granite cirques, chiefly between 6,500 and 7,500 feet, tend to be small, widely scattered, and often bent in gnarled shapes by the wind and poor soil.

Few trees grow between 8,000 and 9,000 feet, the only true alpine zone in the Trinity Alps. Near the highest peaks' summits, where snow persists well into summer and there's more rock than soil, there are only a few stubborn shrubs, lichens, and, for a brief but spectacular period in late summer, bright wildflowers.

The wildflowers of the Trinity Alps could occupy an entire book unto themselves. From late June through September, the Alps are awash in white, yellow, orange, purple, and red blossoms. Many flowers are specific to certain locations (forest fringes, meadows, rocky slopes, etc.) and seasons (early, middle, or late summer), so what you see depends largely on where and when you go. The most dependable flower-viewing time is typically mid-July to mid-August. Some of the more common species include leopard lilies, columbines, angelica, Indian paintbrush, lupines (both yellow and blue), sunflowers, penstemons, asters, and monkshood. One of the most interesting flowering plants in the Alps is the California pitcher plant (*Darlingtonia californica*). This rare insectivorous plant grows in wet meadows at mid-elevations and should be treated with utmost care (don't pick them or trample their habitat).

WILDLIFE

Encountering animals in the wild is one of the most thrilling experiences in the outdoors. Unlike the animals in some of the more heavily visited wilderness areas in the West, the wildlife in the Trinity Alps is still mostly skittish of humans. Consider yourself lucky to see a black bear. The shy bruins, which can be any shade of brown or black or even cinnamon, are quite a sight when they lumber across a high meadow, trying to get out of view.

A more common sight is the Columbian black-tailed deer. These animals are sometimes hard to avoid; they wander into camps in search of handouts and sweaty clothes to chew (they crave the salts). A friend of mine once fell asleep wearing a sweat-soaked cap. She jumped awfully high when she awoke to find a deer nibbling her head.

Other mammals in the region include mountain lions, coyotes, martens, weasels, bobcats, foxes, porcupines, and ringtails. Consider yourself lucky indeed to spot one of these stealthy species. Chipmunks, mice, squirrels, skunks, jackrabbits, and raccoons are much more common, especially in the mid-elevation forests. Bats often can be seen at dusk, swooping low through the twilight as they feed on insects.

Cold-blooded members of the animal kingdom are also well represented in the Trinity Alps. Rattlesnakes, gopher snakes, rubber boas, garter snakes, and lizards (on some trails there seems to be a lizard on every rock) are the most common reptiles. Rattlesnakes tend to remain out of sight in the warm lower elevations and are easily avoided if you spot one; just give them a wide berth or time to get away. As for amphibians, you can find a variety of frogs, salamanders, and newts in the wet meadows, ponds, and lakes throughout the wilderness.

The most eye-catching birds in the Alps are raptors: Hawks, golden eagles, ospreys, and even bald eagles nest and hunt here. Of the ear-catching variety, you might hear the songs of robins, finches, warblers, bluebirds, and jays. Hummingbirds also show up for the summer wildflowers, and the echo of a woodpecker hard at work can often be heard reverberating through the forest. The number and variety of avian species are far too numerous to list here. Dedicated birders should consult a field guide before heading out.

A NOTE ON THE GREEN TRINITIES

The western half of the Trinity Alps Wilderness is often called the "Green Trinities" because it is lower in elevation and more densely forested than the granite heart of the eastern half of the wilderness. Or at least it *was* more densely forested. Wildfires in 2006, 2008, and 2020 charred large portions of this area (see Wildfires below). Like all healthy forests, this one will recover and be green again. Check with rangers on current conditions before you plan a trip here.

Because the Green Trinities lack the alpine lakes and glacier-gouged canyons found in the east, the trails here have retained one of the most important natural wonders in the backcountry: solitude. It wasn't always that way. During the mid- and late 1800s, the New River drainage was a bustling center of mining activity. Today, 21 miles of the stream are included in the National Wild and Scenic Rivers System. Two hikes described in this book (New River Loop and East Fork New River Loop, Hikes 8 and 9) sample some of the scenery and history to be found in the Green Trinities.

In addition to those routes, there are miles of trails that form a maze of possible hikes in the Green Trinities. Extended hikes of a week or more could easily be made along the Salmon Summit, Green Mountain, or Virgin Creek Trails. Keep in mind, however, that trails and trail signs are sometimes not well maintained due to low use (or fire damage). And because of the low elevation (except for a few ridgeline trails, most paths are below 5,000 feet), there are three things you should be aware of: hot weather in summer, poison oak, and rattlesnakes. The first can be avoided by planning an early- or late-season trip; the second and third are best avoided by knowing what they look like and staying alert. (**Note:** The area has been and may continue to be a popular place to grow illegal marijuana crops. If you encounter signs of an illegal marijuana farm, leave the area immediately.) If you want to be alone and don't mind forgoing the lakes and peaks of the Trinity Alps proper, get out a map and plan a trip here.

THE BIGFOOT TRAIL

It takes many years and much passion to create a new long trail. One such effort—the Bigfoot Trail—has emerged since this guide was first written, and it crosses the heart of the Trinity Alps. The 360-mile Bigfoot Trail starts near the Yolla Bolly–Middle Eel Wilderness and heads north, ending near Redwood National and State Parks near Crescent City. En route, it passes through six wilderness areas, one national park, one state park, and forests that harbor thirty-two species of conifers. In the Trinity Alps the Bigfoot Trail crosses the wilderness from Canyon Creek to Trail Creek, linking both popular destinations (Stuart Fork, Caribou Lake) and rarely traveled ones (Bear Creek, Packers Peak). Thru-hikers on the Bigfoot Trail are in for a treat. Check out www.bigfoottrail.org for more information.

WILDFIRES

In recent years, wildfire season in the West has gotten longer and more intense. The heart of the Trinity Alps—and thus most of the hikes in this guidebook—have been spared, but there have been a few close calls. In 2020, shortly before this edition was finished, two wildfires burned in Trinity. The Fox Fire burned just over 2,000 acres on the north side of Fox Creek Lake, and the Red Salmon Complex burned some 145,000 acres in the Shasta-Trinity, Klamath, and Six Rivers National Forests. The Red Salmon fire burned much of the Green Trinities, in the northwest corner of the wilderness. Keep in mind that hiking through wildfire-scarred terrain can have its own rewards, as you get to witness the rejuvenation at work, but if you want green trees and shade it's best to avoid these areas. I have noted hikes where fire damage might be a concern, but there's no doubt that new fires will occur. Contact the Weaverville Ranger Station (appendix A) for the latest information.

Kalmia Lake is perched high above the Canyon Creek drainage.

TRAIL FINDER

BEST LAKES
1 Grizzly Lake
2 Papoose Lake
4 Canyon Creek Lakes
11 Stuart Fork (Emerald and Sapphire Lakes)
14 Smith and Morris Lakes
19 Lake Anna
27 Foster Lake
34 Caribou Lakes

BEST HIKES FOR WILDFLOWERS
1 North Fork Trinity River to Grizzly Lake
17 Long Canyon
19 Lake Anna Loop
20 Swift Creek
21 Bear Basin–Granite Lake Loop
30 Union Creek
47 Pacific Crest Trail

BEST HIKES FOR VIEWS
16 Granite Peak Trail
21 Bear Basin–Granite Lake Loop
27 Foster Lake Loop
33 Tri-Forest Peak–Deer Creek Loop
34 Caribou Lakes
38 Billys Peak Lookout
40 Bear Lakes
44 East Boulder and Upper Boulder Lakes
47 Pacific Crest Trail

BEST HIKES FOR SOLITUDE
2 Rattlesnake Creek to Papoose Lake
15 Stoney Ridge Trail
23 Poison Canyon
30 Union Creek
31 Bullards Basin–Sunrise Creek Loop
32 Ward Lake Loop

LAKE FINDER TABLE

HIKE	LAKE	ELEVATION	ACRES	DEPTH	WHY GO
35	Adams	6,300'	1.00	16'	Good for small children; nice day hike if you're short on time.
13	Alpine	6,150'	14.00	26'	Pretty detour off busy Stuart Fork; good off-trail exploring.
19	Anna	7,550'	4.00	56'	Great swimming in unique red-rock setting; good wildflowers on the hike in.
40	Big Bear	5,800'	28.00	73'	Beautiful views from classic granite cirque; visit two companion lakes.
15, 19	Billy-Be-Damned	7,400'	0.75	9'	Good solitude on a rocky terrace high above Bowerman Meadow.
5	Boulder Creek	5,750'	5.00	17'	Camp on granite slabs with great view of Sawtooth Mountain.
25	Boulder (Big)	6,100'	8.00	27'	Good base camp or day hike for families and novice hikers.
25	Boulder (Little)	6,350'	4.50	19'	Easy hike to a pretty lake with good swimming.
44	Boulder (East)	6,700'	32.00	60'	Unique setting in an open, grassy basin overlooking Scott Valley.
45	Boulder (Middle)	6,500'	6.50	12'	Good base camp for hikers on the Pacific Crest Trail.
45	Boulder (West)	7,000'	7.00	29'	Excellent solitude near Scott Mountain crest.
4	Canyon Creek (Upper)	5,690'	25.00	86'	Spectacular granite setting with great views; several waterfalls on hike in.
34	Caribou	6,850'	72.00	72'	Jaw-dropping scenery with excellent swimming and camping.
27, 28	Conway	6,850'	1.00	3'	Good solitude at lily pad-fringed pond off the beaten track.
17, 18	Deer	7,150'	4.50	19'	Make snow cones in summer at this north-facing basin.
18	Diamond	7,250'	2.50	13'	Great wildflowers and beautiful sunsets at this little gem.
6	East Fork	5,900'	2.00	11'	Isolated lake in a rugged basin; good chance for solitude.
7	East Weaver	6,350'	1.00	12'	Good for families with small children; good day hike destination.
15	Echo	7,250'	2.50	17'	Good chance for solitude and incredible sunsets.
24	Eleanor	4,950'	3.00	10'	Great for anglers who don't want to waste any time hiking.

HIKE	LAKE	ELEVATION	ACRES	DEPTH	WHY GO
11	Emerald	5,500'	21.00	68'	A premier lake in the Trinity Alps; interesting mining relics.
51	Fish	6,000'	3.00	10'	More of a pond than a lake, but it makes a nice day hike.
5	Forbidden	6,250'	1.50	18'	Rugged cirque off the beaten track. Worth it just to say you've been to Forbidden Lake.
27	Foster	7,250'	5.50	20'	Plenty of exploring in the area; one of the best sunset seats in the Trinity Alps.
26	Found	6,600'	2.50	9'	Rugged, isolated setting just stone's throw from busy Big Boulder Lake.
46	Fox Creek	6,600'	9.50	38'	Pleasant camping near the Scott Mountain crest.
21	Granite	6,000'	18.00	64'	Beautiful granite cirque that's relatively easy to get to; it's popular.
1, 52	Grizzly	7,100'	42.00	173'	Tucked between the Trinity Alps highest peak and biggest waterfall. Worth every step.
49	Hidden	6,700'	3.00	15'	Great destination for a short day hike or family with small children.
20	Horseshoe	6,850'	6.00	22'	Swimming and rock scrambling at the head of Swift Creek.
4	Kalmia	7,500'	1.00	13'	Small lake with a big view. Difficult to reach.
4	L or "El"	6,350'	2.00	29'	Good chance for solitude above perpetually crowded Canyon Creek Lakes.
22	Landers	7,100'	6.00	17'	Unique setting with good swimming and peak-bagging potential.
23	Lilypad	6,300'	2.00	8'	Excellent solitude at this shallow lake; good base camp.
27, 28	Lion	7,000'	3.00	37'	A lot of people see this lake but few hike down to it; rugged setting enclosed by cliffs.
42	Log	6,100'	4.6	18'	Private little lake reached by a short, off-trail hike.
50	Long Gulch	6,450'	14.00	21'	Makes a nice stop on a loop that crosses crest of the Salmon Mountains.
18	Luella	6,950'	2.50	13'	Beautiful little lake of cold, clear water perched above Deer Creek.
44	Marshy (Big)	6,400'	5.50	15'	Good place to find solitude a short way from Pacific Crest Trail.
46	Mavis	6,700'	3.50	16'	A pretty place to base camp on north side of the Scott Mountains.
39	McDonald	6,100'	4.00	15'	Good option for exploring while at Stoddard Lake.
43	Mill Creek	6,600'	3.00	16'	A short hike to a small lake with a good chance for solitude.
11	Mirror	6,600'	14.00	25'	Spectacular setting in the granite heart of the Trinity Alps. Tough hike.

HIKE	LAKE	ELEVATION	ACRES	DEPTH	WHY GO
14	Morris	7,350'	3.50	31'	Idyllic lake tucked just below the summit of Sawtooth Mountain. Challenging hike.
2	Papoose	6,600'	28.00	70'	Great swimming and rock scrambling at granite-enclosed lake.
7	Rush Creek (Upper)	6,950'	2.00	44'	Tough hike to a sheer-walled basin; guaranteed cold water in August.
20	Salmon	7,150'	1.50	13'	Good chance for solitude; great view of Caribou Mountain.
11	Sapphire	6,100'	43.00	200'	Classic alpine setting in heart of Trinity Alps. Great swimming.
46	Section Line	7,100'	2.50	10-15'	Scenic off-trail exploring on north side of the Scott Mountains.
24	Shimmy	6,400'	1.50	10'	Easy day hike with views of Trinity Lake.
14	Smith	6,950'	24.00	167'	Spectacular alpine setting near summit of Sawtooth Mountain. Rough off-trail hike.
34	Snowslide	6,700'	10.00	42'	Pretty lake in the popular Caribou Basin.
48	South Fork (Upper)	6,720'	6.40	34'	Larger of two companion lakes perched on Scott Mountain crest.
39	Stoddard	5,900'	25.00	84'	Big, forest-fringed lake popular with equestrians and large groups.
29	Sugar Pine	6,600'	9.00	43'	Isolated lake in a beautiful setting high above Coffee Creek.
18	Summit	7,350'	13.00	34'	Stunning blue water; highest lake accessible by trail.
41	Tangle Blue	5,800'	12.00	17'	Easy hike to a pleasant lake; good for families with small children.
26	Tapie	6,500'	1.75	15'	Nice place to explore while in the Boulder Lakes basin.
45	Telephone	6,900'	3.50	30'	Scenic stopover on loop across the Scott Mountain crest.
50	Trail Gulch	6,400'	10.00	17'	Makes a nice stop on a loop that crosses crest of the Salmon Mountains.
30	Union	6,050'	3.50	14'	Good for equestrians; makes a nice early-season hike.
46	Virginia	6,900'	3.00	16'	Scenic off-trail exploring on north side of the Scott Mountains.
20, 32	Ward	7,100'	5.50	23'	Secluded lake at head of Swift Creek; good sunrises nearby.
43	Washbasin	7,000'	11.00	85'	Short hike with good chance of solitude in a pretty, rocky basin.

MAP LEGEND

Interstate Highway		Bridge
State Highway		Building/Point of Interest
County/Forest Road		Campground
Unpaved Road		Pass/Saddle
Featured Trail		Peak/Summit
Trail		Point Elevation
Off–Trail Route		Town
River or Creek		Trailhead
Body of Water		Waterfall
National Park/Forest		

HIKES FROM
CALIFORNIA HIGHWAY 299

Find perfect swimming holes
along Upper Canyon Creek
(Hike 4).

1 NORTH FORK TRINITY RIVER TO GRIZZLY LAKE

This is an outstanding ramble along the idyllic North Fork Trinity River to heavenly Grizzly Lake. You need more than a weekend to do it right, but in return you get to experience both a quiet river drainage and a spectacular lake tucked into a granite cirque below the Trinity Alps' highest peak. There's a shorter route to Grizzly, but hikers who want a deep immersion in the wilderness will love this way in.

Start: Hobo Gulch Trailhead
Type of hike: Backpack; out-and-back
Distance: 37.0 miles
Hiking time: About 4–6 days
Difficulty: Moderate to difficult (The route is long but on generally easy terrain; the last 0.5 mile is difficult.)
Elevation gain: 4,123 feet
Best season: Midsummer through early fall
Canine compatibility: Dogs can do most of this hike, but the final off-trail scramble up to Grizzly Lake is too steep for four-footed friends.
Nearest town: Weaverville
Fees and permits: Free wilderness permit required for overnight visitors; free campfire permits required for fires and camp stoves
Schedule: Trails in the Trinity Alps are always open; however, most trailhead access roads are closed or impassable during winter.
Maps: USGS Thurston Peaks, Cecil Lake, and Thompson Peak; USDAFS Trinity Alps Wilderness
Trail contact: Weaverville Ranger Station: (530) 623-2121; www.fs.usda.gov/stnf
Parking and trailhead facilities: Campground, outhouse, and ample parking at the trailhead. The only water available is in the North Fork of the Trinity River. Treat all water sources in the wilderness.

FINDING THE TRAILHEAD

From Weaverville drive 15 miles west on CA 299 to the turnoff for Old Helena (an old mining town, largely abandoned) and turn right (north) onto CR 421 (East Fork Road). Follow signs to Hobo Gulch Campground and Trailhead, 16 miles away on steep, unpaved FR 34N07Y. GPS: N40 55.61916′ / W123 9.16224′

THE HIKE

If I were handed the raw materials—blocks of granite, sweet clear water, permanent snowfields, idyllic meadows, majestic waterfall—and allowed to assemble them however I pleased, I would come up with something that looks very much like Grizzly Lake. Perched on a glacier-gouged shelf below 9,002-foot Thompson Peak with a 100-foot waterfall cascading from its sheer outlet and jaw-dropping vistas everywhere you look, Grizzly Lake is a Hollywood set designer's vision of what a quintessential mountain lake should look like—but Grizzly is real.

Of course, if this were a Hollywood version of an alpine lake, there'd also be an easy way to get here. Fortunately, there's not. A lot of hikers find their way to Grizzly, but you can rest assured that no one gets here without breaking a sweat. The shortest way to Grizzly is a sneak route via China Spring Trail (Hike 52). The steep, 6.7-mile trail starts near Cecilville and enables hikers to reach Grizzly in one day.

Grizzly Falls makes for a grand welcome to the Grizzly Lake basin.

Before the China Spring Trail was built, however, the only route to Grizzly Lake was this 18.5-mile trek from Hobo Gulch along the North Fork Trinity River. It still may be the best way. The route is mostly level and incredibly picturesque for the first 12 miles, offering a leisurely stroll through magnificent wilderness, past historic cabins, and along the lush North Fork banks, accompanied by some of the best stream fishing in the

Trinity Alps—all without the crowds that typically march over the China Spring Trail every summer weekend. (**Note to anglers:** Check with the California Department of Fish and Wildlife before casting a line. The North Fork is subject to fishing restrictions to protect endangered species.)

From the Hobo Gulch Trailhead, hike north on the North Fork Trail (12W01) along the North Fork of the Trinity River. The path meanders along the idyllic creek through shady woods of Douglas fir, ponderosa and sugar pines, oaks, madrone, and dogwood. Just 0.9 mile from the trailhead, arrive at a three-way trail junction. The Backbone Creek Trail heads uphill to the right (east) and eventually ends at an old cabin site. To the left (west) is the North Fork Low Water Trail, which also leads to the Whites Creek Trail. The Low Water Trail crosses the river, so stay on the main path if you want to keep your feet dry.

Continuing on the North Fork Trail, the path climbs a little but mostly just hugs the east bank of the North Fork. The parklike walking is pleasant and easygoing. You may spot modern-day miners plying the river in wet suits and operating high-tech dredges.

At 5 miles you arrive at Rattlesnake Camp, a large forested flat at the confluence of Rattlesnake Creek and the North Fork Trinity River. The North Fork Trail (the route to Grizzly Lake) lies to the left (north); the Rattlesnake Creek Trail veers to the right (northeast) and ascends to Papoose Lake.

Take the left fork and immediately cross Rattlesnake Creek, a wide stream that could pose problems at high water. Just after the ford, the trail climbs a set of dusty switchbacks to gain a line high above the North Fork. Once around the nose of the ridge, an easy contour leads north across a wooded hillside with good views of the river below and a gentle grade that makes it easy to enjoy the scenery.

At 7.1 miles the trail dips down to river level again and arrives at the Morrison Gulch Trail junction on a shady bench next to the water. A sign at the fork indicates Rattlesnake Lake to the left (up Morrison Gulch to the northwest) and Grizzly Lake to the right (north). Rattlesnake Lake, which is not much more than a glorified puddle up on Limestone Ridge, probably gets as many visitors in two years as Grizzly Lake gets on a holiday weekend.

Continuing on the North Fork Trail, ascend above the river again; then stroll upstream to a wide, level bench called Pfeiffer Flat. In the center of the grassy glade, shaded by mature ponderosa pines, Douglas fir, and incense cedar, stands Jorstad Cabin. The historic structure is a testament to the tough folks who carved a living out of the wilderness long before the advent of Gore-Tex and freeze-dried food. Willard Jorstad and his wife, Adzie, built the cabin in 1937, and Willard lived here until he reached his 80s (Jorstad recorded an entertaining account of their first year here in his book *Behind the Wild River*). A few outbuildings and fencing still remain, and the trail passes through an old wooden gate on the way through the meadow. Jorstad wrote of discovering this spot: "Imagine a broad flat along the river, fairly open, set about with giant firs and pines, parklike in appearance, covered with grass growing out of a bed of fertile soil. What a find!"

Continue north on the level, streamside trail. Soon the path reaches the confluence of the North Fork and Grizzly Creek and veers right (east) to follow Grizzly Creek to its namesake lake. The path starts climbing a little more earnestly along Grizzly Creek, but the elevation is still relatively low (just 3,600 feet). Oak and maple are mixed liberally with the pine and fir. You can also see a number of tailing piles from the mining done along Grizzly Creek.

The trail now climbs moderately but steadily to a junction with the Moliter–Cold Springs Trail and Bobs Farm Trail (Hike 3) at 12.8 miles. On the west side of Mill Gulch, the Moliter–Cold Springs Trail climbs north over the Salmon River Divide. On the east side of the gulch, the Bobs Farm Trail (signed "Papoose Lake and Specimen Creek") heads south. Some hikers like to use this route to make a loop back to Hobo Gulch by way of Papoose Lake; others swear they'll never set foot on the trail again. I fall into the former camp, but I freely admit that you have to be very open-minded to appreciate the redeeming qualities of Bobs Farm Trail, which in spots is a trail in name only.

The next 1.5 miles of the North Fork Trail contour steadily along the north bank of Grizzly Creek in mixed-forest cover high above the water. At 14.3 miles from Hobo Gulch, the path meets the junction with the China Spring Trail (11W08). It's just under 3 miles from here to the trailhead at China Gulch, but bear in mind that nearly every yard of that is steep, steep, steep (up and down).

The last 4 miles of trail to Grizzly Meadows may seem like twice that distance if you're doing it at the end of a long day. The path parallels the ever-steepening Grizzly Creek drainage on its final journey southeast to its source at the head of the canyon. Several small waterfalls, lush gardens of ferns and berries, and welcome vistas up and down the drainage soon appear. At the top of a rocky outcropping, get your first glimpse of the cirque above Grizzly Lake, with Thompson Peak and its snowfields towering over the basin.

After several more tantalizing glimpses, the path crosses a series of lush emerald meadows and deposits you in the heart of Grizzly Meadows amid stands of red and white fir, summer wildflowers galore, granite-lined glades, and the crash of Grizzly Falls. The lake is hidden above the sheer cliff ahead, up where the falls pour from the sky. There's a way up there, but even the forest service hesitates to call it a trail.

The agency calls it the Grizzly Scramble, which means that a route exists but you'll need your hands free to scramble up it. From the meadow, cairns lead up the left (east) side of the boulder field. Before the base of the falls, the route veers left (east) and climbs a loose talus slope up the side of the canyon. Pick your way up through the rock band (that's the scramble part); then traverse upward and back to the southwest to reach lake level, 0.5 mile and 800 feet above the canyon floor. You should arrive at the shore near the top of the waterfall. There are campsites scattered around the shore, on both sides of the outlet stream, but they are close to the lake; for more privacy and to reduce impact on the lake, it's better to overnight along Grizzly Creek, in the meadow below the lake. The lower campsites also eliminate the need to carry a heavy pack up the Grizzly Scramble and serve up a great view of the waterfall.

Use extreme caution crossing the stream above the falls while exploring the lake basin. Icy water fed by the glacieret on Thompson Peak (a fast-melting remnant of the last period of glaciation, about 10,000 years ago) fills the 42-acre lake. Swimming is excellent if you can bear the temperature; on most summer days, sun-baked granite slabs are in abundance if you can't. A sparse scattering of stunted fir and mountain hemlock grows in the rocky basin, but mostly it's just rock and snow and water. Gray and massive Thompson Peak, the highest summit in the Trinity Alps at 9,002 feet, looms over it all. Experienced peak baggers will have no problem finding a line to the top of Thompson; the obvious ridgeline approach is on the west side. That's also the best route to take for a day hike to high and lonely Lois Lake. When on the ridge, turn right instead of left and take a short hike to where you can view the lake. Small and stark, Lois is good for bragging rights but not much else.

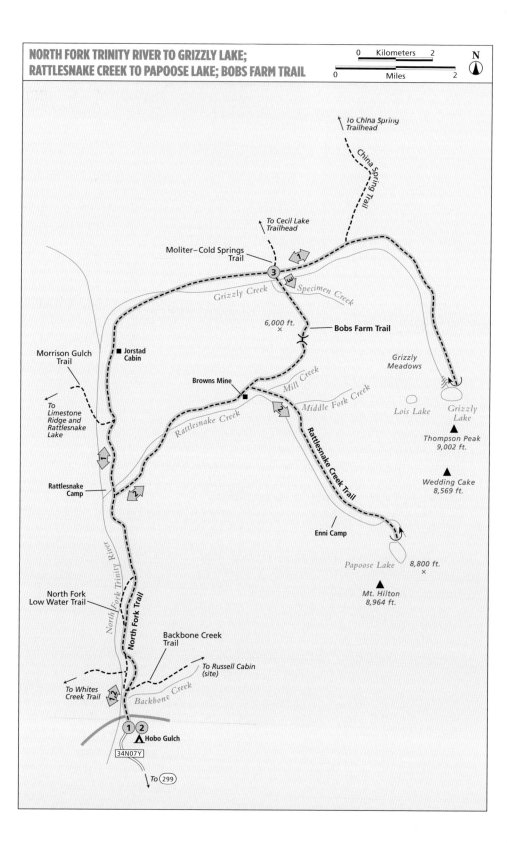

0   Kilometers   2

0   Miles   2

N

To China Spring
Trailhead

China Spring Trail

To Cecil Lake
Trailhead

Moliter–Cold Springs
Trail

3

Grizzly Creek

Specimen Creek

6,000 ft.
×

Bobs Farm Trail

Grizzly
Meadows

Jorstad
Cabin

Morrison Gulch
Trail

Browns Mine

Mill Creek

To
Limestone
Ridge and
Rattlesnake
Lake

Middle Fork Creek

Lois Lake

Grizzly
Lake

Rattlesnake Creek

Thompson Peak
9,002 ft.

Rattlesnake Creek Trail

Rattlesnake
Camp

Wedding Cake
8,569 ft.

Enni Camp

North Fork Trinity River

Papoose Lake   8,800 ft.
×

Mt. Hilton
8,964 ft.

North Fork
Low Water Trail

North Fork Trail

Backbone Creek
Trail

To Russell Cabin
(site)

To Whites
Creek Trail

Backbone Creek

1 2

Hobo Gulch

34N07Y

To 299

Grizzly Lake sits under Thompson Peak, the highest summit in the Trinity Alps.

MILES AND DIRECTIONS

0.0 Start at the Hobo Gulch Trailhead.

0.9 Go straight on the North Fork Trail and follow it to the junction with the Backbone Creek and North Fork Low Water–Whites Creek Trails.

2.8 The North Fork Low Water Trail rejoins the main trail. Stay on the North Fork Trail.

5.0 Arrive at Rattlesnake Camp. The Rattlesnake Creek Trail veers right, to Papoose Lake. Bear left, staying on the North Fork Trail.

7.1 Pass the Morrison Gulch Trail junction. Stay on the North Fork Trail.

9.0 Reach the historic Jorstad Cabin.

12.8 Continue a moderate ascent on the North Fork Trail, passing the Bobs Farm and Moliter–Cold Spring Trail junctions.

14.3 The North Forth Trail meets the China Spring Trail (the shortest route to Grizzly). Stay right.

17.7 Continue on the North Fork Trail to Grizzly Meadows.

18.5 Scramble the steep, rocky slope to Grizzly Lake. Return the way you came.

37.0 Arrive back at the trailhead.

OPTIONS

On the way back from Grizzly Lake, you can make a loop using the Bobs Farm and Rattlesnake Creek Trails. Experienced navigators can also make several off-trail hikes from Grizzly Lake. Besides Thompson Peak, other destinations in the area include Lois, Little South Fork, and Mirror Lakes. Use the map and good judgment: The terrain around these places is steep, wild, and isolated.

2 RATTLESNAKE CREEK TO PAPOOSE LAKE

Explore historic mining relics along Rattlesnake Creek—which is much prettier than the name suggests—and camp at a granite wonderland in the Papoose Lake basin.

(See map on page 6.)
Start: Hobo Gulch Trailhead
Type of hike: Backpack; out-and-back
Distance: 25.6 miles
Hiking time: About 3–5 days
Difficulty: Strenuous due to length and steep, rough going at end
Elevation gain: 3,646 feet
Best season: Midsummer through early fall
Canine compatibility: Yes, though the final steep scramble could be challenging for small or older dogs.
Nearest town: Weaverville
Fees and permits: Free wilderness permit required for overnight visitors; free campfire permits required for fires and camp stoves
Schedule: Trails in the Trinity Alps are always open; however, most trailhead access roads are closed or impassable during winter.
Maps: USGS Thurston, Mount Hilton, and Thompson; USDAFS Trinity Alps Wilderness
Trail contact: Weaverville Ranger Station: (530) 623-2121; www.fs.usda .gov/stnf
Parking and trailhead facilities: Campground, outhouse, and ample parking at the trailhead. The only water available is in the North Fork of the Trinity River.

FINDING THE TRAILHEAD

From Weaverville drive 15 miles west on CA 299 to the turnoff for Old Helena (an old mining town, largely abandoned); turn right (north) onto CR 421 (East Fork Road). Follow signs to Hobo Gulch Campground and Trailhead, another 16 miles away on steep, unpaved FR 34N07Y. GPS: N40 55.61916' / W123 9.16224'

THE HIKE

For years Papoose Lake has managed to fly just under the radar when it comes to renowned Trinity Alps destinations. Overshadowed by more prominent neighbors like Grizzly, Canyon Creek, and Emerald Lakes, Papoose is rarely crowded—but not for lack of charm. The jagged granite cirque above Papoose is drop-dead gorgeous, and the clear, icy water is well worth the final steep scramble up to the lake (calling this last rough segment a trail is a stretch). Along the way you'll hike by many mining relics left along Rattlesnake Creek, a onetime booming center of gold prospecting. Rattlesnake Creek itself tumbles through a deep, lush drainage with mostly pleasant walking.

From the Hobo Gulch Trailhead, hike north on the North Fork Trail (12W01) along the North Fork of the Trinity River. The path meanders along the idyllic creek through shady woods of Douglas fir, ponderosa and sugar pine, oaks, madrone, and dogwood. Just 0.9 mile from the trailhead, arrive at a three-way trail junction. The Backbone Creek Trail heads uphill to the right (east) and eventually ends at an old cabin site. To the left (west) is the North Fork Low Water Trail, which also leads to the Whites Creek Trail. The Low Water Trail crosses the river, so stay on the main path if you want to keep your feet dry.

Papoose Lake is one of Trinity's uncrowded gems.

Continuing on the North Fork Trail, the path climbs a little but mostly just hugs the east bank of the North Fork. The parklike walking is pleasant and easygoing. You may spot modern-day miners plying the river in wet suits.

At 5 miles you arrive at Rattlesnake Camp, a large forested flat at the confluence of Rattlesnake Creek and the North Fork Trinity River. This is a great spot to break up the hike, especially if you got a late start. The route to Grizzly Lake lies to the left (north); the way to Papoose Lake veers to the right (northeast).

Turn right and continue up the south bank of Rattlesnake Creek on the Rattlesnake Creek Trail (11W05). The going is nearly level and mostly shady as you skirt the edge of the creek. After crossing a couple of small tributaries, the trail fords Rattlesnake Creek 1.8 miles from the junction. This is most likely a wet crossing, and the current may be swift in early season. Use caution if the water is high. Maples and oaks line the banks here, and the drainage contains numerous tailing piles (stacks of river boulders left from century-old mining operations).

Now on the north side of the creek, the trail ascends at a very moderate grade through more mixed oak, madrone, fir, and pine woodland. At times the path widens considerably; you can easily imagine wagonloads of equipment and miners plying the route along Rattlesnake Creek. After 1.8 miles of gentle climbing, arrive at Browns Mine, where scattered pieces of such equipment have been left to rust in their wilderness grave. History buffs may want to linger here and try to identify the various machinery, gears, and odd items the miners left behind.

Just beyond Browns Mine, 8.7 miles from the trailhead, arrive at the junction with the Bobs Farm Trail. A left (north) turn here leads steeply uphill to surmount a 6,000-foot ridge separating the Rattlesnake and Grizzly Creek drainages. Mile for mile, it is without doubt one of the most difficult trails in all of the Trinity Alps—and it's also woefully overgrown, making the trail hard to find in addition to being steep. On the plus side, it enables you to make a nifty loop between Papoose and Grizzly Lakes.

Stay right (east) to continue on the Rattlesnake Creek Trail. The path soon crosses Mill Creek (which, should you be in the mood for a serious bushwhack, you could follow to its source at little Lois Lake), then Middle Fork Creek, which rises high on the ridge between Thompson Peak and Wedding Cake. Top off your water bottles before moving on—the next few miles tend to be hot and dry in summer.

The trail climbs along the course of Rattlesnake Creek but stays high above the water, offering only enticing views of the inviting swimming holes in the gorge down below. The ascent steepens at times as you climb through alternating stands of forest cover, berry bushes, and brushy fields of ceanothus and manzanita.

A final push up the narrowing canyon brings you level with Rattlesnake Creek and to the site of Enni Camp ("Enos" on the USGS quad), an overused campsite that marks the end of the Papoose Lake Trail proper. (Overnight at Enni if you don't have time to make the final push in good light.) From here it's a rock-hopping bushwhack up the Papoose Scramble, which is the forest service's official way of saying a trail is not officially a trail. Another faint path leads left from Enni Camp to Bear Valley Meadows, 0.7 mile up the side of the drainage to the north and east.

The path to Papoose Lake continues southeast up the drainage along the north side of the creek, veering away from the water and following the course of a dry gully that runs along the edge of the canyon floor. The route is marked by cairns, but it's easy to lose the path among the downed trees, bushes, and boulders. Just head east along the dwindling strip of land between the creek and canyon wall. After 0.5 mile the route crosses to the south side of the creek at a ford marked (usually) by several cairns.

Once across the creek, follow the faint path up a brushy, exposed slope to the base of a steep headwall guarding the final approach to Papoose Lake. Look for cairns leading the way past a snowmelt pond on a level bench just before what appears to be a sheer cliff. A zigzagging route winds up through the dark band of rock. The ascent is not technical, but it's a good idea to keep your hands free and use caution on the steep scramble. Above this section, the route heads generally left to right as you ascend, veering toward a field of light-colored granite boulders on the southwest side of the canyon. The lake is hidden from view, still high above and to the right (southeast), at the head of the drainage.

To your left (northeast) the outlet from Papoose Lake carves a deep, narrow gorge through naked gray rock. Cairns lead southeast along the lip of the gorge. Even without the cairns the route is obvious; just follow the path of least resistance until you top out on a granite apron at the mouth of the Papoose Lake basin, 12.8 miles from the trailhead.

Here you'll find clear blue water, smooth granite shores, and a spectacular cirque above the lake. Stunted red firs and mountain hemlocks are scattered around the basin, but the shores consist mostly of bare rock and bright-colored wildflowers. Indian paintbrush, scarlet gilia, angelica, and purple monkshood are just a few of the species that bloom here in summer. Smooth slabs of granite slope down to the water's edge. Look for the best campsite among huge boulders at the outlet stream. Find one of the flat ones for your luxurious granite-slab kitchen.

Like the scramble up to the lake? There's plenty more on the ridge (northeast) above Papoose. A stiff climb to the top of the sharp-edged ridgeline will earn you a spectacular view into the head of the Canyon Creek drainage and the heart of the Trinity Alps.

MILES AND DIRECTIONS

0.0   Start at the Hobo Gulch Trailhead.

0.9   Follow the North Fork Trail to the junction with the Backbone Creek and North Fork Low Water–Whites Creek Trails.

2.8   The North Fork Low Water Trail rejoins the main trail. Continue upstream on the North Fork Trail.

5.0   Arrive at Rattlesnake Camp; turn right on the Rattlesnake Creek Trail.

6.8   Follow the Rattlesnake Creek Trail to a ford.

8.6   Reach historic relics at Browns Mine.

8.7   Continue straight on the Rattlesnake Creek Trail to the Bobs Farm Trail junction; bear right.

11.5   Arrive at Enni Camp, with good creek-side camping.

12.0   Ford Rattlesnake Creek again.

12.8   Reach Papoose Lake after a final steep scramble. Return the way you came.

25.6   Arrive back at the trailhead.

OPTIONS

Make a loop over to Grizzly Lake using the Bobs Farm Trail. The detour adds about 25 miles to the route.

3 BOBS FARM TRAIL

This short, steep route linking two of the Trinity Alps' most spectacular destinations is only accessible by foot. It connects the North Fork Trail (Hike 1) and the Rattlesnake Creek Trail (Hike 2), offering ambitious hikers the chance to create a rarely done semi-loop.

(See map on page 6.)
Start: North Fork Trail
Type of hike: Hike-in backcountry connecting trail; one-way
Distance: 4.4 miles
Hiking time: About 3 hours
Difficulty: Strenuous
Elevation gain: 1,900 feet
Best season: Midsummer through early fall
Canine compatibility: Yes
Nearest town: Weaverville
Fees and permits: Free wilderness permit required for overnight visitors; free campfire permits required for fires and camp stoves

Schedule: Trails in the Trinity Alps are always open; however, most trailhead access roads are closed or impassable during winter.
Maps: USGS Thompson Peak; USDAFS Trinity Alps Wilderness.
Trail contact: Weaverville Ranger Station: (530) 623-2121; www.fs.usda .gov/stnf
Parking and trailhead facilities: There's no trailhead parking at either end of Bobs Farm Trail; park at Hobo Gulch Trailhead, where there's a campground, outhouse, and ample parking. The only water available is in the North Fork of the Trinity River.

FINDING THE TRAILHEAD

Bobs Farm Trail runs between mile 12.8 on the North Fork Trail and mile 8.7 on the Rattlesnake Creek Trail. GPS: N41 2.358' / W123 6.489' (junction with North Fork Trail). Drive to the Hobo Gulch Trailhead and then hike to the trail. From Weaverville drive 15 miles west on CA 299 to the turnoff for Old Helena (an old mining town, largely abandoned); turn right (north) onto CR 421 (East Fork Road). Follow signs to Hobo Gulch Campground and Trailhead, another 16 miles away on steep, unpaved FR 34N07Y.

THE HIKE

Any description of the Bobs Farm Trail must start with a disclaimer: Do not attempt this route if you don't like steep, rough hikes. Mile for mile and switchback for switchback, this is one of the most difficult trails in the Trinity Alps. The path is steep, is overgrown in places, and has exposed sections that can be sizzling hot on a summer afternoon. One recent trail report from the Weaverville Ranger District described it as even more overgrown than usual, noting, "A GPS unit helps!"

Even with that disclaimer, Bobs Farm Trail is one of my favorite paths in Trinity Alps. What are its redeeming qualities? First, it allows you to make a spectacular loop between Grizzly and Papoose Lakes with minimal backtracking. Second, it's the only way to see—and appreciate—Bobs Farm, a lonely hillside outpost where long ago an entrepreneurial farmer named Bob grew produce to sell to local miners (or maybe not—it's possible that the legend of Bobs Farm was planted by a miner joking about the hillside's poor agricultural prospects). Finally, and perhaps most important, are the bragging rights: *You hiked Bobs Farm Trail.* If the condition of the path is anything to go on, not many hikers can make that claim.

Connect Papoose Lake (pictured) with Grizzly Lake via the seldom-used Bobs Farm Trail.

Starting at the North Fork end of the trail (11W03), the junction is just a few yards east of Mill Gulch. A couple of well-worn signs indicate the way to Papoose Lake and Specimen Creek (unless signs have changed, expect no mention of Bobs Farm at this end of the trail). Hike south, immediately crossing Grizzly Creek near a little-used campsite; then skirt the edge of Specimen Creek. Instead of crossing the creek here, however, the trail veers left (southeast) and climbs steeply up a dusty, oak-shaded ridge that separates Grizzly and Specimen Creeks. The ascent is short but attention-getting—in places the trail climbs straight up the hillside. By the time you descend the other side of the ridge and cross Specimen Creek, you have a good taste of what's to come. (Be sure to fill up on water before going farther.)

After crossing Specimen Creek, the trail climbs steeply out of the drainage and bends farther southeast, contouring along the base of the mountain across brushy slopes. In places the trail seems to disappear in a dense cover of ceanothus bushes, but it's never so faint that you can't pick it up again on the other side. If it doesn't get you lost, however, this brush-choked section will do a number on bare legs. Long pants are recommended.

Less than 0.5 mile after the creek crossing, the trail turns south and starts climbing in earnest. At times the path ascends what appears to be a primitive form of switchbacks; the idea is there, but they haven't been perfected. The grade is somewhat abated by the old-growth fir forest that dominates the hillside, providing shade and a beautiful, open understory to walk through.

Eventually the trail tops out on the ridgeline separating the Grizzly and Rattlesnake Creek drainages, almost 2,000 feet above your starting point. Enjoy great views of the granite skyline to the east; then descend through manzanita and open slopes to an old hunters' camp in a stand of woods near a spring. Two faint paths cross the short distance between the ridgetop and the camp.

From the camp the trail descends almost due south, winding downhill through a ferny meadow and dropping into thicker forest cover. Don't worry if the spring doesn't look too inviting (it's at the edge of the meadow, just east of the trail); there's plenty of water a few minutes away in the creek at Bobs Farm.

A set of more highly evolved switchbacks leads 0.3 mile down to Bobs Farm. The collection of old machinery and the ruins of a shack are perched on a cramped-looking hillside above a little clear-flowing creek. In summer a profusion of leopard lilies grows on the lush banks.

From here the trail crosses the creek and descends southwest on rocky, dusty switchbacks. The terrain becomes more open and exposed as the path crosses hillsides covered in low-growing manzanita—that makes it sweltering on a hot day but allows for great views. Just over 4 miles from Grizzly Creek, Bobs Farm Trail descends to 4,000 feet (the same elevation you started at) and the junction with the Rattlesnake Creek Trail. Turn left (east) to reach Papoose Lake or right (west) to reach Rattlesnake Camp. Either way, you can start bragging.

MILES AND DIRECTIONS

0.0 Start at the North Fork Trail–Bobs Farm Trail junction.

0.1 Immediately cross Grizzly Creek.

0.8 Continue on Bobs Farm Trail to the Specimen Creek crossing.

2.2 Climb steeply to a ridgetop horse camp/spring.

2.5 Descend to Bobs Farm.

4.4 Continue down to the Rattlesnake Creek Trail–Bobs Farm Trail junction.

4 CANYON CREEK LAKES

This is simply one of the most beautiful hikes in the Trinity Alps, thanks to lush meadows, spectacular waterfalls, gorgeous lakes, and awesome views. For those reasons, plus relatively moderate hiking, it's also one of the most popular. Expect lots of company in summer.

Start: Canyon Creek Lakes Trailhead
Type of hike: Backpack; out-and-back
Distance: 16.0 miles
Hiking time: About 2–4 days
Difficulty: Moderate
Elevation gain: 2,602 feet
Best season: Midsummer through early fall
Canine compatibility: Yes
Nearest town: Weaverville
Fees and permits: Free wilderness permit required for overnight visitors; free campfire permits required for fires and camp stoves

Schedule: Trails in the Trinity Alps are always open; however, most trailhead access roads are closed or impassable during the winter.
Maps: USGS Mount Hilton; USDAFS Trinity Alps Wilderness
Trail contact: Weaverville Ranger Station: (530) 623-2121; www.fs.usda .gov/stnf
Special considerations: No campfires are allowed at any of the Canyon Creek lakes.
Parking and trailhead facilities: Outhouse and parking lot; car camping available at nearby Ripstein Campground

FINDING THE TRAILHEAD

From Weaverville drive 8 miles west on CA 299 to Junction City. Turn right (north) onto paved Canyon Creek Road (CR 401) just before (east of) the bridge over Canyon Creek. Don't count on a sign, but the road is obvious (directly across from the general store). Continue 13.5 miles to the trailhead at the end of the road (all paved but the last mile). Stay right at 10.5 miles and pass the East Fork Lake Trailhead at 11 miles. Next comes a sign commemorating the old mining town of Dedrick, now lost to history, which once did a bustling bit of business on the banks of Canyon Creek. The trailhead is at the end of the road. GPS: N40 53.242' / W123 1.470'

THE HIKE

All of Canyon Creek's attractions—waterfalls, sweeping granite cliffs, sparkling lakes, spectacular views, swimming holes of near-perfect proportions—can be found elsewhere in the Trinity Alps. But you'd be hard-pressed to find anywhere else where they're all packaged into one pleasant hike. **Fair warning:** Such abundance makes Canyon Creek the most popular destination in the wilderness. From the overflowing parking lot at the trailhead to the numerous tents lining the creek along the way, you'll have no illusions about wilderness solitude here on a busy summer weekend.

Nevertheless, Canyon Creek is still one of the most beautiful slices of mountain country you'll ever walk through. And if you plan your trip accordingly (off-season or midweek), you can still see Canyon Creek in all its glory without the crowds. I once spent a few peaceful days here in October without encountering one other person. **Note:** Camp well below the lakes. There are much better campsites along the creek leading up the drainage. The lakes themselves are in granite-lined basins too vulnerable to human impact. Also, campfires are not allowed at the lakes.

The trail hugs Canyon Creek, passing many good campsites and swimming holes.

Two paths start at the trailhead: Canyon Creek and Bear Creek Trails (Bear Creek is a little-used trail that hops over to Stuart Fork). For the Canyon Creek Trail, head north on the well-marked path. The trail ascends gradually through shady, low-elevation vegetation of dogwood, maple, Douglas fir, and oak with a smattering of pine and cedar thrown in. The path dips down to cross Bear Creek and then climbs moderately to a low ridge, continuing north parallel to and high above Canyon Creek's east bank.

It's pleasant going for the next 2.5 miles to McKay Camp. A spur trail to the left (west) leads down to Canyon Creek and McKay Camp, a little island nestled between two arms of the creek. In particularly dry years the water may disappear under the Sinks (a pile of debris from a massive rock fall) just upstream and then reappear at the downstream end of the island. Normally, however, you can expect to see impossibly clear, aquamarine water flowing by the island.

After McKay Camp the trail climbs more steeply on a short series of switchbacks to reach a ledge high above Canyon Creek. The trail crosses a dependable little creek three times as it switchbacks up.

Ascending moderately along the granite-lined ledge, you first hear, then glimpse, the fabled Canyon Creek Falls. The crashing waterfall is commonly called the Lower Canyon Creek Falls to distinguish it from the Middle and Upper Falls, but when most people refer to the Canyon Creek Falls, this is the one they're talking about. Years ago the trail climbed right up Canyon Creek and passed within spitting distance of the falls. Today the path rejoins the creek above the falls, 3.9 miles from the trailhead.

Trail and creek meet at a pleasant site with a mini-falls, a refreshing little swimming hole, and a rather poor trailside campsite marked by weeping spruce. Much better campsites can be found 0.5 mile ahead and for the next 3 miles, in Upper Canyon Creek Meadows and beyond.

Continuing upstream from the falls, the trail meanders alongside the east bank of the now-peaceful creek. The creek winds tranquilly through a lush, parklike forest of incense cedars, ferns, willows, and inviting meadows of corn lilies and mullein. The trail runs mostly level to the base of Middle Canyon Creek Falls, about 5.5 miles from the trailhead. A use trail branches left (west) to the base of the falls, easily accessible through the open understory. To the right (east) is the beginning of a difficult off-trail route to Smith and Morris Lakes.

From the base of the Middle Falls, the Canyon Creek Trail climbs a series of switchbacks to reach the junction with the Boulder Creek Lakes Trail on a level, forested flat 6 miles from the trailhead. A left turn leads 2 miles up to Boulder Creek Lakes and Forbidden Lakes. **Caution:** Canyon Creek is often too high to be crossed safely during the early summer. It's best to plan your trip for July or later.

Past the junction, the Canyon Creek Trail continues north, climbing gently through weeping spruce, ponderosa pine, manzanita, incense cedar, and more meadows. Near the end of a forested flat, after another set of falls and just before the last hill at the base of Lower Canyon Creek Lake, the trail crosses to the west side of the creek. A trail sign

Fall colors and fewer people make autumn a great time to hike Canyon Creek.

Upper Canyon Creek Lake sits amid a granite-lined cirque.

should indicate the crossing, and a couple of downed trees may be present to help keep your feet dry. The old route (which some people still use) goes up the east side of the creek along the falls. The problem with going up the east side is that you have to cross the outlet at the top of the falls—a very bad idea in high water. Hikers have died attempting it. The trail on the west side ascends a series of granite ledges (follow the cairns) and abruptly arrives at Lower Canyon Creek Lake, 7.1 miles from the trailhead.

If all the waterfalls, meadows, and swimming holes weren't enough, the sight from here should make you understand why there may be fifty or more cars at the trailhead on summer weekends. The deep-blue, 14-acre lake sits at an elevation of 5,600 feet in a trough gouged out of smooth slabs of granite. (Avoid camping here; there are virtually no good sites.) The east side of the lake ranges from steep to very steep, with 8,886-foot Sawtooth Mountain towering directly overhead. The west side is littered with sloping granite benches that are perfect for warming yourself after a dip in the cold, clear water. Framed in a notch at the north end of the lake are Thompson Peak and Wedding Cake.

To reach Upper Canyon Creek Lake, simply follow the route on the west side of the basin. Stay high as you work your way northwest through a steep gully to the southwest corner of Upper Canyon Creek Lake.

The upper lake is 400 feet higher, 10 acres bigger, and maybe just a tad more spectacular than its lower companion. A sloping granite dike holds the water back on the south side, sheer slabs of gray rock plunge into the lake's northwest shore, and a lush green meadow surrounds the inlet on the northeast. While it's best to camp along the creek in the valley below, there is a good campsite on the upper lake; it's surrounded by willows at the upper end of the meadow. There's also a small white-sand beach to lounge on, as well as a picturesque little waterfall at the upper end of the meadow. Fishing from the beach and in the deep pool at the base of the waterfall is superb.

Above all loom the secluded headwaters of Canyon Creek, topped by 9,002-foot Thompson Peak and its slightly lower neighbor, 8,592-foot Wedding Cake. If it's solitude you're after, set your sights on the wild, trail-less drainage up ahead. Retrace your path to the trailhead.

MILES AND DIRECTIONS

0.0 Start at the Canyon Creek Lakes Trailhead.

2.5 Follow the Canyon Creek Trail to McKay Camp.

3.0 Pass the Sinks, where Canyon Creek disappears underground in dry years.

3.9 Continue straight to Canyon Creek Falls.

4.5 Reach Upper Canyon Creek Meadows.

5.5 Keep hugging the creek and arrive at Middle Canyon Creek Falls.

6.0 Pass the Boulder Creek Lakes Trail junction (it goes left); stay on the Canyon Creek Trail.

7.1 Continue straight on the Canyon Creek Trail to Lower Canyon Creek Lake.

8.0 Ascend above the first lake to reach Upper Canyon Creek Lake. Return the way you came.

16.0 Arrive back at the trailhead.

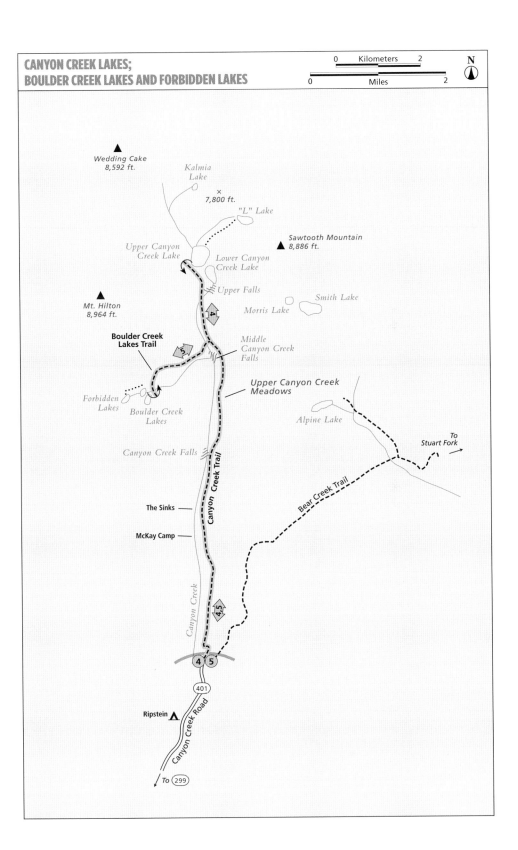

0   Kilometers   2

0   Miles   2

N

▲ Wedding Cake
8,592 ft.

Kalmia
Lake

× 7,800 ft.

"L" Lake

Sawtooth Mountain
▲ 8,886 ft.

Upper Canyon
Creek Lake

Lower Canyon
Creek Lake

Upper Falls

Morris Lake

Smith Lake

▲ Mt. Hilton
8,964 ft.

**Boulder Creek
Lakes Trail**

Middle
Canyon Creek
Falls

Upper Canyon Creek
Meadows

Forbidden
Lakes

Boulder Creek
Lakes

Alpine Lake

To
Stuart Fork

Canyon Creek Falls

Canyon Creek Trail

Bear Creek Trail

The Sinks

McKay Camp

Canyon Creek

4.5

4 5

401

Ripstein ▲

Canyon Creek Road

To 299

OPTIONS

In the upper reaches of the Canyon Creek drainage lie two little lakes rarely seen by the crowds down below. Only experienced hikers should attempt these routes. All travel above Upper Canyon Creek Lake is off-trail.

Side trip to L (also spelled "Ell") Lake (2.2 miles round-trip from Upper Canyon Creek Lake): Cross the outlet at Upper Canyon Creek Lake (carefully) and make your way to the northeast side of the lake. Little 2-acre L Lake lies in the basin that bends around to the northeast, directly below the northwest face of Sawtooth Mountain. Follow cairns up the gully and ascend the south side of the creek tumbling down from L. A mile of fairly easy scrambling and a few steep bands of granite lie between you and the lake. Finally, pick your way through the trees on the basin's west side and discover the aptly named lake at 6,350 feet. The best (somewhat spartan) campsites are on the north shore. Remember: No campfires are allowed.

From a granite seat near the lake's outlet, you look directly across the Canyon Creek drainage at the sheer western wall and steep slopes leading up to 8,964-foot Mount Hilton. The peak was named in honor of James Hilton, who honored Weaverville by comparing the town to the mythical Shangri-La in his book *Lost Horizon*.

L Lake is also a great place to start a hike to the top of 8,886-foot Sawtooth Mountain. The peak, which crowns the divide between Canyon Creek and Stuart Fork drainages, is one of the most dramatic summits in the Trinity Alps. To reach it, hike southeast from L Lake and ascend the obvious line on the mountain's northwest side. The strenuous climb is challenging but not technical. Near the top you'll find a cave. It provides welcome, cooling shade in the heat of summer. **Caution:** The peak's top rock is about 4 square feet. Climbers have been known to have difficulty on the descent of this summit block, so avoid ascending this final scramble if you're not confident in reversing course.

Side trip to Kalmia Lake (about 3.5 miles): This tough scramble is recommended only for strong hikers with good route-finding ability. To reach tiny, 1-acre Kalmia Lake, perched high on the shoulder of an unnamed peak at the head of the Canyon Creek drainage, you've got to tackle the steep gully northwest of L Lake and ascend to the ridge between the Canyon Creek and Stuart Fork headwaters. Follow the ridgeline northwest, up and over the shoulder south of the unnamed peak. Drop down to Kalmia after climbing about 1,500 feet and 1 mile from L Lake. The tiny, shallow lake, gouged into the side of the mountain at 7,500 feet, is so close to Wedding Cake it feels as though you can reach out and grab a slice. One treeless campsite is all you'll find on this gem of a lake. That seems more than sufficient, though, since the lake only has a handful of visitors each season. From here you can scope out Mirror, Sapphire, and Emerald Lakes by climbing to the eastern ridgeline.

Two extremely steep gullies lead from Kalmia down to the headwaters of Canyon Creek. The gullies are not a good way to get down, much less up (retrace your steps to L if you're not comfortable descending the steep, rocky gully). Still, I must admit I was rather pleased with the loop formed by traveling counterclockwise from Upper Canyon Creek Lake to L to Kalmia and back along Canyon Creek. The headwaters along Upper Canyon Creek offer some of the best alpine scenery in the Trinity Alps, with flower-filled meadows, sparkling waterfalls, and amazing vistas in every direction. No maintained trail leads between the upper drainage and Upper Canyon Creek Lake, but you'll pick up cairns and traces of use trails as you get closer to the lake.

5 BOULDER CREEK LAKES AND FORBIDDEN LAKES

These quiet lakes are perched high above the Canyon Creek drainage, with one of the best views of Sawtooth Mountain in the entire wilderness. Though they're a short distance from the most-crowded trail in the Trinity Alps, the pretty little granite basin doesn't get as much traffic as you might expect. Most hikers don't want to leave the cool creek-side walking in the valley in order to tackle a steep climb.

(See map on page 21.)
Start: Canyon Creek Lakes Trailhead
Type of hike: Backpack; out-and-back
Distance: 17.0 miles
Hiking time: About 2–4 days
Difficulty: Moderate, with one steep section (The short, optional off-trail hike to Forbidden Lakes is strenuous due to the terrain.)
Elevation gain: 3,040 feet
Best season: Midsummer through early fall
Canine compatibility: Yes
Nearest town: Weaverville
Fees and permits: Free wilderness permit required for overnight visitors; free campfire permits required for fires and camp stoves

Schedule: Trails in the Trinity Alps are always open; however, most trailhead access roads are closed or impassable during the winter.
Maps: USGS Mount Hilton; USDAFS Trinity Alps Wilderness
Trail contact: Weaverville Ranger Station: (530) 623-2121; www.fs.usda.gov/stnf
Special considerations: No campfires are allowed at any of the Canyon Creek lakes or the immediate vicinity.
Parking and trailhead facilities: The large parking lot has an outhouse; developed car camping available at Ripstein Campground.

FINDING THE TRAILHEAD

From Weaverville drive 8 miles west on CA 299 to Junction City. Turn right (north) onto paved Canyon Creek Road (CR 401) just before (east of) the bridge over Canyon Creek. Don't count on a sign, but the road is obvious (directly across from the general store). Continue 13.5 miles to the trailhead at the end of the road (all paved but the last mile). Stay right at 10.5 miles and pass the East Fork Lake Trailhead at 11 miles. Next comes a sign commemorating the old mining town of Dedrick, now lost to history, which once did a bustling bit of business on the banks of Canyon Creek. The trailhead is at end of the road. GPS: N40 53.242' / W123 1.470'

THE HIKE

Boulder Creek Lakes is a collection of shallow pools and mini-lakes spread over a wide granite bench that hangs above the west side of the Canyon Creek drainage, just 2 miles off the crowded thoroughfare. The hanging cirque is protected by a sheer headwall the trail skirts on the north. It's an impressive sight and makes for a strenuous climb up sunny, exposed switchbacks. Trees are sparse in the lake basin as well, so the shallow water warms up earlier than most lakes in the wilderness. Numerous campsites are located around the main lake and ponds, so the area can absorb a number of groups. Smooth granite slabs offer abundant places to lie down in peace and quiet. (The moss-free slabs

Boulder Creek Lakes overlook the Canyon Creek drainage.

extend into the lake, making great places to lounge half in and half out of the water.) If that's not enough, the Forbidden Lakes hang hidden and mysterious in a concealed cirque above the basin. Who can resist a name like Forbidden Lakes?

Start at the Canyon Creek Trailhead and head north on the well-marked Canyon Creek Trail. The trail ascends gradually through shady, low-elevation vegetation of dogwood, maple, Douglas fir, and oak with a smattering of pine and cedar thrown in. The path dips down to cross Bear Creek and then climbs moderately to a low ridge, continuing north parallel to and high above Canyon Creek's east bank.

It's pleasant going for the next 2.5 miles to McKay Camp. A spur trail to the left (west) leads down to Canyon Creek and McKay Camp, a little island nestled between two clear arms of the creek. In particularly dry years the water may disappear under the Sinks (a pile of debris from a massive rockfall) just upstream and then reappear at the downstream end of the island. Normally, however, you can expect to see impossibly clear, aquamarine water flowing by the island.

After McKay Camp the trail climbs more steeply on a short series of switchbacks to reach a ledge high above Canyon Creek. The trail crosses a dependable little creek three times as you switchback up its course.

Ascending moderately along the granite-lined ledge, you first hear, then glimpse, the fabled Canyon Creek Falls. The crashing waterfall is commonly called the Lower Canyon Creek Falls to distinguish it from the Middle and Upper Falls, but when most people refer to the Canyon Creek Falls, this is the one they're talking about. Years ago the trail climbed right up Canyon Creek and passed within spitting distance of the falls. Today the path rejoins the creek above the falls, 3.9 miles from the trailhead.

Trail and creek meet at a pleasant site with a mini-falls, a refreshing little swimming hole, and a rather poor trailside campsite marked by weeping spruce. Much better campsites can be found 0.5 mile ahead and for the next 3 miles, in Upper Canyon Creek Meadows and beyond.

Continuing upstream from the falls, the trail meanders alongside the east bank of the now-peaceful creek. The creek winds tranquilly through a lush, parklike forest of incense cedars, ferns, willows, and inviting meadows of corn lilies and mullein. The trail runs mostly level to the base of Middle Canyon Creek Falls, about 5.5 miles from the trailhead. A use trail branches left (west) to the base of the falls, easily accessible through the open understory. To the right (east) is the beginning of a difficult off-trail route to Smith and Morris Lakes.

From the base of the Middle Falls, the Canyon Creek Trail climbs a series of switchbacks to reach the signed junction with the Boulder Creek Lakes Trail on a level, forested flat 6 miles from the trailhead.

At the junction turn left (west) and proceed over a little rise before reaching Canyon Creek just upstream from the falls. Cross to the west side of the creek. In low water you can keep your feet dry with some creative boulder-hopping, but use caution when the water's high—the falls isn't far away. Go farther upstream to cross if needed, or simply come back another time if it's not safe. (Refill your water bottles here; there's no water on the steep hillside ahead.)

Once across the creek the trail heads south and then west through mixed conifers and alongside a secluded little meadow. (The trail heading north from the crossing leads to campsites along Canyon Creek.) Climb moderately, parallel to and above Boulder Creek, which remains a good distance to the south.

After leaving the last of the meadows behind, the trail climbs more steeply up the north side of the drainage. There are great views of the headwall below the lake, but the shadeless trail is rough and rocky. The switchbacks soon lead to a granite slope that rises to the lip of the basin; from there it's just a matter of following cairns around the north side. Though you can see the lake from here, you can't go directly to it because a wide and deep chasm lies in the way. The cairns lead to the western, narrow edge of the ravine, where you can cross the little stream it contains. Continue from there to Boulder Creek Lakes, 2 miles from the junction (8 miles from the trailhead).

The wide, spacious basin has only a few Jeffrey pines and weeping spruce. Mostly it's just granite, water, and views. According to a few Sawtooth aficionados, the Trinity Alps' best view of Sawtooth Mountain is from here. It's also a good place to eye one of several off-trail routes up to Smith Lake, on the opposite side of the Canyon Creek drainage.

To reach the Forbidden Lakes, aim for the notch in the canyon above and to the west, where a stream emerges. If the route looks forbidding, maybe that's how the lake got its name. (Not everyone thinks it's so bad; some people—and maps—identify Lower Forbidden Lake as Upper Boulder Creek Lake.) In any case, the way up isn't too difficult. Cairns lead up the north side of the outlet; look for a path that starts where you crossed the ravine on the way in. On the south side, boulder-hop and scramble your way up to the notch; then push through the bushes to the lower lake. Either way you go, the last 100 yards is going to be a bushwhack.

Lower Forbidden Lake is a picturesque little slip of a thing, tucked between high, steep walls that barely let much sunshine in even in midsummer. In the far west side of the basin that holds Upper Forbidden Lake, expect to find late-season snow and a little meadow that remains emerald green well into September. The two lakes lie side by side at 6,250 feet, with not much more than rocks and cold water and a view of Sawtooth Mountain framed in the outlet notch—a truly wonderful place.

If you like to scramble over the granite high country, explore the largely untraveled terrain above Boulder Creek Lakes. It's possible to climb nearby Mount Hilton (8,964 feet, second highest in the Trinity Alps) from here. Bring plenty of water.

Upper Forbidden Lake frames one of the area's best views of Sawtooth Mountain.

MILES AND DIRECTIONS

0.0   Start at the Canyon Creek Trailhead.

2.5   Follow Canyon Creek Trail to McKay Camp.

3.0   Pass the Sinks, where the creek may disappear underground in dry years.

3.9   Continue straight to Canyon Creek Falls.

4.5   Stay on the creek-side trail and continue upstream to Upper Canyon Creek Meadows.

5.5   Keep hugging the creek and arrive at Middle Canyon Creek Falls.

6.0   Arrive at Boulder Creek Lakes Trail junction; go left.

8.0   Climb steeply to Boulder Creek Lakes.

8.5   Ascend off-trail to Forbidden Lakes. Return the way you came.

17.0   Arrive back at the trailhead.

OPTIONS

Canyon Creek Lakes (2 miles from the trail junction on Canyon Creek): You can also make a difficult, off-trail journey to **Smith Lake** by scaling the drainage directly across from the Boulder Creek drainage.

6 EAST FORK LAKES

This secluded granite cirque has a shallow little lake at its base—and zero crowds. It's not as spectacular as its neighbors, but it offers wilderness solitude that in other places would require a much longer hike.

Start: East Fork Lakes Trailhead
Type of hike: Day hike or backpack; out-and-back
Distance: 10.4 miles
Hiking time: About 1–3 days
Difficulty: Moderate
Elevation gain: 2,758 feet
Best season: Midsummer through early fall
Canine compatibility: Yes
Nearest town: Weaverville
Fees and permits: Free wilderness permit required for overnight visitors; free campfire permits required for fires and camp stoves
Schedule: Trails in the Trinity Alps are always open; however, most trailhead access roads are closed or impassable during winter.
Maps: USGS Rush Creek Lakes and Dedrick; USDAFS Trinity Alps Wilderness
Trail contact: Weaverville Ranger Station: (530) 623-2121; www.fs.usda.gov/stnf
Special considerations: The access road is closed Oct 30 to May 1.
Parking and trailhead facilities: Parking available but no facilities. The nearest developed campgrounds are just a few miles away. Ripstein Campground is located 2 miles farther north on Canyon Creek Road; Junction City Campground is on CA 299 west of Junction City.

FINDING THE TRAILHEAD

From Weaverville drive 8 miles west on CA 299 to Junction City. Turn right (north) onto paved Canyon Creek Road (CR 401) just before (east of) the bridge over Canyon Creek. Don't count on a sign, but the road is obvious (directly across from the general store). Drive north 11 miles to the signed turn for the East Fork Lakes Trailhead on FR 35N47Y. Turn right (east) and continue up the unpaved road. Stay left at the fork at 1.2 miles. Arrive at the signed trailhead at 2 miles. GPS: N40 51.043' / W123 1.306'

THE HIKE

East Fork Lakes is one of those lost-and-forgotten corners of the Trinity Alps. The small lake is not much more than a pond, really, tucked up in a pretty but isolated basin on the north side of Monument Peak. This obscurity is highlighted by the multitude of people who drive by the trailhead each summer. The East Fork Lakes Trail is on the way to Canyon Creek, which means 99.9 percent of the people who pass the trailhead just keep on going. Prefer solitude with your scenery? Just hang a right at the sign for East Fork Lake and rest assured no one is likely to follow. Expect overgrown trail, especially toward the end.

The East Fork Lakes Trail (9W22) zigzags steeply uphill through a low-elevation mixture of oak, madrone, and brush. The path soon settles into a more moderate grade, climbing past old mining relics as it switchbacks up the slope. Watch for an obscure, unmarked fork 0.5 mile in. The well-defined main trail goes right (north). At 0.8 mile

East Fork Lake is not as dramatic as its neighbors, but it's also not as crowded.

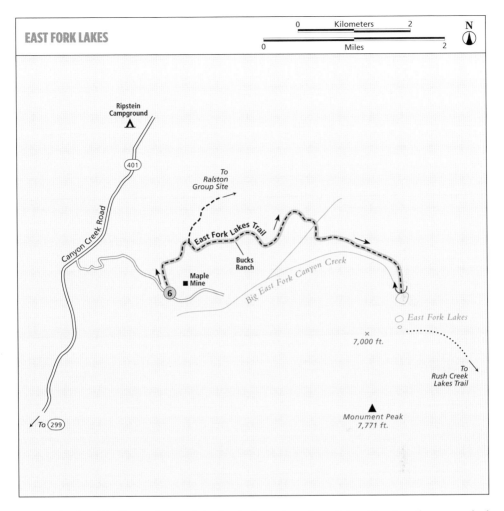

0   Kilometers   2

0   Miles   2

N

Ripstein
Campground

401

To
Ralston
Group Site

Canyon Creek Road

East Fork Lakes Trail

Bucks
Ranch

Maple
■ Mine

6

Big East Fork Canyon Creek

East Fork Lakes

×
7,000 ft.

To
Rush Creek
Lakes Trail

To 299

▲
Monument Peak
7,771 ft.

gain the ridgeline and turn right (east) along the spine of the ridge (another unmarked path goes west).

The sparse forest becomes denser as you ascend, with more pines appearing with the elevation gain. At another fork located just over 1 mile in, the main trail is signed (right/east) where it follows a gentle contour with good views across the drainage. (The left fork leads north 1 mile to Ralston Group site.) Just over 2 miles from the trailhead, arrive at the old Bucks Ranch site, where traces of an ancient flume lead to a perennial creek, the trail's first dependable water source.

Break into an open and sunny section after the creek crossing. This part of the trail, though not long, is hot and dry in summer. The tread is steep and rocky, lined by man-zanita, and exposed to the sun. Fortunately, the path soon reenters the canyon bottom, where a cool forest of cedar, fern, and alder lines Big East Fork Canyon Creek.

The last mile of trail may be overgrown in places—a sign of just how few hikers make it up here. Finally, climb steeply to the south and reach the top of a granite shelf where East Fork Lake is cupped in a grass-and boulder-lined bed gouged into the narrow canyon. Take a seat on the lip of granite and enjoy the views down the drainage or relax and enjoy the picturesque cascade of the lake's inlet stream.

The cirque above the lake is a gradual slope of sweeping gray granite blessed with an inviting, level bench. No trail leads to it, but with some creative rock hopping, it's not difficult to pick your way up the boulder fields and brushy slopes to get there, though you do have to fight your way through a few dense thickets to get beyond East Fork Lake. Stick to the slope on the east side of the inlet creek.

It's worth the effort. The bench harbors a hanging garden of wildflowers, emerald meadows, fir and hemlock trees, a waterfall, and several delightful ponds of crystal-clear water. It's because of these ponds that some maps call the basin East Fork *Lakes*. Hike up to the ridgeline on either side for spectacular views.

MILES AND DIRECTIONS

0.0   Start at the East Fork Lakes Trailhead.

0.2   Follow the East Fork Lake Trail to the Maple Mine.

2.1   Reach historic artifacts at Bucks Ranch.

5.2   Continue ascending to East Fork Lake. Return the way you came.

10.4 Arrive back at the trailhead.

OPTIONS

Rush Creek Lakes: A difficult off-trail route to Rush Creek Lakes is possible for ambitious hikers. Go over the ridge southeast of East Fork Lake and descend to the Rush Creek Lakes Trail.

7 EAST WEAVER LAKE; RUSH CREEK LAKES

Part 1 of this hike (East Weaver Lake) is an easy day hike or good family overnight. It's not a spectacular destination, but it takes only about 30 minutes to reach. Part 2 (Rush Creek Lakes) accesses a sparkling little chain of lakes set deep in the jaws of a rocky cirque. The scenery is dramatic, and so is the hike to get there. The off-trail descent to the lakes is very steep, with loose rock, so only attempt it if you're comfortable with the terrain. That said, the hike can be a lot of fun if you like getting off the beaten track.

Start: East Weaver Lake Trailhead
Type of hike: Day hike or backpack; out-and-back
Distance: 8.0 miles
Hiking time: About 1–3 days
Difficulty: Easy to East Weaver Lake; strenuous to Rush Creek Lakes, with the steep descent from Monument Peak
Elevation gain: 2,198 feet
Best season: Midsummer through early fall
Canine compatibility: Yes
Nearest town: Weaverville
Fees and permits: Free wilderness permit required for overnight visitors; free campfire permits required for fires and camp stoves
Schedule: Trails in the Trinity Alps are always open; however, most trailhead access roads are closed or impassable during winter.
Maps: USGS Rush Creek Lakes; USDAFS Trinity Alps Wilderness
Trail contact: Weaverville Ranger Station: (530) 623-2121; www.fs.usda .gov/stnf
Parking and trailhead facilities: Ample parking and a picnic area. You could throw a sleeping bag on the ground here (the sunsets are extraordinary), but there are no facilities or water.

FINDING THE TRAILHEAD

The journey to the trailhead is a trip in itself. In fact, some people drive the 9 miles up to the fire lookout on top of Weaver Bally Mountain just to watch the sunset. From Weaverville drive west on CA 299 (but not too fast; the turn is on the edge of town). Turn right (north) onto Memorial Drive, just past the Trinity County Office of Education, and proceed a few blocks to the beginning of unpaved Weaver Bally Road (FR 33N38). Go straight (north) and gain 5,000 feet over the next 9 miles. The road is rough but passable for passenger cars. Numerous poorly marked forest roads can be confusing; the main road should be obvious, but go uphill if you're unsure. The trailhead is on the right, just before the fire lookout at the end of the road. GPS: N40 48.547' / W122 59.668'

THE HIKE

The Rush Creek Lakes (there are four, plus assorted ponds) are close to Weaverville as the bird flies, but birds are about all you'll find here on most days. People just don't seem to believe the kind of spectacular scenery found in Rush Creek Lakes' craggy cirque could be so close to town. (**Note:** This off-trail route is my favorite way to the lakes, but it's not the only way. Hikers who don't like steep, brushy, off-trail scrambles should use the

Rush Creek Lakes Trail. However, this route has also become overgrown due to lack of maintenance; while not as steep, it's still very challenging.)

The trailhead elevation and the elevation at Upper Rush Creek Lake are nearly the same (just under and just over 6,900 feet, respectively), but in between you descend 600 feet, ascend 1,200 feet, then drop another 600 feet to end up where you started in terms of altitude.

In terms of scenery, you enter another world. The trail starts on a brushy, exposed ridge on the side of Weaver Bally Mountain and finishes with a steep scramble down a rock-strewn chute to the rugged interior of the Rush Creek basin. The descent doesn't require any technical skills or equipment, just caution.

There are three reasons to take the Weaver Bally (off-trail) route to Rush Creek Lakes instead of using the Rush Creek Lake Trail (Hike 10). First, it's simply shorter and more elegant. It shaves 3 miles off the maintained route and lets you drop into the basin from above—always a nice way to finish a hike. Second, the route passes within a few hundred feet of Monument Peak's craggy summit. If you came the other way, you might never make the climb all the way up to the peak from the lake, and that would be a shame. Finally, the Rush Creek Lakes Trail itself is a waterless route that's decidedly unpleasant compared with the region's better trails.

From the East Weaver Lake Trailhead, walk east on the signed East Weaver Lake Trail (10W11). Almost immediately the path leads past the remains of a ridgetop track cut during efforts to stop the 1987 East Fire. A forest service sign explains that fire crews prepared to set a backfire here as the wildfire approached from Bear Gulch. Fortunately, the fire was controlled before it crossed the ridge, so they didn't have to.

After passing the East Fire sign (stay right), the trail veers east across slopes of ceanothus and manzanita. You soon reach a prominent shoulder above East Weaver Lake; the trail turns sharply left to contour around the basin above the north side of the lake and drops down on steep, rocky switchbacks. The ridge is a good place to pause and survey the route ahead.

Below is East Weaver Lake, 1 mile from the trailhead. The little 1-acre lake is more of a stop along the route than a destination itself, though people often come here for an easy day hike. The one and only campsite is away from the lake's north end, about 100 feet. It's in a protected, forested site. There's no fishing in the lake, but there's cell reception. It's one of the few lakes in the Trinity Alps where you can call home from your sleeping bag.

To the south are the road you came up on and a view of Weaverville. To the northeast lie 7,771-foot Monument Peak and the high ridge between you and Rush Creek Lakes. Once you're standing on the low spot on that ridge, the lake will be at your feet.

First you must descend into (and out of) the drainage below East Weaver Lake. Follow the trail downhill to its junction with the Bear Gulch Scramble, 0.5 mile past the lake (the junction is signed; turn left, or west). After eyeing that ridge next to Monument Peak, don't be discouraged by this initial descent—and don't be tempted to save yourself some climbing by leaving the trail early and cutting across the brush-covered slope. It's not a shortcut. I tried it once and had nothing but manzanita wounds to show for the effort.

After turning onto the Bear Gulch Scramble, head uphill through shady forest cover and small meadows. The path wanders up a dry creek bed for a short way (usually marked by a cairn) and then continues up steep, rocky switchbacks for the final push to the ridge between the Bear Gulch and East Weaver Creek drainages.

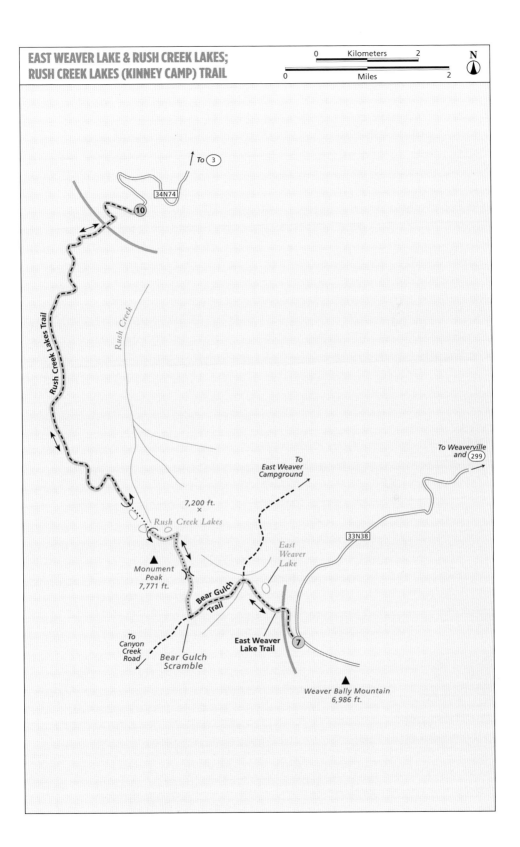

A short detour leads to this view from Monument Peak.

From here it's an easy 1 mile along the ridgeline and up to the base of Monument Peak. The Bear Gulch Scramble drops down the hill to the west, while you head cross-country to the north. The off-trail route passes right along the burn line from the 1987 fire, past charred logs and giant firs felled by the firefighters, and up to the ridge just east of Monument Peak. A fairly obvious use trail ascends through mature firs to the ridgeline, though the "trail" is steep and has very little zig or zag (and is badly eroded because of it); this is a good place to spread out and make your own, better, trail.

Once atop the ridge, it's a matter of controlling your descent to Upper Rush Creek Lake. Two extremely steep chutes lead down to the lake. Take it slow. A granite "island" midway down forces you right or left; the right side is much steeper.

The upper lake itself has icy blue water and a pleasing mixture of evergreens and rock terraces. The 2-acre lake sits at 6,950 feet, and its craggy, high-walled basin keeps the sun out and the water chilly all summer. In fact, the basin often holds snow until late summer.

Head downcanyon through the basin to explore the other Rush Creek Lakes. The ponds and 1-acre lakes are spread out in a curving basin that bends north and then east. No maintained trail leads between them.

On the way in or out, don't pass up the chance to scramble up Monument Peak. The 7,771-foot summit commands a 360-degree view of northwest California: the Trinity Alps, Mount Shasta, Lassen Peak, and a bird's-eye view of Rush Creek Lakes. A use trail marked by cairns leads up the ridge to the base of the peak. The final push to the summit is on huge blocks of rock, one of which supports a small white cross that reads "Soaring with the Eagles."

MILES AND DIRECTIONS

0.0   Start at the East Weaver Lake Trailhead.

1.0   Descend to East Weaver Lake. (Option: Turn around here for an easy 2 -mile hike.)

1.5   Go left and uphill on the Bear Gulch Trail.

2.5   Start the off-trail route by navigating the ridgeline and heading toward Monument Peak.

4.0   Descend steeply to Upper Rush Creek Lake. Return the way you came.

8.0   Arrive back at the trailhead.

8 NEW RIVER LOOP

History buffs and solitude lovers will appreciate this hike. The route winds through wild canyon country to a historic mining district that long ago was a bustling center of activity. *Note:* In 2020, a wildfire burned through this area; check with rangers for current conditions before heading out.

Start: New River Trailhead
Type of hike: Backpack; lollipop
Distance: 23.4 miles
Hiking time: About 2–4 days
Difficulty: Moderate
Elevation gain: 3,000 feet
Best season: Summer through early fall
Canine compatibility: Yes
Nearest town: Willow Creek
Fees and permits: Free wilderness permit required for overnight visitors; free campfire permits required for fires and camp stoves

Schedule: Trails in the Trinity Alps are always open; however, most trailhead access roads are closed or impassable during winter.
Maps: USGS Jim Jam Ridge and Dees Peak; USDAFS Trinity Alps Wilderness
Trail contact: Weaverville Ranger Station: (530) 623-2121; www.fs.usda .gov/stnf
Parking and trailhead facilities: Parking and an outhouse. The nearest developed campground is at Denny.

FINDING THE TRAILHEAD

From Hawkins Bar (on CA 299, 10 miles east of Willow Creek), drive north on Denny Road (CR 402). Continue for 20 miles, past a USDA Forest Service campground (at 18 miles) and the tiny settlement of Denny. It's slow going on the twisting, winding road. At 21.5 miles from the highway, turn left (west) at the sign for New River Trailhead (FR 7N15). Continue 6 miles on the unpaved road (the way is marked by trailhead signs). The trailhead is at the end of the road, 27.5 miles from CA 299. GPS: N40 59.923' / W123 20.710'

THE HIKE

This journey into the heart of the "Green Trinities" is dramatically different from the classic hikes in the better-known eastern part of the wilderness. Rather than the high alpine lakes, granite peaks, and glacier-gouged valleys that draw alpine fans to the east side, the west side of the wilderness is a land of thick-forested mountains and wild river canyons where few people venture. Elevations in the Green Trinities tend to be a little lower (and temperatures a little warmer), wildlife more wild, and trails a lot less traveled. (**Note:** This area was affected by several wildfires in the last two decades, with a major blaze burning through as recently as 2020. Check with rangers on habitat recovery and trail conditions before a trip here.)

But it wasn't always that way. In the late 1800s the New River drainage was home to a number of mining settlements. Old Denny boasted 500 residents in its heyday. Due to the rugged, remote nature of the drainage, it was the last major river in the region that prospectors explored (hence the name New River). Once discovered, however, New River became a center of mining activity, with bustling communities at New River City (now called Old Denny), White Rock City, and Marysville. After a half century of quiet, the

Green Trinities again attracted cash-hungry entrepreneurs. In the 1970s and 1980s, the area became a popular place to grow illegal marijuana crops (if you encounter an illegal marijuana farm, leave the area immediately).

Except for a few miles of trail, the hike is chiefly below 4,000 feet. The low elevation means there are three things you should be aware of: hot weather in midsummer, poison oak, and rattlesnakes. The first can be avoided by planning an early- or late-season trip; the second and third are best avoided by staying alert. Despite the lack of lakes, water is plentiful along the route. Creeks and streams are sparkling clear, with refreshing swimming holes and year-round flows. In fact, an abundance of water poses the only problem with hiking this route too early in the year. The ford at Virgin Creek, 2.8 miles in, may be uncrossable in high water. Check with the ranger station before heading out.

The hike starts on the New River Trail (7E05), meandering along the canyon high above the river and heading north up the drainage. The vegetation at this low elevation is a mix of oak, madrone, maple, and dogwood, with a fir thrown in here and there for good measure. The initial hike is an easy stroll downhill and along the river.

At 2.8 miles arrive at the junction of Virgin and Slide Creeks (which form New River). You'll see evidence of an old flume and historic mining camps. The trail jogs to the left (west) to cross Virgin Creek slightly upstream from the confluence. If you can cross here, you should have no problem at the route's other crossings. On the opposite bank, ascend immediately to a trail junction marked "Soldier Creek" to the left (west) and "Old Denny" to the right (east). Turn right toward Old Denny on the Slide Creek Trail (12W03).

Climb the point of a spur ridge separating Virgin and Slide Creeks; then amble up and down along Slide Creek for 2.6 miles. The forest is still a mix of oak, maple, and fir through here, with plenty of good swimming holes along the way. At the confluence of Slide and Eagle Creeks, 5.4 miles from the trailhead, arrive at another junction. To the right (east) is the Slide Creek Trail; to the left (north) is the Eagle Creek Trail (8E11), signed "Battle Creek–Salmon Summit." The Eagle Creek Trail is the path you'll use to return to this point.

To continue the loop segment in the recommended direction, turn right and stay on the Slide Creek Trail. You descend and cross Eagle Creek a few hundred yards upstream from the confluence of the two creeks. From the crossing it's a steep haul up and over the ridge separating the drainages, then another pleasant hike along and above the course of Slide Creek (with a few more uphill sections thrown in here and there, but nothing difficult). Top off your water bottles at the crossing; the next few miles are apt to be dry.

Just under 3 miles from the last junction, drop down to a grassy flat along Slide Creek. More well-preserved mining relics litter the clearing (look for an intact wood-and-metal hand truck). Past the mining camp, the trail climbs moderately and crosses a couple of small tributaries, one of which boasts an ancient wooden bridge that's suitable only for looking at—not walking on. After crossing a fern-filled meadow about 0.2 mile beyond the camp, arrive at a somewhat confusing trail junction. To the right (south) is Emigrant Creek Trail (8E05), signed "Milk Camp–Pony Creek." The left (east) fork that goes straight is the trail to Old Denny. Apparently unsigned at first, you'll spot a "Mary Blaine Meadows" sign soon after you start uphill. (**Note:** Signs come and go in the wilderness, so be alert and consult your map if the route is not clear.)

Climb moderately but steadily for about 2 miles, reaching an elevation where pine, fir, and incense cedar start dominating the forest, then arrive at Old Denny in a wooded flat

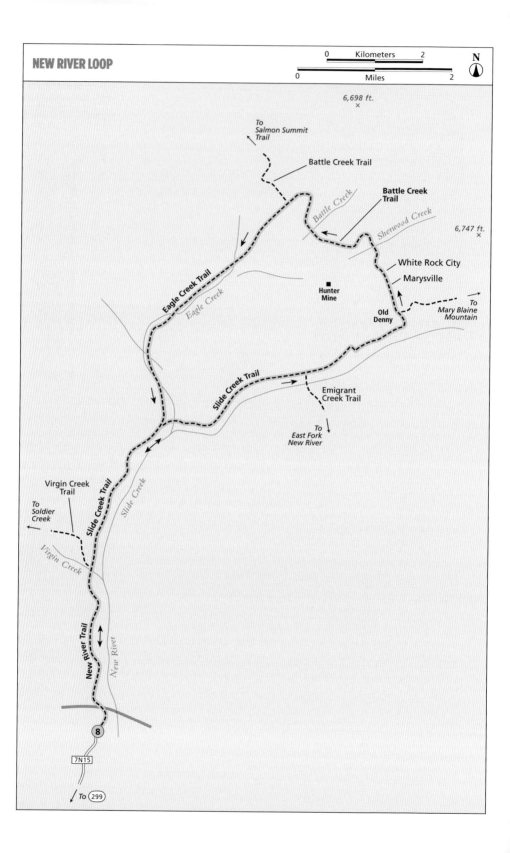

Kilometers

Miles

N

6,698 ft.
×

To
Salmon Summit
Trail

Battle Creek Trail

Battle Creek
Trail

Battle Creek

Sherwood Creek

6,747 ft.
×

White Rock City

Marysville

Eagle Creek Trail

Eagle Creek

Hunter
Mine

Old
Denny

To
Mary Blaine
Mountain

Slide Creek Trail

Emigrant
Creek Trail

To
East Fork
New River

Virgin Creek
Trail

To
Soldier
Creek

Slide Creek Trail

Slide Creek

Virgin Creek

New River Trail

New River

8

7N15

To 299

Old Denny was once a busy mining town with more than 500 people.

high above Slide Creek. A weathered sign tells you the short version of the town's history: founded by Clive Clements in 1882, originally called New River City, abandoned in 1920. Looking around the wild setting, it's hard to imagine that 500 people lived here at the start of the twentieth century. Water is available from a spring 50 yards east of the Old Denny sign.

The trail heads north from Old Denny, climbing switchbacks to a ridgetop junction. Another ancient sign points right (east) to Mary Blaine–Cinnabar and left (north) to Marysville. The Cinnabar Mine, just 1 mile away toward the crest of the Salmon Mountains, is a great place to explore if you have time. This route continues north through Marysville (not much to see) and White Rock City (lots of artifacts and nice views). The White Rock City site is perched high on the ridgeline, a more aesthetically pleasing location than Old Denny's cramped forest quarters, and water is available from nearby Sherwood Creek. If you want to explore another old mine site, look for an unmarked trail (no longer on current forest service maps) heading west just after you pass Marysville. The path leads 1 mile to the Hunter Mine. There are enough relics and mines in the immediate vicinity to keep history buffs busy for a couple days. Use caution around old mine sites, which may be unstable and dangerous.

To continue the loop, head north and west from White Rock City on what is now the Battle Creek Trail (8E19). The trail crosses Sherwood Creek and descends on moderate switchbacks to cross Battle Creek, less than 2 miles from White Rock City. Partway down, an indistinct and overgrown path veers right (north) from a sharp bend in the wide track and cuts across the hillside to reach the Battle Creek crossing. The section of trail between here and Eagle Creek, just over the ridge to the southwest, is likely to be overgrown and sometimes difficult to follow.

After the creek crossing, climb a rocky slope 0.5 mile to reach the crest of the ridge between Battle and Eagle Creeks. Arrive at a poorly marked junction on the forested crest. To the right (north) Battle Creek Trail leads north along the ridge to the spine of the Salmon Mountains. To the left (south) the Eagle Creek Trail (8E11) heads downhill to the southwest and an eventual meeting with Eagle Creek. A broken sign indicates that Slide Creek lies in that direction. The Eagle Creek Trail plunges straight over the side of the ridge and then immediately turns south to begin a sloping descent into the drainage. The trail steepens on a rocky, open hillside before finally leveling off in the wild, forested terrain at the bottom of the canyon. The path may be indistinct here (look for cairns), but the drainage naturally funnels you down to Eagle Creek (stay right, or west, and you'll run into it). The trail crosses to the west side of Eagle Creek just upstream from the confluence with Battle Creek, less than 2 miles from the ridgetop trail junction. From here the path is once again easy to follow.

The next 3.3 miles is another up-and-down affair as the creek-side trail parallels the course of Eagle Creek. Plenty of water, inviting swimming holes, and a return to oak-and-maple woodland highlight the delightful little stream. The path crosses Eagle Creek two more times on the way down the drainage. Look for an ancient wooden ladder in a flat near one of the crossings. Arrive at the Slide Creek trail junction, 18.2 miles from the beginning. Turn right and retrace your steps to the trailhead.

MILES AND DIRECTIONS

0.0 Start at the New River Trailhead.

2.8 Go straight on the New River Trail to the Slide Creek Trail and Virgin Creek Trail junctions.

5.4 Take the Slide Creek Trail and continue to the Eagle Creek Trail junction. Stay right.

7.9 Follow the Slide Creek Trail past the Emigrant Creek Trail.

10.5 Arrive at historic Old Denny.

10.8 Pass the Mary Blaine–Cinnabar Trail and Battle Creek Trail junctions.

11.0 Follow the Battle Creek Trail to Marysville.

11.2 Continue to White Rock City.

14.0 Take the Eagle Creek Trail downhill and follow its namesake creek.

18.2 Arrive at the Slide Creek Trail junction; go right.

20.6 Follow the New River Trail back to the trailhead.

23.4 Arrive back at the trailhead.

OPTIONS

From Old Denny, follow signs to Mary Blaine Meadows–Cinnabar Mine to reach the Salmon Summit Trail (12W02), which runs along the spine of the Salmon Mountains and can be used to make a longer loop connecting with the Battle Creek Trail.

A 40-plus-mile loop can be created by linking the Salmon Summit Trail with the Virgin Creek Trail.

Yet another loop can be made by heading east on the Salmon Summit Trail and linking the Mullane Corral, Pony Creek, and Emigrant Creek–Milk Camp Trails.

The possibilities are endless in this corner of the Trinity Alps. Just study the map, and rest assured that no matter where you go, you're not likely to have company.

9 EAST FORK NEW RIVER LOOP

This rugged route dips into the canyons of the remote Green Trinities, where you'll find solitude and quiet riverside camps. Note: Wildfires in 2006, 2008, and 2020 severely burned parts of this area; check with rangers for current conditions before heading out.

Start: East Fork New River Trailhead
Type of hike: Backpack; lollipop
Distance: 19.8 miles
Hiking time: About 2–4 days
Difficulty: Moderate
Elevation gain: 3,900 feet
Best season: Summer through early fall
Canine compatibility: Yes
Nearest town: Willow Creek
Fees and permits: Free wilderness permit required for overnight visitors; free campfire permits required for fires and camp stoves

Schedule: Trails in the Trinity Alps are always open; however, most trailhead access roads are closed or impassable during winter.
Maps: USGS Cecil Lake and Dees Peak; USDAFS Trinity Alps Wilderness
Trail contact: Weaverville Ranger Station: (530) 623-2121; www.fs.usda .gov/stnf
Parking and trailhead facilities: Ample parking, a horse corral, and an outhouse. Nearest developed campground is at Denny.

FINDING THE TRAILHEAD

From Hawkins Bar (on CA 299, 10 miles east of Willow Creek), drive north on Denny Road (CR 402). Continue for 20 miles, past a forest service campground and the small settlement of Denny. It's slow going on the twisting, winding road. Four miles past Denny, cross New River and proceed on unpaved FR 7N01 (stay left at a signed fork). The trailhead is at the end of the road, 7.5 miles from the Denny campground. GPS: N40 58.795' / W123 19.062'

THE HIKE

The East Fork New River is a smaller version of the New River drainage: a deep and shady canyon, dotted with oak, maple, and madrone at the lower elevations, leading up to a rugged, untraveled pine- and fir-forested wilderness at the higher end. It's a fine sampling of the "Green Trinities," the western part of the Trinity Alps known for its thick-forested mountains (notwithstanding recent wildfire activity), wild river canyons, and solitude. As along New River, you come across a few old mining relics along the East Fork (though not nearly as many). Numerous connections to a maze of little-used trails make it easy to disappear for a couple of weeks if that's your desire. You won't find the spectacular lakes and peaks of the eastern Trinity Alps here. What you will find is wilderness with a capital W, where you're more likely to come across a bear than another backpacker. Most two-legged visitors are hunters who come here in the fall and a few modern-day prospectors who work active mining claims. **Note:** This area was burned by several wildfires over the last two decades. The 2020 Red Salmon Fire came right up to the edge of this hike but spared most of the route. Check current conditions before heading out.

Much of this hike is below 4,000 feet. The low elevation means there are three things you should be aware of: hot weather in midsummer, poison oak, and rattlesnakes. The

A bridge crosses the East Fork New River at the start of this hike.

first can be avoided by planning an early- or late-season trip; the second and third are best avoided by knowing what they look like and staying alert. Despite the lack of lakes, water is plentiful along the route. Creeks and streams are sparkling clear, with refreshing swimming holes and year-round flows.

From the trailhead the East Fork New River Trail (12W08) descends to a solid wood-and-steel bridge, where you cross the East Fork New River and switchback up the canyon wall before heading northeast along the river. The gentle ascent meanders along the north bank for 2 miles, winding under shady stands of deciduous trees and alternating between water-side hiking and climbing the canyon wall above the river. Swimming holes appear regularly along the course of the hike, and you're never far from water. In early summer the first section of this hike can be like walking through a green leafy tunnel; in the fall you walk on a carpet of red and gold. Here and in numerous other places along this hike, you see mine tailings and other remnants of mining activity.

At 2.5 miles from the trailhead, arrive at a trail junction on a level bench near the confluence of East Fork New River and Pony Creek (the sign may be on the ground). The Pony Creek Trail (12W07) veers left (north); the East Fork Trail continues straight (east) along the canyon bottom. It's 2.3 miles up Pony Creek to Lake City if that's where you're headed. To do this route in the recommended direction, stay right and follow the East Fork Trail. You return to this point via the Pony Creek Trail and Lake City (don't be confused by the name; Lake City is a historic site).

Just after the junction, cross the East Fork on a wood-and-steel bridge and then continue up the drainage on the south bank. Ignore the unmarked paths that meander along the riverbank; they're left over from old mining activity. In 0.5 mile pass the signed junction with the Semore Gulch Trail (8E08) on the right. Stay left and descend to the East Fork, where for the first time you need to cross it without benefit of a bridge. The crossing should pose no problem at normal water levels, but beware when runoff is high in the early season.

Back on the north bank, climb an open, brushy slope and continue upstream. The canyon becomes rocky and narrow through here, with a deep swimming hole tucked into a bend in the river. The trail climbs moderately through the forested canyon, crossing the East Fork twice more in quick succession near the confluence with the South Fork of the East Fork New River, then crossing it one last time just below the confluence with Cabin Creek. The trail leaves the East Fork and follows Cabin Creek for about 1 mile. Just before starting the climb out of the Cabin Creek drainage, cross and recross the creek, then head uphill to the north.

On the short but steep ascent—the first real climb of the hike—you break out of the forest and pass through a rocky, open clearing with the first good view of your surroundings. To the south is the imposing hulk of 6,870-foot Cabin Peak. Once on top of Blue Ridge, 7.7 miles from the trailhead, you have an unobstructed vista of the East Fork drainage, as well as the sea of forested ridgelines that make up the Green Trinities.

On the crest of Blue Ridge is the Mullane Corral Trail junction (12W04). The East Fork Trail goes right (east) here, running along the ridgetop to Green Mountain Trail (12W09) on the crest of Limestone Ridge. (The route is also known as the New River Divide Trail because this ridge separates the New River drainage from that of the North Fork Trinity River.) Rattlesnake Lake is 2 miles away from the junction on Limestone Ridge. The "lake" is really not much more than a mud puddle, so only hang a right here for one of two reasons: (1) You want to camp at Rattlesnake Camp (where a spring offers the only water in the vicinity) and watch the sunset over the New River drainage; or (2) you want to extend this hike by following the Green Mountain Trail north to the Salmon Summit Trail, picking up the Mullane Corral Trail for the return (adds about 12 miles). You also may want to allow time to scramble up the easy summit of nearby Cabin Peak (with a view so good it used to host a fire lookout).

Staying left (north) at the junction, follow the Mullane Corral Trail down the north side of Blue Ridge, which the trail descends as abruptly as it climbed the south side. The trail up and over the ridge is not always obvious, but the route is generally marked with rock ducks and blazes. Keep your map handy and you shouldn't have a problem.

A 1,200-foot descent brings you quickly to the East Fork again, where you cross the stream and climb the ridge between East Fork and Pony Creek. After 2 miles of moderate climbing with plenty of great views, arrive at the signed junction with the Pony Creek Trail. This junction affords another opportunity for side trips to Pony Lake (a little pond, difficult to reach because there's no trail) or the historic sites of Mullane Corral and Election Camp.

Election Camp, just a couple of miles north of the junction, has an interesting story behind it. After a fire burned nearby Lake City to the ground, the displaced miners had nowhere to vote in the upcoming 1864 presidential election. According to local lore, miners wanted to cast their votes for President Lincoln, so they arranged to have the election in the forest at a major trail junction. A hollow cedar tree was used for a ballot box, and upwards of 300 miners participated in the election.

To complete the East Fork loop, turn left (southwest) onto Pony Creek Trail and contour through mixed forest dominated by mature fir and incense cedar. The trail follows

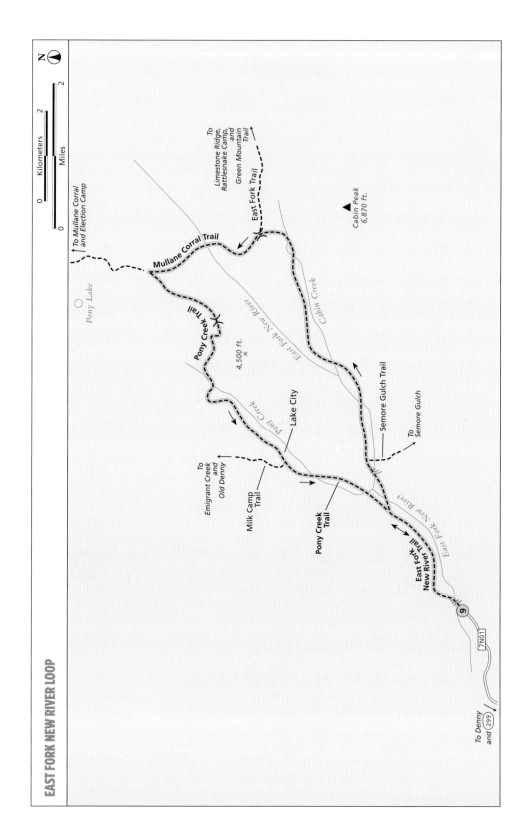

To Mullane Corral and Election Camp

Pony Lake

Mullane Corral Trail

To Limestone Ridge, Rattlesnake Camp, and Green Mountain Trail

East Fork Trail

Pony Creek Trail

East Fork New River

4,500 ft.

Cabin Peak 6,870 ft.

Cabin Creek

Lake City

Pony Creek

Semore Gulch Trail

To Semore Gulch

To Emigrant Creek and Old Denny

Milk Camp Trail

Pony Creek Trail

East Fork New River Trail

East Fork New River

7N01

To Denny and 299

N

Kilometers
0   2

Miles
0   2

a mostly level contour around the point of the ridge, serving up more great views along the open, rocky crest before finally plunging over the side and dropping down to Pony Creek. The path is easy to follow as you return to the land of oaks and maples.

At Pony Creek, hop across the water and follow the trail downhill along the stream. An easy 1.8-mile descent leads downstream, past more swimming holes and mining relics, plus a cabin of more recent vintage used by owners of a current mining claim. Lake City, a mining settlement founded in the 1850s, is in a clearing high above Pony Creek, just before the Milk Camp Trail junction. There's not much left here, but you can still see an old sign on a tree that identifies the site. As many as 1,500 miners lived here in the early 1860s. The town was never rebuilt after its destruction in 1863.

On the west side of the clearing, the Milk Camp Trail (8E16) turns north and heads uphill (eventually connecting with Slide Creek in the New River drainage). Go left (south) at the signed junction to stay on the Pony Creek Trail. Continue an easy 2.2 miles downhill (with one climb over a spur ridge), crossing the creek two times, to the junction with the East Fork Trail. Retrace the first 2.5 miles back to the trailhead.

MILES AND DIRECTIONS

0.0 Start at the East Fork New River Trailhead.

0.4 Cross a footbridge over the East Fork New River.

2.5 At the Pony Creek Trail junction, stay right on the East Fork Trail.

3.2 Stay left at the Semore Gulch Trail junction, continuing on the East Fork Trail.

7.7 Turn left onto the Mullane Corral Trail.

10.2 Turn left onto the Pony Creek Trail.

15.0 Arrive at historic Lake City, an old, long-abandoned mining camp.

15.1 Stay left at the Milk Camp Trail junction.

17.3 Turn right onto the East Fork Trail and retrace your route to the trailhead.

19.8 Arrive back at the trailhead.

OPTIONS

Numerous connecting trails along this route offer extended trips into the rugged drainages of the Green Trinities. For a scenic loop that runs along the spine of Limestone Ridge, follow the Green Mountain Trail to Salmon Summit Trail, and then return via the Mullane Corral Trail.

HIKES FROM CALIFORNIA HIGHWAY 3

Get this view of Sapphire Lake on an off-trail scramble to Mirror Lake (Hike 11).

10 RUSH CREEK LAKES (KINNEY CAMP) TRAIL

This tough ridgeline hike is one of two ways to Rush Creek Lakes. It's not as scenic as the off-trail trek, and it's longer and often overgrown, but it requires no tricky scrambling or complicated navigation.

(See map on page 33.)
Start: Rush Creek Lakes Trailhead
Type of hike: Backpack; out-and-back
Distance: 14.4 miles
Hiking time: About 2–4 days
Difficulty: Strenuous
Elevation gain: 3,500 feet
Best season: Midsummer through early fall
Canine compatibility: Yes
Nearest town: Weaverville
Fees and permits: Free wilderness permit required for overnight visitors; free campfire permits required for fires and camp stoves

Schedule: Trails in the Trinity Alps are always open; however, most trailhead access roads are closed or impassable during winter.
Maps: USGS Rush Creek Lakes; USDAFS Trinity Alps Wilderness
Trail contact: Weaverville Ranger Station: (530) 623-2121; www.fs.usda.gov/stnf
Parking and trailhead facilities: Limited parking for up to 6 cars. The closest developed campground is Rush Creek, just 2.5 miles south on CA 3.

FINDING THE TRAILHEAD

From Weaverville drive 10 miles north on CA 3 to the signed turn for the Rush Creek Lakes Trail. Turn left (west) onto FR 34N74 and proceed 2 miles to the trailhead. GPS: N40 50.163' / W122 53.962'

THE HIKE

The Rush Creek Lakes (there are four, plus assorted ponds) are close to Weaverville as the bird flies, but birds are about all you'll find here on most days. Maybe people just don't believe the kind of spectacular scenery found in Rush Creek Lakes' craggy cirque could be so close to town. This is the on-trail route to Rush Creek Lakes. The other route is 3 miles shorter but requires a steep off-trail scramble that some hikers may prefer to avoid. If you want to visit this beautiful chain of lakes but would like to hike on a trail (albeit extremely overgrown in places), use the Rush Creek Lakes Trail (10W10), sometimes called the Kinney Camp Trail. This route has its own drawbacks, but steep scrambling is not among them. The Rush Creek Lakes Trail has a poor reputation because it follows a ridgeline instead of a drainage bottom. It's hot in the summer, waterless, exposed, and generally held in low regard by rangers and hikers alike (though there are some good views). There is also abundant poison oak along the first 2 miles. Wear long pants for hacking through the brush.

On the plus side, the trail deposits you safely in the Rush Creek Lakes basin without the elevator-like descent of the off-trail route. And you'll probably have the path all to yourself. Just carry plenty of water.

Climb the ridge above Rush Creek Lakes for a bird's-eye view of the basin.

From the trailhead the path winds uphill through mixed forest that at least provides some welcome shade. Ascending higher, the trail heads northwest, climbing the spine of a ridge and eventually bending around to the west. It's a straightforward ascent most of the way, though because of low use, the trail is not high on the forest service's list of maintenance priorities. Trail reports in 2019 and 2020 said the trail was particularly overgrown in the last mile.

To add insult to injury, the trail dips down several hundred feet and climbs back up again just before arriving at the basin. Reach Lower Rush Creek Lake at 6.5 miles.

If you still have the energy, make your way another 0.7 mile to the uppermost lake in the chain, where you'll find the best swimming and coldest water. The maintained trail ends at the first lake; use caution negotiating the rocky terrain between the lakes.

MILES AND DIRECTIONS

0.0   Start at the Rush Creek Lakes Trailhead.

6.5   Reach the lowermost Rush Creek Lake.

7.2   Make your way off-trail to the uppermost Rush Creek Lake. Return the way you came.

14.4 Arrive back at the trailhead.

OPTIONS

Monument Peak is within reach, but you'll have to ascend the steep gully used in the off-trail route (Hike 7). If the summit is your real goal, approach it from the East Weaver Lake Trailhead.

11 STUART FORK TO EMERALD AND SAPPHIRE LAKES

Together with Canyon Creek and Caribou Lakes, Stuart Fork forms the Holy Trinity of the Trinity Alps' most spectacular drainages. Emerald and Sapphire Lakes, at the head of the canyon, are the crown jewels of the wilderness. Not surprisingly, this is a popular destination.

Start: Stuart Fork Trailhead
Type of hike: Backpack; out-and-back
Distance: 29.0 miles
Hiking time: About 4–8 days
Difficulty: Moderate (strenuous for last optional off-trail mile to Mirror Lake)
Elevation gain: 3,300 feet
Best season: Midsummer through early fall
Canine compatibility: Yes
Nearest town: Weaverville
Fees and permits: Free wilderness permit required for overnight visitors; free campfire permits required for fires and camp stoves

Schedule: Trails in the Trinity Alps are always open; however, most trailhead access roads are closed or impassable during winter.
Maps: USGS Siligo Peak, Mount Hilton, Caribou Lake, and Rush Creek Lakes; USDAFS Trinity Alps Wilderness
Trail contact: Weaverville Ranger Station: (530) 623-2121; www.fs.usda.gov/stnf
Special considerations: No campfires are allowed at any of the lakes in the Stuart Fork drainage.
Parking and trailhead facilities: Parking only; camping, toilets, and water are available at the adjacent Bridge Camp Campground.

FINDING THE TRAILHEAD

From Weaverville drive 13 miles north on CA 3 to Trinity Alps Road (FR 35N33Y). Turn left (west) just beyond a highway bridge and proceed 3.5 miles to the trailhead (the last mile is unpaved but easily passable to passenger cars). The road passes through Trinity Alps Resort, a collection of private cabins on the banks of Stuart Fork. The road dead-ends at the trailhead, 100 yards after passing Bridge Camp Campground. GPS: N40 52.975' / W122 55.540'

THE HIKE

Stuart Fork Trail is like a highway into the heart of the Trinity Alps; it leads swiftly and smoothly into the inner sanctum of the wilderness. The trail seems to whisk you right up the drainage, through oaks and maples, into mixed conifers, past peaceful meadows, and finally to the treeless granite splendor of the Stuart Fork headwaters, tucked into a deep, glacier-carved gap in the wild terrain between Thompson Peak, Sawtooth Mountain, and Sawtooth Ridge. All the while you follow the spectacular course of Stuart Fork, one of the largest rivers in the Trinity Alps proper.

Expect plenty of company in summer. You'll know what to expect by the number of cars at the trailhead, so if what you see gives you pause, consider relocating to a less popular trail. (Though not as busy in the fall, hunting season brings extra visitors since Stuart Fork is a popular destination among deer hunters.) Also like Canyon Creek and Caribou Lakes, there's a good reason people flock here. And with plenty of dispersed campsites

Emerald Lake is the first lake you encounter at the head of Stuart Fork.

between Morris Meadow and Portuguese Camp, the drainage can absorb a lot of visitors. (Avoid camping at Emerald and Sapphire Lakes, which have only poor, fragile sites and very little room.) From a base camp in Morris Meadow, you can make any number of day hikes into the surrounding wilderness.

The path starts out wide and level, following an old dirt road to the wilderness boundary at Cherry Flat. This first mile crosses private property—well marked, with white "Trail" signs indicating the way at all junctions. The road ends after the wilderness boundary, and you start climbing moderately on the well-trodden trail, paralleling Stuart Fork as you head northwest. The river remains below as you travel up the east bank, but water is readily available in tributaries like Salt, Little Deep, and Deep Creeks and others, all the way up. (Be sure to treat all water.)

After ascending a moderate grade, return to river level and enjoy easy walking on a path shaded by fir, incense cedar, maples, dogwoods, and both sugar and ponderosa pines. If you got a late start (coming or going), there are many fine riverside campsites on the east bank of Stuart Fork between here and Oak Flat, an oak-and conifer-forested bench 4.5 miles from the trailhead. Just before Oak Flat the trail dips down to cross Deep Creek on a footbridge. An inviting swimming hole awaits at the base of a waterfall here, but swim at your own risk—the current can be swift, and the rocks downstream are treacherous. Pause for a moment on the bridge and gaze up Deep Creek. If you tire of the human company in Stuart Fork and want to be truly alone for a while, bushwhack your way up Deep Creek; you won't see another soul until you arrive at Siligo Meadows, several steep and trail-less miles away. Good luck.

Reach the signed junction for Alpine Lake 5 miles from the trailhead. A left turn here leads to the beginning of the Bear Creek Trail, which connects the Stuart Fork drainage to the Canyon Creek Trailhead, and Alpine Lake via the Alpine Lake Trail. Alpine Lake

Mirror Lake lies at the very top of the Stuart Fork drainage.

(or just before it, to be accurate) is the most popular jumping-off point for the off-trail route to Smith and Morris Lakes. The Bear Creek Trail is across the river, and fording Stuart Fork at high water should not be taken lightly. Use good judgment at all creek crossings.

To continue up Stuart Fork, stay right (north) at the junction. Walking up a gentle grade, look for signs of Buckeye and La Grange Ditches, which carried water from this drainage to mining operations miles away. The trail follows the historic Buckeye Ditch in some places, and you can see the last vestiges of the once-lengthy flume. The Buckeye Ditch, which carried water to a mining operation some 40 miles away, was reputed to be one of the longest such flumes ever constructed. During the miners' heyday, a wagon road led all the way up Stuart Fork.

The path proceeds moderately for the next several miles, climbing a few switchbacks in and out of tributaries when necessary but generally maintaining the gentle grade Stuart Fork is known for. Salt Creek is the next major tributary. Look for a few pieces of weathered, long-abandoned lumber on the forested hillside after Salt Creek. Next comes Deer Creek, just over 7 miles from the trailhead. Cross Deer Creek on a solid steel bridge. There's a refreshing swimming hole here if it's a hot day. Return to the ledge above Stuart Fork after climbing out of the Deer Creek drainage and bend farther east, out of sight of the river.

Arrive at the Deer Creek Trail junction 8 miles from the trailhead. This trail (9W17A) climbs east up the Deer Creek drainage to a beautiful, secluded canyon with a good chance for solitude (before it reaches the popular Four Lakes Loop). You can also access the northern spur of the Deer Creek Trail (9W17) at another junction in Morris Meadow, a short distance ahead.

Soon after the Deer Creek junction, you start seeing the beginnings of Morris Meadow; then, just after the northern spur of the Deer Creek Trail, you enter the lower end of Morris Meadow proper (about 9 miles from the trailhead). The idyllic meadow fans out in green splendor from here, serving up one of the best late-summer wildflower displays in the Trinity Alps. Yarrow, Indian paintbrush, lupine, and lush grasses grow in profusion throughout the wide valley. Campsites are liberally sprinkled in the forested fringes. A little island of pine and cedar sits at the head of the meadow where you come in, and the historic Morris Meadow horse camp lies on the western edge of the clearing. Water may be available in meadow streams, or you may have to trek over to Stuart Fork, which is hidden in dense trees on the west side of the valley.

Be wary of rattlesnakes, which are notoriously plentiful in the area (I seem to see one on every trip). It's likely that too many campers dropping crumbs have increased the local rodent population, which in turn has drawn the snakes. Ditto the local bears, which come to munch on unprotected food everywhere from Bridge Camp at the trailhead to Sapphire Lake. On one memorable afternoon trail run along Stuart Fork, I nearly ran head-long into a bear, which also was lumbering along at a good clip. Our paths were about to intersect when we saw each other, put on the brakes, and narrowly avoided disaster.

Ambitious bushwhackers who want to use Bear Gulch to reach Smith Lake should start their trek here. A number of use trails meander north through Morris Meadow to the upper end, where the main trail picks up again near an impressive double-trunked ponderosa pine. Enter the forest proper and pass another pile of historic lumber on the left, as well as more campsites and good access to the river. The trail winds up the drainage, passing through shady forest, brushy slopes, and lush glens of ferns and wildflowers.

As the canyon starts bending from north to west, bigger and bigger views of the granite peaks and ridges hanging over the headwaters start to open up. Alder, maple, and wildflowers of several persuasions turn some parts of the trail into a green jungle

Get this view of Sapphire Lake on an off-trail scramble to Mirror Lake.

Stuart Fork leads straight into the heart of the wilderness.

in midsummer. Portuguese Camp, a historic Stuart Fork camp that offers the last good site to pitch a tent before the lakes, is located just before the junction with the Caribou Scramble.

At the signed junction with the Caribou Scramble, at a rocky intersection 12.1 miles from the trailhead, stop and contemplate the route up to Sawtooth Ridge. You better have a good idea of what lies above before you set out for the saddle between Stuart Fork and Caribou Lakes. Some one hundred switchbacks and 2,500 feet of elevation gain are

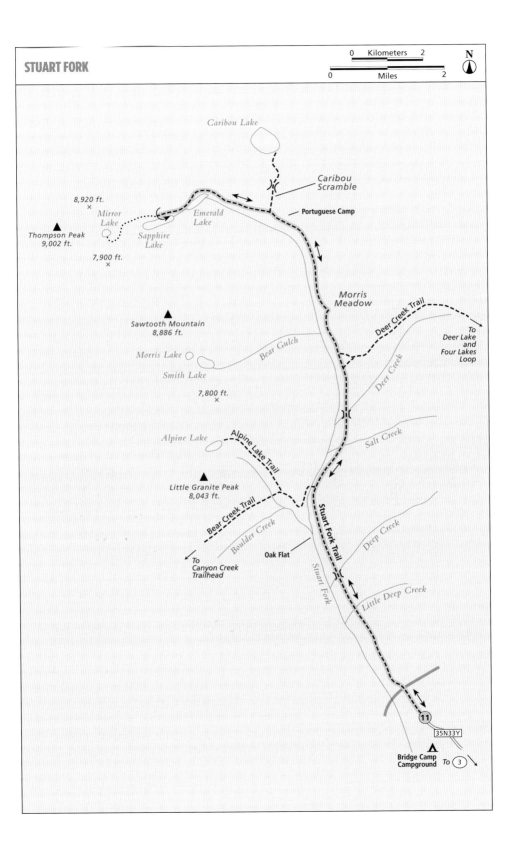

Caribou Lake

Caribou Scramble

Portuguese Camp

8,920 ft. ×

Mirror Lake

Emerald Lake

Thompson Peak 9,002 ft.

Sapphire Lake

7,900 ft. ×

Morris Meadow

Deer Creek Trail

To Deer Lake and Four Lakes Loop

Sawtooth Mountain 8,886 ft.

Bear Gulch

Morris Lake

Deer Creek

Smith Lake

7,800 ft. ×

Salt Creek

Alpine Lake

Alpine Lake Trail

Little Granite Peak 8,043 ft.

Bear Creek Trail

Stuart Fork Trail

Boulder Creek

Deep Creek

To Canyon Creek Trailhead

Oak Flat

Stuart Fork

Little Deep Creek

11

35N33Y

Bridge Camp Campground

To 3

0   Kilometers   2

0   Miles   2

N

Storm clouds gather over Emerald and Sapphire Lakes.

packed into the shadeless, waterless route above. The view from up there is spectacular; just start early and carry plenty of water if you decide to do it.

After the Caribou junction the Stuart Fork Trail continues to bend west and starts climbing more steeply toward the head of the canyon, now plainly visible through breaks in the trees. The last mile is steep and rocky and offers little shade. A crystal-clear spring flows across the trail and helps take the bite out of the climb. On the way up this last haul, you can glimpse to your left (south) the deep gorge cut in the rocky canyon by the Stuart Fork headwaters emerging from the lip of Emerald Lake. Save time to explore the waterfalls and pools down there before leaving. The trail gains the top of Emerald's granite dike at the lake's northeast corner, passing through a sparse stand of firs and an overused campsite before winding over the last few boulders and arriving at water's edge 14 miles from the trailhead.

Twenty-one-acre Emerald Lake lives up to the promise of its name: cold, clear water; granite piled on granite; and the mass of Sawtooth Mountain's northern shoulder towering overhead. Remnants of the dam built by miners are still visible along Emerald's eastern shore. There are two campsites at Emerald Lake, but they're both small and overused and don't offer much privacy. It's much better to camp below the lake and visit on a day hike. Also, remember that fires are prohibited in the lake basin.

To reach Sapphire Lake, make your way around Emerald's north shore on a rough trail marked by cairns. After passing through a stand of trees above the lake's northeast corner, cross the boulder piles where a trail has been literally blasted into the rock. The granite-lined path switchbacks steeply up the north side of Sapphire's outlet (the lake is 600 feet higher than Emerald). On the way, look for rusty remains of the heavy equipment laboriously dragged in here a century ago, as well as still-solid remnants of the dam at Sapphire Lake's eastern edge.

The 43-acre lake is sunk into a narrow east–west trough in the canyon, with stunning views at both ends and jumbled piles of blindingly white granite around the shoreline. Caesar Peak looms over the western edge of the cirque, where Mirror Lake lies concealed in a hidden basin, and Sawtooth Ridge dominates the eastern vista, where Stuart Fork drainage falls away precipitously. The visible evidence left behind by the glacier that carved out this basin is impressive enough, but just as astounding is what you can't see, in the depths below Sapphire's surface. The blue water is 200 feet deep, which makes it the deepest lake in the Trinity Alps. The camping situation is similar to Emerald: very limited, and really not the best choice given the area's high use in summer.

MILES AND DIRECTIONS

- 0.0   Start at the Stuart Fork Trailhead.
- 4.1   Cross Deep Creek.
- 4.5   Pass late-start campsites at Oak Flat.
- 5.0   Stay right at the Bear Creek Trail junction.
- 8.0   Stay left at the Deer Creek Trail junction.
- 8.8   Arrive at sprawling Morris Meadow, with many good campsites.
- 11.9 Reach Portuguese Camp, another good base camp before the trail climbs to the lakes in the upper drainage.

12.1   Stay left at the junction with the Caribou Scramble.

14.0   Reach Emerald Lake.

14.5   Reach Sapphire Lake. Return the way you came.

29.0   Arrive back at the trailhead.

OPTIONS

Stuart Fork drains the heart of the Trinity Alps and has arteries connecting with a number of the area's other drainages. Alpine Lake, Caribou Lakes, and Deer Creek are all easily reached via trails. A long loop back to the Stuart Fork Trailhead can be made by linking the Deer Creek, Stonewall Pass, and Weber Flat Trails (requires several miles of walking on roads at the end). Experienced hikers will find off-trail routes to Canyon Creek Lakes, Smith Lake, and Grizzly Lake.

Off-trail to Mirror Lake: No maintained trail leads to little Mirror Lake, in a secluded cirque at the upper end of the Stuart Fork canyon, 1 mile farther and 500 feet higher than Sapphire Lake. Mirror Lake sits atop a steep formation of vertical cliffs and narrow gullies. The difficult, off-trail approach keeps at bay most of the visitors who come as far as Emerald and Sapphire Lakes.

Start the route to Mirror by traversing the south shore of Sapphire, boulder hopping to the west end of the lake. From there, there are two ways to go. Aim for the 50-foot waterfall on the north side of the basin if you prefer the short and steep route. Pass just beneath the falls and continue around to the southwest, where you can scramble up the ledges to a chimney that allows passage (barely) to the top. This is by no means the best way, just the shortest.

The safer and slightly longer route simply follows the talus field up the south side of the basin toward a permanent snowfield and then up to the lake. At the west end of Sapphire, stay low and pick your way across the drainage to the talus-filled gully, then boulder-hop the rest of the way up to Mirror Lake's lonely cirque.

Mirror Lake is aptly named. Gaze at its smooth waters on a calm, still evening and you will find one of the most perfect reflections in the Trinity Alps. Numerous peaks clutter the nearby skyline, and Mirror Lake manages to gather them all in. The lake has a few stunted foxtail pines and hemlocks, but it's mostly bare rock and water, with several granite islands breaking the surface of the clear, shallow lake. There are no established campsites.

12 DEER CREEK TRAIL

Use this connecting trail between Stuart Fork and the Four Lakes Loop to create a longer route or just add a slice of solitude to any trek. This backcountry trail is accessible only by foot.

Start: Deer Creek Trail junction, 8.0 miles from the Stuart Fork Trailhead
Type of hike: Hike-in backcountry connecting trail; one-way
Distance: 5.5 miles
Hiking time: About 3–5 hours
Difficulty: Moderate
Elevation gain: 1,800 feet
Best season: Midsummer through early fall
Canine compatibility: Yes
Nearest town: Weaverville
Fees and permits: Free wilderness permit required for overnight visitors; free campfire permits required for fires and camp stoves

Schedule: Trails in the Trinity Alps are always open; however, most trailhead access roads are closed or impassable during winter.
Maps: USGS Siligo Peak; USDAFS Trinity Alps Wilderness
Trail contact: Weaverville Ranger Station: (530) 623-2121; www.fs.usda .gov/stnf
Parking and trailhead facilities: None, this backcountry trail is only accessible by foot. If you approach from Stuart Fork Trailhead, camping, toilets, and water are available at the adjacent Bridge Camp Campground.

FINDING THE TRAILHEAD

 The Deer Creek Trail runs between mile 8 on the Stuart Fork Trail and the Four Lakes Loop at the head of Deer Creek drainage. Start at either end. The description here is from Morris Meadow. GPS: N40 57.839' / W122 56.944' (first junction in Morris Meadow). See Hikes 11, 17, and 21 for the best routes to reach Deer Creek.

THE HIKE

The Deer Creek Trail links Stuart Fork to the Four Lakes Loop. It can also be used to create a number of routes that start and end at the Long Canyon, Swift Creek, and Big Flat Trailheads. This description starts in Morris Meadow on the Stuart Fork Trail.

Approaching from the south, you reach the first of two trail junctions for the Deer Creek Trail (9W17) 8 miles from the Stuart Fork Trailhead. The next junction is just before the lower end of Morris Meadow. Turn right (east) here and begin a steep climb over the ridge that separates the Stuart Fork and Deer Creek drainages. A series of switchbacks leads up the slope; then you crest the ridgeline and start a much more moderate ascent along the course of Deer Creek. Forest cover is a shady mixture of mature ponderosa and sugar pines, Douglas fir, and incense cedar.

Three miles from Morris Meadow, reach Willow Creek and the junction with the Tri-Forest Peak Trail. This little-used path leads up to a pass at the base of Tri-Forest Peak and then on to Big Flat Trailhead, 8 miles away. The pass affords easy access to spectacular views along Sawtooth Ridge and makes a good day hike if you base camp along Deer Creek.

Continuing along the Deer Creek Trail, a very pleasant 1.5 miles of streamside hiking brings you to Deer Creek Camp. Look for beautiful gardens of leopard lilies and other

Use Deer Creek Trail to access a quiet, forested corner of the wilderness.

wildflowers that grow in little riots of color along the creek. The path crosses Deer Creek twice in quick succession just before arriving at historic Deer Creek Camp, a series of old hunting and cow camps spread out along the north bank of the creek. The cows are long gone, but the area is still a popular base camp for hunters and horsepackers.

The junction with the Black Basin Trail (9W12) is located on a rocky flat near the beginning of an open meadow at the southeastern end of Deer Creek Camp. The little-used Black Basin Trail leads uphill and connects with two paths that cross the divide between Deer Creek and Swift Creek drainages. Anyone looking for solitude will find it up there.

The Deer Creek Trail continues southeast from the junction, skirting the edge of the first of a series of beautiful meadows leading up to the head of the canyon. The open valley affords great views of Seven Up and Siligo Peaks at the head of the drainage. A few hundred yards from the junction, the trail crosses the creek for the last time and ascends a moderately rising slope past more wildflowers and great views up and down the valley.

The final mile brings you to a spectacular meadow sprawling across the entire breadth of the valley. Little Round Lake (not named on some maps) sits in the southwest corner of the meadow. From here you have three trail junctions from which to choose. Two junctions are for the Four Lakes Loop, which continues up to Deer Lake or Luella Lake and circles Siligo Peak. The first fork, 0.3 mile before you reach the upper meadow, is an unmarked junction with a spur trail that forks right (southwest). This faint path is an old trail that connects with the Four Lakes Loop on the west side of the valley, on the way to Luella Lake. The second junction with the Four Lakes Loop is at the head of valley, where the steep ascent to Deer Lake starts. Just before the second intersection with the Four Lakes Loop, you arrive at the Granite Lake Trail, which heads east over Seven Up Pass to Granite Lake and eventually Swift Creek.

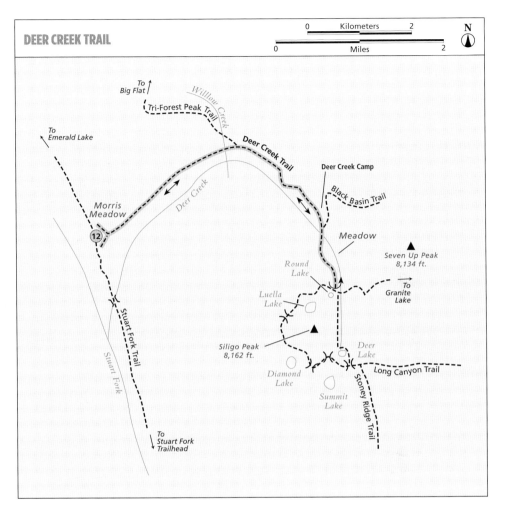

DEER CREEK TRAIL

MILES AND DIRECTIONS

0.0 Start at the Morris Meadow–Stuart Fork Trail.

3.0 Stay right at the Willow Creek Trail junction.

4.5 Arrive at Deer Creek Camp, a good place to base camp in the drainage.

4.6 Stay right at the Black Basin Trail junction.

5.5 Arrive at the Granite Lake Trail–Four Lakes Loop Trail junction.

OPTIONS

Use Deer Creek Trail to connect with the Four Lakes Loop and climb Siligo Peak. In the other direction, follow Deer Creek to Morris Meadow in the Stuart Fork drainage. From there you can access Emerald and Sapphire Lakes. To get farther off the beaten track, take the Black Basin Trail and explore the ridge between Deer Creek and Swift Creek. Or make a loop by hiking down Swift Creek and then returning to Deer Creek via Granite Lake.

13 ALPINE LAKE

Take this scenic detour off the popular Stuart Fork Trail to reach a lake that gets much less traffic than the star attractions farther up the main drainage. Brave an early-season crossing of Stuart Fork (carefully!) and you'll have Alpine Lake to yourself.

Start: Stuart Fork Trailhead
Type of hike: Backpack; out-and-back
Distance: 16.6 miles
Hiking time: About 2–4 days
Difficulty: Moderate
Elevation gain: 3,400 feet
Best season: Midsummer through early fall
Canine compatibility: Yes
Nearest town: Weaverville
Fees and permits: Free wilderness permit required for overnight visitors; free campfire permits required for fires and camp stoves

Schedule: Trails in the Trinity Alps are always open; however, most trailhead access roads are closed or impassable during winter.
Maps: USGS Siligo Peak; USDAFS Trinity Alps Wilderness
Trail contact: Weaverville Ranger Station: (530) 623-2121; www.fs.usda .gov/stnf
Parking and trailhead facilities: Ample parking. Camping, toilets, and potable water are available at the adjacent campground.

FINDING THE TRAILHEAD

From Weaverville drive 13 miles north on CA 3 to Trinity Alps Road (FR 35N33Y). Turn left (west) just after a highway bridge and proceed 3.5 miles to the trailhead (the last mile is unpaved but easily passable to passenger cars). The road passes through Trinity Alps Resort, a collection of private cabins on the banks of Stuart Fork. The road dead-ends at the trailhead, 100 yards after passing Bridge Camp Campground. GPS: N40 52.975' / W122 55.540'

THE HIKE

The trail to Alpine Lake has a split personality. First comes an easy, mostly level stroll along the shady banks of Stuart Fork; second, the route climbs sharply up dry, brush-choked, rocky slopes. The lake itself is not the least bit schizophrenic—just pure, tranquil mountain splendor. If you don't want to lug your pack up the final steep 3 miles, Alpine Lake makes a great day hike from a number of streamside camps along Stuart Fork. Most of the traffic on the Stuart Fork Trail is heading for Emerald and Sapphire Lakes, so making a detour to Alpine is often a good way to leave the crowds behind.

The path starts out wide and level, following an old dirt road to the wilderness boundary at Cherry Flat. This first mile crosses private property—well marked, with white "Trail" signs indicating the way at all junctions. The road ends after the wilderness boundary, and you start climbing moderately on the well-trodden trail, paralleling Stuart Fork as you head northwest. The river remains below as you travel up the east bank.

After ascending a moderate grade, return to river level and enjoy easy walking on a path shaded by fir, incense cedar, maples, dogwoods, and both sugar and ponderosa pines. If you got a late start (coming or going), there are many fine riverside campsites on the east bank of Stuart Fork between here and Oak Flat, an oak- and conifer-forested bench 4.5

Scramble up the ridge above Alpine Lake for this commanding view.

miles from the trailhead. Just before Oak Flat, the trail dips down to cross Deep Creek on a footbridge. An inviting swimming hole awaits at the base of a waterfall here, but swim at your own risk—the current can be swift, and the rocks downstream are treacherous.

At the signed junction for Alpine Lake (mile 5), turn left and proceed downhill to a crossing of Stuart Fork. This ford is the crucial factor in reaching Alpine Lake in early season (the current is typically too high and swift to cross before sometime after June, when runoff subsides). Use extreme caution. If the water is too high but you are nonetheless determined to reach Alpine Lake, you can bypass the ford by starting at the Canyon Creek Trailhead and using the Bear Creek Trail to reach the Alpine Lake Trail. This route is only 2 miles longer than starting at the Stuart Fork Trailhead, but it's much steeper—you have to cross the ridge between the Canyon Creek and Stuart Fork drainages—and rarely maintained. (Expect to negotiate your way under, over, and around downed trees. If you care about trail conditions, check with rangers before attempting the Bear Creek Trail, as it's not likely to be maintained.)

Once you're safely across Stuart Fork, the trail climbs away from the creek on an easy contour to the south; it then turns northwest just before reaching Boulder Creek and ascends more steeply. Just under 1 mile from Stuart Fork, arrive at a fork in a small clearing next to a large snag. Canyon Creek is straight (west) on the Bear Creek Trail; Alpine Lake lies to the right (north).

Turn right on the Alpine Lake Trail. It's only 2.6 miles from here to Alpine Lake, but the hike may seem quite a bit longer on a hot, sunny afternoon.

Climbing generally northwest through a mixed forest of oak and conifers, the trail follows the course of Alpine Lake's outlet creek to its source. Unfortunately, the path stays well east of the creek, keeping the refreshing stream at arm's length for most of the way. You have one opportunity to fill your water bottles when the trail nearly touches the creek in the first mile. Use it.

The final 1.5 miles climb steadily through manzanita and ceanothus. The rocky, brush-covered tread has a southern exposure, so you can expect the final push to be brutally hot

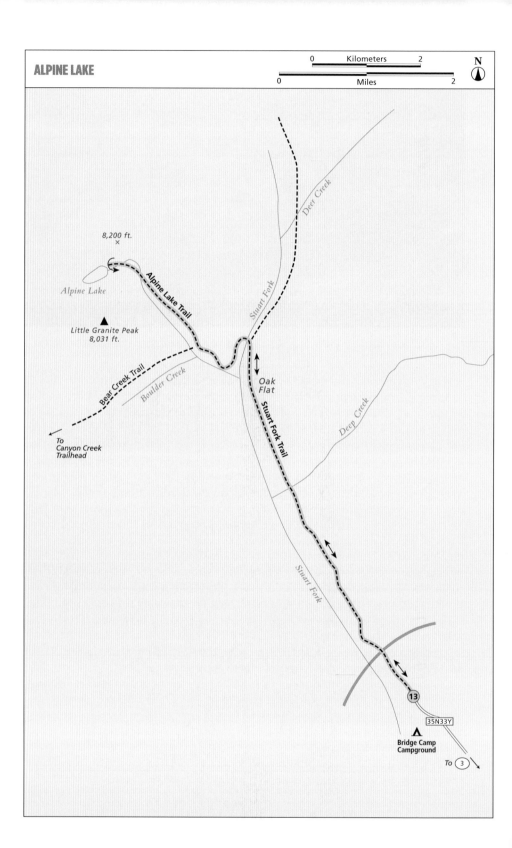

0   Kilometers   2

0   Miles   2

N

8,200 ft.
×

Alpine Lake

Alpine Lake Trail

▲ Little Granite Peak
8,031 ft.

Bear Creek Trail

Boulder Creek

Stuart Fork

Oak
Flat

Deer Creek

Deep Creek

To
Canyon Creek
Trailhead

Stuart Fork Trail

Stuart Fork

13

35N33Y

Ⓐ
Bridge Camp
Campground

To ③

Alpine Lake offers a quiet refuge close to busy Stuart Fork.

on a sunny summer afternoon. A quarter mile before reaching the lake, the trail crosses the outlet stream for the first time. The creek crossing is just upstream from a series of pretty cascades and tremendous views down the Stuart Fork drainage. Hikers looking for the off-trail route to Smith and Morris Lakes (Hike 14) should turn right (north) at the rock cairns just before the creek crossing.

The last few hundred yards of the trail traverse a series of open, rocky benches and grass-fringed ponds. Just before reaching the lake, look for a rock cairn that marks the last crossing of the outlet creek. (If you miss this last creek crossing, you'll soon run into a wall of steep boulders and head-high brush.) Once on the north side of the stream, follow an obvious path through a lush green meadow and arrive at the narrow, southeast end of the lake.

Alpine Lake sits in a narrow, steep-sided basin topped by a jumble of gray granite crags. Little Granite Peak (8,031 feet) is almost directly south of the lake. A sparse forest of stunted fir and weeping spruce grows on the southern side of the 14-acre lake, while rocks, wildflowers, and shoreline meadows dominate the northern side. There are a few poor campsites near the outlet and better sites at the far (southwest) end. Reach them by hiking along the north shore. Expect excellent fishing and swimming. Return the way you came.

MILES AND DIRECTIONS

0.0   Start at the Stuart Fork Trailhead.

4.1   Cross Deep Creek.

4.5   Continue past Oak Flat.

5.0   Turn left on the Bear Creek Trail and cross Stuart Fork.

5.7   Turn right on the Alpine Lake Trail.

8.3   Reach Alpine Lake. Return the way you came.

16.6 Arrive back at the trailhead.

OPTIONS

Experienced hikers can make their way off-trail to Smith and Morris Lakes, as well as Sawtooth Mountain.

14 SMITH AND MORRIS LAKES

This tough hike requires a steep off-trail climb, with both terrain and navigation challenges. The reward? One of the prettiest lakes in the wilderness—a deep-blue gem tucked under the soaring granite of Sawtooth Mountain.

Start: Stuart Fork Trailhead
Type of hike: Backpack; out-and-back or possible loop
Distance: 20.6 miles via Alpine Lake (recommended route)
Hiking time: About 4–7 days
Difficulty: Strenuous
Elevation gain: 5,100 feet
Best season: Midsummer through early fall
Canine compatibility: Yes, though the off-trail section can be rough and hot on paws.
Nearest town: Weaverville
Fees and permits: Free wilderness permit required for overnight

visitors; free campfire permits required for fires and camp stoves
Schedule: Trails in the Trinity Alps are always open; however, most trailhead access roads are closed or impassable during winter.
Maps: USGS Siligo Peak; USDAFS Trinity Alps Wilderness
Trail contact: Weaverville Ranger Station: (530) 623-2121; www.fs.usda .gov/stnf
Parking and trailhead facilities: Ample parking. Camping, toilets, and potable water are available at the adjacent campground.

FINDING THE TRAILHEAD

From Weaverville drive 13 miles north on CA 3 to Trinity Alps Road (FR 35N33Y). Turn left (west) just beyond a highway bridge and proceed 3.5 miles to the trailhead (the last mile is unpaved). The road passes through Trinity Alps Resort, a collection of private cabins on the banks of Stuart Fork. The road dead-ends at the trailhead, 100 yards after passing Bridge Camp Campground. GPS: N40 52.975' / W122 55.540'

THE HIKE

If there were a queen of the Trinity Alps, her throne would be somewhere in the vicinity of Smith Lake. Perched on a majestic bench below Sawtooth Mountain, in the granite heart of the Alps, the lake and its cirque have natural wonders like a queen has jewels: A misty waterfall pours over a cliff at the inlet; the sun rises over the awesome canyon of Stuart Fork; the jagged profile of Sawtooth towers overhead. Seat yourself on a slab of gray granite near the lake's outlet and you'll feel like royalty indeed.

The admission price? Dense brush and steep granite slopes surround Smith like a mountainous moat. No trail leads to the basin. Only hikers who are experienced with route finding and comfortable with off-trail travel should attempt this hike. Though not technical, some of the hiking gets quite steep.

ALPINE LAKE ROUTE

This is by far the most popular way to reach Smith Lake. You'll hike 8 miles on good trail to within spitting distance of Alpine Lake, then head cross-country to Smith. It's only 2.2 miles from the Alpine Lake Trail to Smith Lake, but most hikers take several hours

Smith Lake sits in a granite bowl beneath Sawtooth Mountain.

to complete the off-trail route. From the Stuart Fork Trailhead, the path starts out wide and level, following an old dirt road to the wilderness boundary at Cherry Flat. This first mile crosses private property—well marked, with white "Trail" signs indicating the way at all junctions. The road ends after the wilderness boundary, and you start climbing moderately on the well-trodden trail, paralleling Stuart Fork as you head northwest. The river remains below as you travel up the east bank.

After ascending a moderate grade, return to river level and enjoy easy walking on a path shaded by fir, incense cedar, maples, dogwoods, and both sugar and ponderosa pines. Just before Oak Flat the trail dips down to cross Deep Creek on a footbridge.

At the signed junction for Alpine Lake (mile 5), turn left and proceed downhill to a crossing of Stuart Fork. This ford is the crucial factor in reaching Alpine Lake in early season (the current is typically too high and swift to cross before sometime after June, when runoff subsides). Use extreme caution.

Once you're safely across Stuart Fork, the trail climbs away from the creek on an easy contour to the south; it then turns northwest just before reaching Boulder Creek and ascends more steeply. Just under 1 mile from Stuart Fork, arrive at a fork in a small clearing next to a large snag. Canyon Creek is straight (west) on the Bear Creek Trail; Alpine Lake lies to the right (north).

Turn right on the Alpine Lake Trail. It's only 2.6 miles from here to Alpine Lake.

Climbing generally northwest through a mixed forest of oak and conifers, the trail follows the course of Alpine Lake's outlet creek to its source. You have one opportunity to fill your water bottles when the trail nearly touches the creek in the first mile. Use it.

A quarter mile before reaching the lake, the trail crosses the outlet stream for the first time. The creek crossing is just upstream from a series of pretty cascades and tremendous views down the Stuart Fork drainage. The off-trail route to Smith and Morris Lakes starts here, 0.25 mile before Alpine Lake (just before the trail crosses the outlet creek).

Find little Morris Lake on a scramble above Smith Lake.

Head north, up the drainage. Cairns lead the way. Thick brush here used to make this the most difficult part of the route, but depending on recent traffic, you'll likely find a reasonably worn path leading through the bushes. (Look for bushes that have been trimmed with ratchet pruners. The end-cuts of the brush will show you the way.) Once through the brush, continue north up steep granite slabs and over the ridge; then make your way down and across an open cirque to the outlet of Smith Lake. This high, north-facing part of the route is often snow-covered until August. Be prepared.

CANYON CREEK ROUTE

The approach hike to this route is shorter and easier than the Alpine Lake route, but the final 2 miles are harder. Start at the Canyon Creek Trailhead and follow the Canyon Creek Trail north. The trail ascends gradually through shady, low-elevation vegetation of dogwood, maple, Douglas fir, and oak with a smattering of pine and cedar thrown in. Continue 2.5 miles to McKay Camp. A spur trail to the left (west) leads down to Canyon Creek and McKay Camp, a little island nestled between two clear arms of the creek. After McKay Camp, the trail climbs more steeply on a short series of switchbacks to reach a ledge high above Canyon Creek.

Ascending moderately along the granite-lined ledge, you first hear, then glimpse, the fabled Canyon Creek Falls. Continuing upstream from the falls, the trail meanders alongside the east bank of the now-peaceful creek. The trail runs mostly level to the base of Middle Canyon Creek Falls, about 5.5 miles from the trailhead (0.5 mile before reaching the junction with the Boulder Creek Lakes Trail junction). A use trail branches left (west) to the base of the falls, easily accessible through the open understory. To the right (east) is the beginning of the difficult off-trail route to Smith and Morris Lakes.

Your route lies up the big drainage to the east. Good luck with the brush guarding the entrance. After the initial bushwhack (bring plenty of bandages), it's a fairly straightforward scramble up the south side of the drainage and around the head of the canyon. (The

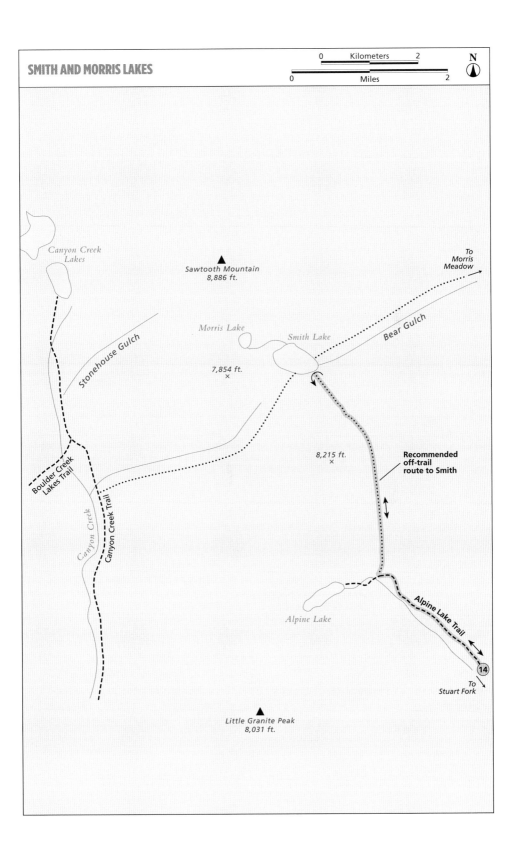

Kilometers

Miles

N

Canyon Creek
Lakes

Sawtooth Mountain
8,886 ft.

To
Morris
Meadow

Morris Lake

Smith Lake

Bear Gulch

Stonehouse Gulch

7,854 ft.
×

Boulder Creek
Lakes Trail

8,215 ft.
×

Recommended
off-trail
route to Smith

Canyon Creek

Canyon Creek Trail

Alpine Lake

Alpine Lake Trail

14

To
Stuart Fork

Little Granite Peak
8,031 ft.

The off-trail hike to Smith Lake crosses slopes of broken granite.

route never drops down to the gully at the bottom.) As an alternative, gluttons for steep stuff can continue up Canyon Creek another 1 mile to Stonehouse Gulch. This sheer gully leads to the ridge above Morris Lake, from where you can descend into the basin (for extremely experienced hikers only).

BEAR GULCH ROUTE

This route has the longest approach hike (12 miles), but in some ways it's the most elegant way to reach Smith: Just hike up its outlet creek. From Morris Meadow in Stuart Fork, battle your way through the brush to gain the granite slopes of Bear Gulch and then climb the north side of the creek. Watch for plentiful rattlesnakes in this area. I've never hiked this route and have heard only bad things about it. But some people like a challenge.

SMITH LAKE

Whichever way you choose to get here, allow plenty of time to enjoy this beautiful basin once you arrive. The steep-sided, 24-acre lake takes time to explore (just making your way around its shores requires some effort). On a hot day, try swimming to the base of the 50-foot waterfall cascading into the lake. There are a number of excellent campsites located along the benches above the lake to the southeast, as well as near the outlet.

Above Smith Lake lies tiny Morris Lake, a little gem of a pond hanging on a bench that feeds Smith Lake's inlet stream. Morris has stunning campsites as well. Above Morris Lake the granite soon gives way to sky. The ridgeline above Morris leads to the steep, craggy slopes of 8,886-foot Sawtooth Mountain.

A few stunted firs and mountain hemlocks grow in the basin, but mostly it's a world of rock and water. In late summer, wildflowers thrive in colorful little mini-gardens where seeps and soil combine to create the right environment. One of my most cherished memories of the Trinity Alps is an evening I spent next to one of these little gardens. My soon-to-be wife and I sat on a slab of granite and watched a bald eagle hunt for trout as the evening light turned the gray rocks red and orange.

MILES AND DIRECTIONS

- **0.0** Start at the Stuart Fork Trailhead.
- **4.5** Pass Oak Flat.
- **5.0** Continue on Bear Creek Trail.
- **5.7** Arrive at Alpine Lake Trail.
- **8.1** Take the off-trail route to Smith Lake.
- **9.1** Reach the saddle above Smith Lake.
- **10.3** Arrive at Smith Lake.
- **20.6** Arrive back at the trailhead.

OPTIONS

Ambitious hikers can make a loop by combining two of the routes described above.

15 STONEY RIDGE TRAIL

Want a trail all to yourself? This steep, dry path is your ticket. Basically, it's a backdoor route to beautiful Siligo Meadows and the Four Lakes Loop, which can also be reached by the more popular (and more scenic) Long Canyon Trail. But Stoney Ridge is worth knowing about for solitude seekers—and anyone who wants the most direct route to Echo Lake.

Start: Stoney Ridge Trailhead
Type of hike: Backpack; out-and-back
Distance: 17.0 miles
Hiking time: About 2–4 days
Difficulty: Strenuous
Elevation gain: 4,000 feet
Best season: Midsummer through early fall
Canine compatibility: Yes
Nearest town: Weaverville/Trinity Center
Fees and permits: Free wilderness permit required for overnight visitors; free campfire permits required for fires and camp stoves

Schedule: Trails in the Trinity Alps are always open; however, most trailhead access roads are closed or impassable during winter.
Maps: USGS Siligo Peak and Covington Mill; USDAFS Trinity Alps Wilderness
Trail contact: Weaverville Ranger Station: (530) 623-2121; www.fs.usda .gov/stnf
Special considerations: The access road is closed Oct 30 to May 1.
Parking and trailhead facilities: Ample room for parking but no facilities. The closest developed campground is at Stoney Point on CA 3.

FINDING THE TRAILHEAD

From Weaverville drive 15 miles north on CA 3 to the signed turnoff for the Stonewall Pass Trailhead. The dirt road is on the left (west), just past Trinity Alps Road and before the Stoney Creek swim area. Proceed 6 miles up the road (FR 35N72Y) to the trailhead. Stay right at 4.3 and 5.3 miles on the well-marked road. GPS: N40 52.950' / W122 52.520'

THE HIKE

From the trailhead the path climbs a seemingly endless staircase of switchbacks (about 6 miles) through mixed forest, brushy slopes, and high meadow. The moderate grade of the switchbacks eases the pain, but expect a hot, tough hike on a midsummer day.

So why use the Stoney Ridge Trail? Solitude, first and foremost. The route gets much less traffic than nearby Long Canyon. And because Echo Lake and Van Matre Meadows are the first things you encounter at the end of the hike, as opposed to the last if you're coming from Long Canyon, fewer people visit these areas. For peak baggers, there's also the added allure of three 8,000-foot summits within easy striking distance: Red Mountain (7,928 feet), Granite Peak (8,091 feet), and Middle Peak (8,095 feet).

The Stoney Ridge Trail (9W21) starts uphill and trends generally northwest up the flanks of Red Mountain. The mountain is named for the reddish peridotite rock of which it's composed. The mixed-conifer forest is similar to other areas of the Trinity Alps, but the red rock lends a remarkably different feel to Stoney Ridge.

Grab a seat at Echo Lake for a sweet sunset.

Past logging has left a relatively young and open forest of fir, incense cedar, and pine at the lower elevations. The trail is laid atop a soft cushion of duff. After 1 mile of gradual but steady ascent, the forest cover gets thicker and shadier and the trail gets noticeably steeper. Look for a seasonal creek decorated with dogwood, incense cedar, and fern near the wilderness boundary. The first dependable water source comes shortly after, at 2 miles. There isn't much water along the Stoney Ridge Trail, so fill up at one of these early streams if your bottle needs topping off.

A long contour east around the shoulder of the ridge reveals a fine view of Trinity Lake. Climbing steadily, the route gets sunnier; manzanita lines both sides of the trail. You soon get your first good view of Red Mountain, still high above. The junction with the Granite Peak Trail is at 4 miles. The junction is not well marked, but you can see a fairly obvious path leading northeast away from the main trail. A right at the fork leads east across a gully (dry by late season) and up the side of Granite Peak. Stoney Ridge Trail continues to the left and northwest.

A quarter mile after the junction, the trail arrives at Red Mountain Meadow (elevation 6,900 feet). The fringes of the meadow offer the first place to camp on the route, though the scenery is a notch below the meadows on the other side of Stonewall Pass. The sunrise from here is spectacular, though.

From the meadow the trail winds the rest of the way through open, rocky terrain to Stonewall Pass, elevation 7,400 feet. Allow time for a long break on the pass; your legs will probably need it anyway. The pass commands an incredible view directly into the heart of the Trinity Alps. Looking north, the vista includes Middle Peak, Gibson Peak, Siligo Peak, Sawtooth Mountain, and Little Granite Peak. At your feet lie the emerald-green fields of Van Matre Meadows. Interspersed among the meadows are little subalpine ponds that keep the grasses green all summer long. The ponds are filled with life—like the mountains' own tide pools—and great care should be taken in exploring this fragile environment.

Stonewall Pass does, indeed, have a stone wall running along it. The fence and a few remnants of barbed wire remain from the time when cattle were allowed to munch on the lush meadows.

Solitude seekers will find plenty of privacy in Van Matre Meadows.

A steep descent on rocky tread leads down into the drainage below Echo Lake. The trail levels out after 0.5 mile and crosses a creek and then the outlet from Echo. These small streams, along with the tributary arising in Siligo Meadows, join to form Deep Creek, which drains the entire basin at your feet. Downhill from here lies one of the Trinity Alps' truly wild and half-forgotten corners. Deep Creek, with no formal trail and very little human traffic, remains off the map in all but the most literal way.

No maintained trail leads to Echo Lake, but if you're anxious to reach the lake, you can pick your way 0.3 mile up the rocky, boulder-strewn outlet, which you cross before heading uphill again toward Little Stonewall Pass. For the more leisurely route, stay on the trail as it climbs up to Little Stonewall Pass on the way to Siligo Meadows and beyond. But don't go over the pass. Just before Little Stonewall, an obvious use trail heads right (southeast) across a level area that holds a snowmelt pond (it shrinks to a mudflat by late summer). Pick your way across the meadow and through the boulder field on the other side of the pond. Just over the rise lies Echo Lake.

Though Echo Lake is only a couple miles from the Four Lakes Loop and Long Canyon, both of which host a stream of hikers all summer long, Echo doesn't get nearly as much attention as its neighbors. In this case, ignorance is not bliss.

The forest service's *1984 Trinity Alps Wilderness* map (no longer in print) had a brief description of each lake in the Alps. The map pegs Echo at 2.5 acres and 7,250 feet and then notes simply: "Many daytime activities possible in the surrounding area. Sunsets

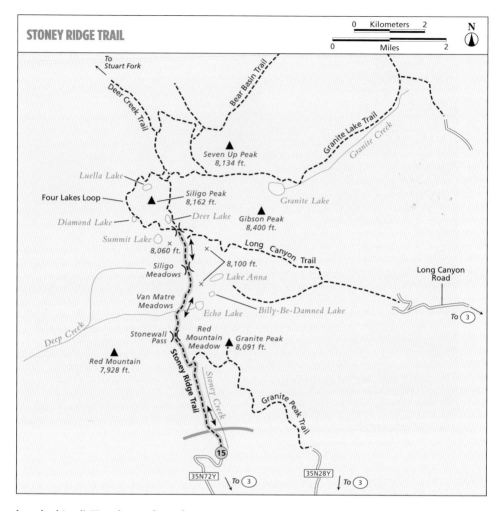

breathtaking." Translation from forest service speak into plain English: No fewer than six lakes, five peaks, four sprawling meadows, and three of the most stunning canyons in the Trinity Alps are within striking distance of Echo Lake. The lake itself sits in a rocky cirque perched on the north side of Middle Peak. Only a few stunted firs and mountain hemlocks grow in the basin, but summer flower gardens around the east side of the lake are glorious. The inlet is a gurgling, crystal-clear creek that tumbles through a slide of rocks and tiny pockets of meadow grass. The balcony of red rock on Echo's western edge offers a magnificent view of wild Deep Creek drainage and Sawtooth Mountain. Finally, topography has conspired to place the setting sun directly in the V-notch cut by Echo's outlet. Take a seat on the eastern side of the bowl and watch the sun slip into the perfectly cut notch and disappear in a blaze of glory. Breathtaking indeed.

To reach the Four Lakes Loop from Echo Lake, return to the Stoney Ridge Trail and continue north, over Little Stonewall Pass and down into Siligo Meadows. The trail descends on rocky switchbacks to the bottom of the drainage and then crosses a small stream in a stand of trees (this is the headwaters of Deep Creek). More alpine "tide pools" dot the meadows downstream from the crossing.

Across the creek, the sometimes-obscure trail is on the west side of the wide meadow. Old cattle paths can make the going a little confusing in this area. Fortunately, the route is easy to see. Once you come down from Little Stonewall Pass and cross the creek, look up to the head of the drainage. The saddle on the left (northwest) is Deer Creek Pass; the saddle on the right (northeast) is Bee Tree Gap. Midway up the valley you reach a signed junction. The right fork leads to Bee Tree Gap and Long Canyon; the left fork leads to Deer Creek Pass and the beginning of the Four Lakes Loop. Another spur trail at the top of the valley links the two passes. Both saddles are just under 2 miles from Echo Lake.

MILES AND DIRECTIONS

0.0   Start at the Stoney Ridge Trailhead.

4.0   Pass the Granite Peak Trail junction; stay left.

4.2   Arrive at Red Mountain Meadow, with camping options for late starters.

6.0   Continue over Stonewall Pass.

6.7   Arrive at Echo Lake.

7.1   Cross Little Stonewall Pass.

8.0   Descend to Siligo Meadows.

8.5   Climb to Deer Creek Pass. Return the way you came.

17.0   Arrive back at the trailhead.

OPTIONS

Start at Deer Creek Pass (described above) and descend 100 yards to the beginning of the Four Lakes Loop, a beautiful trail that circles Siligo Peak.

Side trip to Lake Anna and Billy-Be-Damned Lake: The shortest way to reach Lake Anna and Billy-Be-Damned Lake is through the narrow gap directly east of Echo Lake. There's no trail on the rocky scramble across the ridge, but the route is fairly obvious (and very steep; use caution due to loose rock and turn back if you're not comfortable). From the east side of Echo Lake, pick your way up the rocky slope to the narrow notch on the ridgeline, directly above the lake. After stopping for a moment to admire a perfect view of Mount Shasta, contour north across the open, rocky slope to little Billy-Be-Damned Lake (7,400 feet elevation; 1 acre).

Billy-Be-Damned is set in a treeless basin on a dramatic ledge overlooking Bowerman Meadows. Colorful wildflowers dot the rocky cirque in midsummer; views are spectacular, and it's a fine place to wile away a day in the Trinity Alps. A rock dam forms the eastern edge of the lake and offers an incredible throne-like seat from which to watch the sunrise. Beneath your throne there's nothing but 1,000 feet of pure mountain air between you and the meadow far below.

Lake Anna is across one more ridge to the north. Follow the use trail north over the grassy ridge between the lakes; then pick your way down the rocky slope to Lake Anna. The lakes are about 0.5 mile apart. Anna, 4 acres of deep-blue paradise, is one of the best swimming lakes in the Alps. Take a dip in the sparkling turquoise water; then lay your body out on Anna's sun-warmed rocks, feel your goose bumps melt away, and just try to imagine a place you'd rather be.

16 GRANITE PEAK TRAIL

Score one of the area's top views from 8,091-foot Granite Peak. This is a steep hike—with no lake or good camping—so it's best done as a day hike.

Start: Granite Peak Trailhead
Type of hike: Day hike; out-and-back
Distance: 8.4 miles
Hiking time: About 5–8 hours
Difficulty: Strenuous
Elevation gain: 4,400 feet
Best season: Midsummer through early fall
Canine compatibility: Yes
Nearest town: Weaverville/Trinity Center
Fees and permits: Free wilderness permit required for overnight visitors; free campfire permits required for fires and camp stoves

Schedule: Trails in the Trinity Alps are always open; however, most trailhead access roads are closed or impassable during winter.
Maps: USGS Covington Mill; USDAFS Trinity Alps Wilderness
Trail contact: Weaverville Ranger Station: (530) 623-2121; www.fs.usda .gov/stnf
Parking and trailhead facilities: There's ample parking at the trailhead (on an old logging landing), though there is no water or camping facilities. Two USDA Forest Service campgrounds, Bushytail and Minersville, are nearby on CA 3.

FINDING THE TRAILHEAD

From Weaverville drive 18 miles north on CA 3 to the signed turn for Granite Peak Trail (FR 35N28Y). Turn left (west) and proceed 3 miles to the dead-end trailhead. GPS: N40 53.177' / W122 50.76185'

THE HIKE

If you're a glutton for punishment and a pushover for great views, you'll love the hike to Granite Peak. Rising 4,400 feet in 4.2 miles, the route is like one long Stairmaster to the sky, but the view from the top of the 8,091-foot peak is worth every grueling step. All of the inner Trinity Alps, as well as Mount Shasta, Lassen Peak, and Trinity Lake are laid out before you like a relief map of rock and water. Granite Peak is a popular summit hike for two simple reasons: It's the only peak over 8,000 feet in Trinity with a trail to the top, and it's relatively accessible, with a shorter approach compared to the backcountry peaks elsewhere in the wilderness.

Most people tackle Granite Peak as a day hike, but you can definitely lay your sleeping bag out if you want to sleep with your head in the stars. If you do, you'll get a small taste of what it was like for those who spent their summers up here on the old (now gone) Granite Peak fire lookout. Water is available along the way (but not on top).

The Granite Peak Trail (9W18) starts wide and steep on an old jeep track, climbing steadily northwest through mixed forest of Douglas fir, incense cedar, and sugar pine. Oak, madrone, and dogwood also grow at this lower elevation.

Look back over your shoulder as you climb. There's a nice view of Mount Shasta every time the trees open up. After about 1 mile the wide track gives way to real trail—a well-defined path that snakes upward in a series of seemingly endless switchbacks. Cross East

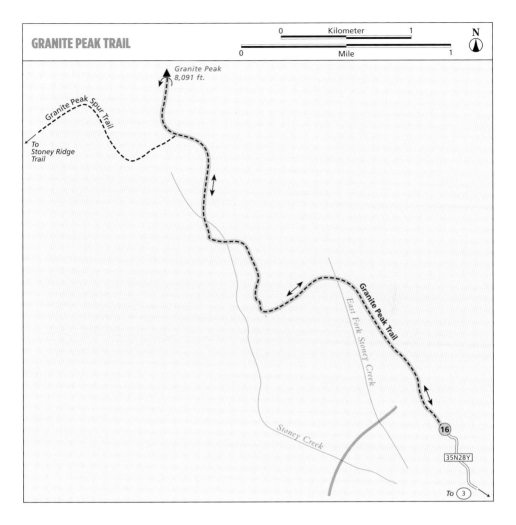

Fork Stoney Creek just before the wilderness boundary; then continue the zigzagging ascent through open, mature forest dotted with large boulders.

At 2.5 miles from the trailhead, the path enters a steep, rocky gully. For the next 0.5 mile it's more steep switchbacks, but now the route hugs the gully, meandering back and forth through wildflowers, stands of brush and ferns, and green grassy glades. This idyllic setting helps somewhat to alleviate the disappointment you feel when you reach what looks like the summit straight above you. It's not.

After the false summit, climb 0.5 mile to the junction with the spur trail to Stoney Ridge. A left (west) turn here leads to Red Mountain Meadow and the Stoney Ridge Trail (just over 1 mile away). (Tip: You can also climb Granite Peak via Stoney Ridge and camp in Red Mountain Meadow along the way. I highly recommend this alternative route if you want to make it an overnight. See the Stoney Ridge Trail hike.) Stay straight (north) to reach the old lookout site at the trail's end, 4.2 miles from the trailhead.

Leopard lilies grow in wet areas throughout the Trinity Alps.

MILES AND DIRECTIONS

0.0   Start at the Granite Peak Trailhead.

1.4   Arrive at East Fork Stoney Creek and continue up.

1.5   Pass the wilderness area boundary.

3.9   Stay straight at the junction for the Stoney Ridge spur trail.

4.2   Reach Granite Peak. Return the way you came.

8.4   Arrive back at the trailhead.

OPTIONS

The only option from Granite Peak is a side trip to Red Mountain Meadow by way of the spur trail to Stoney Ridge, which offers fine camping on the south side of Stonewall Pass. You can reach Van Matre and Siligo Meadows by going over Stonewall Pass, but it makes more sense to use the Stoney Ridge Trail if that's your destination.

17 LONG CANYON

This canyon boasts one of the best summer wildflower shows in the Trinity Alps. It's also the most direct route to the Four Lakes Loop, a popular trail that circles Siligo Peak and its four scenic lakes.

Start: Long Canyon Trailhead
Type of hike: Day hike or backpack; out-and-back
Distance: 13.6 miles (plus optional 5.2-mile Four Lakes Loop)
Hiking time: About 1–5 days
Difficulty: Moderate
Elevation gain: 3,900 feet
Best season: Midsummer through early fall
Canine compatibility: Yes
Nearest town: Weaverville/Trinity Center
Fees and permits: Free wilderness permit required for overnight

visitors; free campfire permits required for fires and camp stoves
Schedule: Trails in the Trinity Alps are always open; however, most trailhead access roads are closed or impassable during winter.
Maps: USGS Siligo Peak and Covington Mill; USDAFS Trinity Alps Wilderness
Trail contact: Weaverville Ranger Station: (530) 623-2121; www.fs.usda .gov/stnf
Parking and trailhead facilities: Ample parking but no facilities. There are numerous forest service campgrounds nearby on CA 3.

FINDING THE TRAILHEAD

From Weaverville drive 24 miles north on CA 3 to the signed Long Canyon turnoff. Turn left (west) onto Long Canyon Road (CR 115) and proceed 3 miles to the trailhead, bearing right at the signed fork just before the trailhead. Long Canyon Road is unpaved after the first mile. GPS: N40 55.380' / W122 48.789'

THE HIKE

Despite the name, a colorful array of summer wildflowers and fantastic views can make Long Canyon seem entirely too short. If it's wildflowers you're after, late July is your best bet for hitting Long Canyon at its peak.

Water is readily available at numerous stream crossings (purify all water) along the Long Canyon Trail (9W14). From the trailhead begin walking west with a short uphill push on a wide, smooth track. This initial climb is only a few hundred yards, but it gives a good taste of what's to come.

After the brief ascent, the route levels out on a narrower path. The trail is shaded by mixed forest of fir, pine, and incense cedar. The route parallels but remains high above the East Fork of Stuart Fork for just under 1 mile, climbing very gradually and crossing two tributaries in short succession.

Shortly after crossing the second tributary, the trail turns uphill (northwest) and ascends to a junction with the Bowerman Meadows Trail, 1.3 miles from the trailhead. To continue up Long Canyon from the junction, bear right at the fork and start climbing. The trail ascends steeply on a series of switchbacks and then climbs more moderately after reaching a meadow marked by a grandfather incense cedar—one of the biggest I've ever seen in the Trinity Alps. Cross two small, flower-crowded creeks shortly after the meadow; then climb gradually to a pleasant, stream side clearing, just under 3 miles from

Siligo Meadows offers a quiet detour at the end of the Long Canyon Trail.

the trailhead. In midsummer this spot boasts a lovely little garden of leopard lilies and other wildflowers.

The trail then continues up the north bank of the creek, with Bee Tree Gap, the pass at the head of Long Canyon, coming into view for the first time. You're now in Long Canyon proper. Sheer walls rise on either side as the trail ascends the ravine. Lake Anna is behind the ridge on the left (south); Granite Lake is behind the ridge on the right (north).

Bee Tree Gap may look close in the clear alpine air, but it's still a steep 2 miles away. As you continue up, look for colorful explosions where little streams nourish sprays of monkshood, leopard lilies, Indian paintbrush, and scarlet gilia. Just before reaching the top of the meadow, the trail descends briefly on rocky tread to cross the creek at the bottom of the canyon, passes a golden field of yellow lupine, and then climbs the south wall on several switchbacks to a hanging meadow. Most years, an icy stream emerges from under a snowbank here. It's a welcome spot for a rest (and maybe a snowball fight) on a hot day.

A miniature forest of western pasque flowers (mountain anemones) makes this a particularly idyllic spot. In late summer the anemones turn into tiny imitations of Dr. Seuss's Truffula trees. (There's no record of Dr. Seuss having been in Long Canyon, but the resemblance is uncanny.) The steep gully up the south side of the canyon is the off-trail route to Lake Anna (see the Lake Anna Loop hike).

The Long Canyon Trail turns back to the north, contours up to the heart of the canyon, and then bends west for the final push to Bee Tree Gap. The little stream in this uppermost meadow is the last chance for water. The trail climbs through rocks on the south side of the upper canyon and then ascends two steep switchbacks to the saddle. Enjoy your much-deserved rest—and the awesome views—on Bee Tree Gap. You can see the striking difference between two different geological features that nearly come together here: red metamorphic rock to the south and gray granite to the north. You'll also see remnants of barbed-wire fencing still hanging from a few trees near the pass, relics from the era when cattle grazed here (no longer allowed).

Drop into Deer Lake at the end of the Long Canyon Trail.

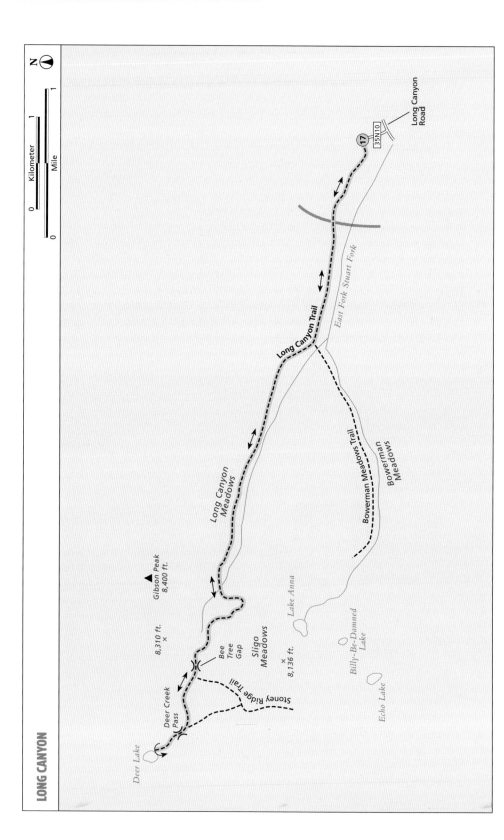

LONG CANYON

N

| 0 | Kilometer | 1 |
| 0 | Mile | 1 |

17

35N10

Long Canyon Road

Long Canyon Trail

East Fork Stuart Fork

Long Canyon Meadows

Bowerman Meadows Trail

Bowerman Meadows

Gibson Peak 8,400 ft.

8,310 ft. ×

Bee Tree Gap

Sligo Meadows

Deer Creek Pass

Stoney Ridge Trail

× 8,136 ft.

Lake Anna

Billy-Be-Damned Lake

Deer Lake

Echo Lake

To reach the Four Lakes Loop from the saddle, bear right on the signed trail to Deer Creek Pass. The left fork heads down into Siligo Meadows and then over Little Stonewall Pass, passing within a stone's throw of Echo Lake. A detour to Echo Lake is well worth the time if you want more solitude than you're likely to find on the Four Lakes Loop. If you go this way, note the enormous foxtail pines; one has an average diameter of more than 8 feet.

The route to Deer Creek Pass follows an easy path that dips down and then up across the top of the basin, leading 0.8 mile to the saddle above Deer Lake. The view from the pass is even better than the one you just left behind, with Deer Lake literally at your feet, Siligo Peak to the west, and the pristine wilderness of Deer Creek drainage falling away to the north. (Siligo Peak is the gray summit between Deer and Diamond Lakes, not the unnamed red peak rising immediately above the pass you're standing on.)

Steep switchbacks lead 0.7 mile down to the shoreline of Deer Lake, passing the Four Lakes Loop junction on the way. The red talus slopes above the north-facing basin usually hold snow until late summer. Sitting at 7,150 feet, Deer is a pretty little 4.5-acre lake with emerald-green grass around most of its shoreline and, in late summer, an eye-catching display of blue gentians on its western edge. The basin is nearly treeless, with just a few foxtail pines on its northeastern side. Walk up the granite shelf to the north for excellent views down the Deer Creek drainage and into the heart of the Trinity Alps.

MILES AND DIRECTIONS

0.0   Start at the Long Canyon Trailhead.

1.3   Pass the junction with the Bowerman Meadows Trail. Stay right.

4.0   Pass the start of the off-trail route to Lake Anna. Stay on the Long Canyon Trail. (The route to Lake Anna shoots steeply up the gully to your left.)

5.3   Arrive at Bee Tree Gap. The trail descends and crosses the top of the drainage to Deer Creek Pass.

6.1   Reach Deer Creek Pass.

6.8   Reach Deer Lake. Return the way you came.

13.6 Arrive back at the trailhead.

OPTIONS

The four lakes at the end of the hike (Deer, Summit, Diamond, and Luella) are linked by the aptly named Four Lakes Loop (Hike 18). The 5.2-mile roller coaster of a path is a stunning trail by any standard and has become one of the more popular destinations here. And no surprise why: It boasts more views per mile than just about any other trail in the Trinity Alps, with many good swimming, fishing, and camping opportunities along the way. You can also make a side trip to Echo Lake on the Stoney Ridge Trail by veering south at Bee Tree Gap and going over Little Stonewall Pass. To make a loop back to the trailhead, you can hike cross-country to Lake Anna (Hike 19) and then follow the Bowerman Meadows Trail to its junction with the Long Canyon Trail.

18 FOUR LAKES LOOP

This stunner circles Siligo Peak, dipping in and out of four distinctive cirques, each with its own lake. It's short and can easily be done as a day hike while you're base camping nearby along Deer Creek or in Siligo Meadows (or at a nearby lake such as Granite, Echo, or Anna). No matter which route you take to get here, expect company.

Start: Deer Lake or Deer Creek, wherever you approach from
Type of hike: Hike-in backcountry trail, accessible from several trailheads; loop
Distance: 5.2 miles
Hiking time: About 1-3 days
Difficulty: Moderate
Elevation gain: 2,000 feet
Best season: Midsummer through early fall
Canine compatibility: Yes
Nearest town: Weaverville/Trinity Center
Fees and permits: Free wilderness permit required for overnight

visitors; free campfire permits required for fires and camp stoves
Schedule: Trails in the Trinity Alps are always open; however, most trailhead access roads are closed or impassable during winter.
Maps: USGS Siligo Peak quad; USDAFS Trinity Alps Wilderness map
Trail contact: Weaverville Ranger Station: (530) 623-2121; www.fs.usda .gov/stnf
Parking and trailhead facilities: None, this is a backcountry trail you approach on foot.

FINDING THE TRAILHEAD

Use the Long Canyon, Stoney Ridge, Granite Lake, or Deer Creek Trails to access the Four Lakes Loop. GPS: N40 56.526' / W122 53.421' (junction above Deer Lake). The most popular (and shortest) approach is via Long Canyon (see Hike 17 for driving and trail directions).

THE HIKE

The Four Lakes Loop is one of those alpine delights that is so well arranged it almost seems unnatural. If Disneyland designed a trail, this would be it (though maybe without the steep bits). The Four Lakes Loop roller coasters around 8,162-foot Siligo Peak—dipping in and out of four cirques, skirting four inviting lakes, and presenting more views per mile than any other hike in the Trinity Alps.

This trail is best done as a day hike while base camping in one of the drainages or at one of the lakes nearby. End the day (or start it) with a walk up Siligo Peak and you will definitely sleep well that night. Like all beautiful places with a good trail, this one attracts plenty of visitors. In recent years social media fame has made the Four Lakes Loop one of the more popular hikes in Trinity. Go on a weekday or in fall if you want a better chance of solitude. Avoid camping at the lakes along the loop. There's very little space, and the fragile environment has suffered from the impact.

This description starts at the Four Lakes Loop junction above Deer Lake. The closest access is from the Long Canyon Trailhead.

On the south side of Deer Lake, midway up the slope to Deer Creek Pass, go west on the Four Lakes Loop Trail (9W13) toward Summit Lake. The loop can be hiked in either direction. There's no obvious advantage to either.

Diamond Lake is midway around the Four Lakes Loop.

After turning onto the Four Lakes Loop, start the traverse across a broad talus slope above Deer Lake. Beautiful bouquets of rock fringe, veronica, and Indian paintbrush bloom among the reddish rocks in July and August. The north-facing cirque often holds snow well into summer. The path is carved directly into the rocky hillside, but a moderate grade makes for easy walking until you get to the final, sandy switchbacks that lead up to the saddle. Near the start of the switchbacks, you can still see remnants of the old trail that plunged almost straight down the hillside to the lake.

Once you gain the saddle, it's an easy 0.5-mile descent to Summit Lake. The startlingly clear blue water of Summit—at 7,350 feet and 13 acres, the highest and biggest of the four lakes—is perched in a basin of red metamorphic rock. The lake appears to sit in a volcanic crater, but in fact it's in a glacier-carved bowl like other lakes in the Trinity Alps.

Before descending to the lake, take a look up the hill to the right (north). This is the way up Siligo Peak. Scattered use trails lead to a steep but nontechnical walk up the 8,162-foot peak. On top of Siligo you can see three of the four lakes on the loop (Luella remains hidden to the north). The 360-degree view encompasses Sawtooth Mountain to the west, Seven Up Peak to the east, and Mount Shasta and Lassen Peak on the eastern horizon. (**Note:** When in the Trinity Alps, if you can see Mount Shasta, you'll generally have good cell phone reception.) As far as peak-bagging goes, Siligo offers more view for the effort than just about any other summit in the Trinity Alps.

Back down on the main path, descend 0.25 mile west to a signed junction with a spur trail that leads down a series of switchbacks to Summit Lake. It's a favorite base camp for horsepackers, but there are a few good camps for backpackers on the opposite end of the lake from where the horses might be.

The forested north shore offers easy access to the clear blue water. Swimming is superb—and cold—all summer long. A steep, rocky slope and a nameless 8,061-foot red peak dominate the other side of the lake. The only water available is usually from the lake itself. (There's no inlet, and the outlet runs only in early season, though you can find a dependable little stream in the meadow to the west below the lake.)

Return to the main trail above Summit Lake and head left (west) on an easy 0.25-mile leg to the saddle above Diamond Lake. From the pass, descend a staircase of switchbacks

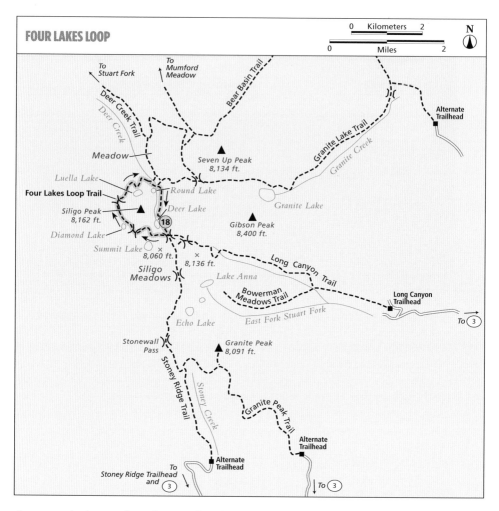

0   Kilometers   2

0   Miles   2

N

To Stuart Fork

To Mumford Meadow

Bear Basin Trail

Alternate Trailhead

Deer Creek Trail

Deer Creek

Granite Lake Trail

Granite Creek

Meadow

Seven Up Peak 8,134 ft.

Luella Lake

Four Lakes Loop Trail

Round Lake

Granite Lake

Siligo Peak 8,162 ft.

Deer Lake

18

Diamond Lake

Gibson Peak 8,400 ft.

Summit Lake

8,060 ft.

8,136 ft.

Long Canyon Trail

Siligo Meadows

Lake Anna

Long Canyon Trailhead

Bowerman Meadows Trail

East Fork Stuart Fork

To 3

Echo Lake

Stonewall Pass

Granite Peak 8,091 ft.

Stoney Ridge Trail

Stoney Creek

Granite Peak Trail

Alternate Trailhead

Alternate Trailhead

To Stoney Ridge Trailhead and 3

To 3

down a rocky, barren slope decorated with bright-colored summer flower gardens. Diamond Lake sits in a grassy bowl on a shelf overlooking Stuart Fork and the heart of the Trinity Alps. A castle-like rock on the western edge of the lake offers an incredible throne from which to watch the sun go down over Sawtooth Mountain.

To continue on the loop, follow the trail north through a lush meadow sloping away from the lake; then start climbing as the path contours north up the hill into mixed forest (stock up on water before leaving the lake, as nothing dependable lies between here and Luella). After 0.5 mile several moderate switchbacks lead northeast up to the third pass on the loop.

A grassy, tree-shaded saddle offers another spectacular place to rest and enjoy expansive views before dropping down to little Luella Lake. Looking east across Deer Creek drainage, you're looking directly at Seven Up Peak (named for a card game, not the soft drink). The reddish, rounded summit is distinctly different from nearby Gibson Peak (sharp gray granite), though Seven Up is often confused with its granite neighbor. You can also see the route to Granite Lake—a seemingly endless series of switchbacks carved into the eastern side of the drainage. The sight should give you a good idea of what lies between you and Deer Creek far below.

Summit Lake is part of what some call the "Red Trinities."

Descend on moderately steep switchbacks that zigzag down to little Luella, 1 mile below. Luella is tucked into a treeless, rocky shelf midway down the canyon wall (just under 7,000 feet elevation). The 2.5-acre lake rivals Summit Lake for the clearest water in the Alps.

To reach Deer Creek and complete the loop, continue east on the trail as it descends another series of switchbacks. A gradual descent to the south finally brings you to the canyon floor at the head of a large meadow. An unmarked trail to the northeast is just a spur trail that joins Deer Creek Trail down the canyon. Continue southeast, rounding the meadow near a creek that meanders through the deep grass. The source of the pretty little creek is Round Lake—a beautiful but tiny pond that stretches the definition of "lake" (and makes one wonder why this isn't called the Five Lakes Loop).

Follow the path through the meadow to a signed junction at the edge of Deer Creek. Turn right (south) to return to Deer Lake and complete the loop. A left turn leads north down the Deer Creek Trail to Stuart Fork. Just 100 yards north is the junction with the Granite Lake Trail, which leads over the ridge to Swift Creek.

Heading south on the Four Lakes Loop, you begin the only really challenging section of the hike. It's only 1 mile from here to Deer Lake, but it's all uphill. Fill up your water bottles before starting. The first part of the ascent is shaded by mixed forest, but the final push up to the lake can be sunny and hot. Cool off in Deer Lake before returning to your starting point.

MILES AND DIRECTIONS

0.0   Start at the Four Lakes Loop junction above Deer Lake.

1.0   Reach Summit Lake.

1.9   Arrive at Diamond Lake.

3.5   Arrive at Luella Lake.

4.2   Reach the Deer Creek Trail junction.

5.2   Arrive back at Deer Lake.

19 LAKE ANNA LOOP

You'll need basic route-finding skills for this (partially) off-trail hike. The reward? A turquoise-colored gem in a red-rock basin, with great views and great swimming.

Start: Long Canyon Trailhead
Type of hike: Backpack; lollipop or out-and-back
Distance: 9.3 miles (lollipop); 9.0 miles (out-and-back)
Hiking time: About 3–5 days
Difficulty: Strenuous
Elevation gain: 3,900 feet
Best season: Midsummer through early fall
Canine compatibility: Yes
Nearest town: Weaverville/Trinity Center
Fees and permits: Free wilderness permit required for overnight visitors; free campfire permits required for fires and camp stoves
Schedule: Trails in the Trinity Alps are always open; however, most trailhead access roads are closed or impassable during winter.
Maps: USGS Covington Mill and Siligo Peak; USDAFS Trinity Alps Wilderness
Trail contact: Weaverville Ranger Station: (530) 623-2121; www.fs.usda .gov/stnf
Parking and trailhead facilities: Ample parking but no facilities. There are numerous forest service campgrounds nearby on CA 3.

FINDING THE TRAILHEAD

From Weaverville drive 24 miles north on CA 3 to the signed Long Canyon turnoff. Turn left (west) onto Long Canyon Road (CR 115) and proceed 3 miles to the trailhead, bearing right at the signed fork just before the trailhead. Long Canyon Road is unpaved after the first mile. GPS: N40 55.380' / W122 48.789'

THE HIKE

You'll find great swimming in lakes all over the Trinity Alps. But it's hard to beat the cool water and warm red rocks of Lake Anna on a summer afternoon. The sedimentary rock, so unlike the white granite found nearby, forms a swollen lip of a dike on the lake's east side, just above a 1,000-foot drop to Bowerman Meadows. The effect is like an alpine infinity pool, with blue water that's 56 feet deep and clear all the way down. It should be no surprise that visitors have come here with grand plans for further exploration, only to come under Anna's spell and never get beyond the basin.

A summer garden of wildflowers lines the inlet, which runs through a lush meadow a few hundred feet above the lake and then tumbles down a rocky cascade to the shore. The basin commands one of the best sunrise views in the Alps, with Mount Shasta in the picture if you climb up the west side of the cirque (where you can also likely get cell reception). Within easy day-hiking distance are Billy-Be-Damned and Echo Lakes, as well as Siligo Meadows and the Four Lakes Loop.

What's the catch? There's no trail to Lake Anna, and it's a steep haul from every side. Only hikers who are comfortable with route finding and steep scrambling should attempt this hike. The loop route described here goes up Long Canyon, off-trail up an unnamed gully to Lake Anna, and then back through Bowerman Meadows. The off-trail descent from Lake Anna to Bowerman Meadows is steep and rough. You can avoid it by returning the way you came. (The Long Canyon route is slightly longer but definitely easier.)

Lake Anna's blue water and red rock make for great swimming and lounging.

Start the hike at the Long Canyon Trailhead and begin walking west with a short uphill push on a wide, smooth track. After a brief ascent, the route levels out on a narrower path shaded by mixed forest of fir, pine, and incense cedar. The route parallels but remains high above the East Fork of Stuart Fork for just under 1 mile, climbing very gradually and crossing two tributaries in short succession.

Shortly after crossing the second tributary, the trail turns uphill (northwest) and ascends to a junction with the Bowerman Meadows Trail, 1.3 miles from the trailhead. (If you plan on returning via Bowerman Meadows and it's early season, scout the creek crossing here before moving on. You don't want to go all the way around and then find you can't cross the creek here.) Bear right at the fork and start climbing. The trail ascends steeply on a series of switchbacks and then climbs more moderately after reaching a meadow marked by a grandfather incense cedar. Cross two small, flower-crowded creeks shortly after the meadow; then climb gradually to a stream side clearing, just under 3 miles from the trailhead. A lovely little garden of leopard lilies and other wildflowers blooms here in midsummer.

The trail continues up the north bank of the creek, with Bee Tree Gap, the pass at the head of Long Canyon, coming into view for the first time. Sheer walls rise on either side as the trail ascends the ravine. Lake Anna is behind the ridge on the left (south).

Leave the trail when you arrive at the base of a steep gully leading up the south wall of Long Canyon, about 4 miles from the trailhead. The gully is easy to identify, because you cross from the north side of Long Canyon to the south side immediately before reaching its base. After crossing the creek at the bottom of Long Canyon, ascend switchbacks to the meadow hanging midway up the south wall of the canyon. Most years, a snowbank fills the rocky bench gouged into the side of the canyon. The Long Canyon Trail jogs right and continues west, ascending the upper drainage to Bee Tree Gap. The route to Lake Anna lies directly ahead, up the steep, rocky chute that leads out of Long Canyon. Once atop the ridge, you drop into Anna from above.

Billy-Be-Damned Lake hangs over Bowerman Meadows.

If the snowbank is present, use caution: The stream running under the snow can under-cut the seemingly stable field and leave it dangerously thin (the snow is easy to walk around). Once in the gully proper, traces of user trails and cairns may appear, but it's simply a matter of ascending the steep chute to the saddle about 500 feet and 0.5 mile above. Midsummer wildflowers on the grassy slope west of the streambed take the sting out of this tough climb.

Once you gain the ridge above Lake Anna, the deep-blue water is at your feet. The 4-acre lake sits at 7,550 feet, and all you have to do is descend a couple hundred feet to get there.

So steep is the drop from Lake Anna's outlet, the red rock–blue water basin seems to hang on the side of the mountain. The view down to Bowerman Meadows is spectacu-lar, especially during a full moon: Sit on the naked red rocks on a warm summer evening and watch the lunar show at your feet.

While at Lake Anna, be sure to explore the upper basin (great sunrise and sunset views of Mount Shasta). Shallow, seldom-seen Billy-Be-Damned Lake is directly over the ridge to the south, just 15 minutes away. The shallow little (less than 1 acre) puddle is in a

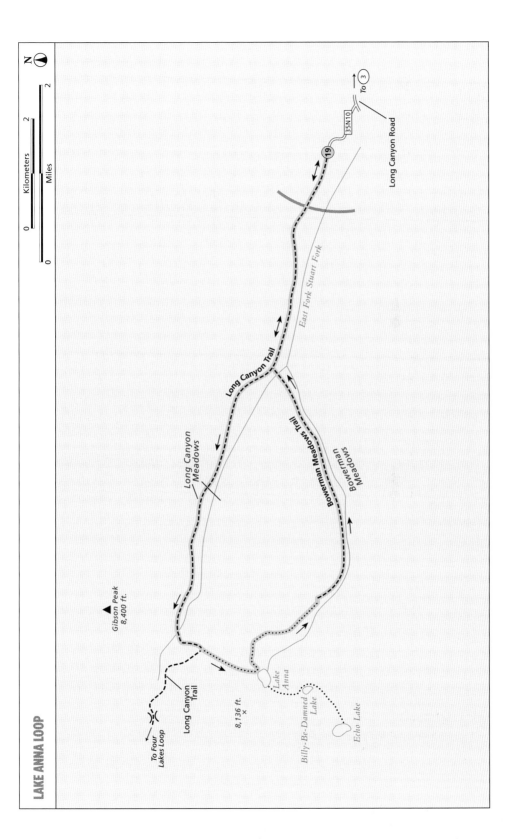

LAKE ANNA LOOP

To Four Lakes Loop

Long Canyon Trail

Gibson Peak
8,400 ft.

8,136 ft.
×

Lake Anna

Billy-Be-Damned Lake

Echo Lake

Long Canyon Meadows

Long Canyon Trail

Bowerman Meadows Trail

Bowerman Meadows

East Fork Stuart Fork

19

35N10

To 3

Long Canyon Road

Kilometers
0   2

Miles
0   2

N

rock-lined basin with a red-rock dike that almost matches Anna's (with a similar drop). You can reach Echo Lake via a steep talus slope southwest of Billy-Be-Damned. The chute leads up to a narrow notch in the ridge and then down another steep slope on the other side (less than 0.5 mile between lakes.) No maintained trails lead between Lake Anna, Billy-Be-Damned Lake, and Echo Lake, but the routes are easy to follow in the near treeless basins (only Anna has a few sparse stands of any size).

To return to the trailhead via Bowerman Meadows, thread your way through the boulders above the northeast corner of Lake Anna. Emerge on the shoulder of the ridge northeast of the steep outlet; then pick your way down the brushy slopes to the meadow nearly 1,000 feet below. I find that working your way east affords the gentlest grade. However, some Anna fans swear by the rocky route along the near-vertical outlet below the lake. (Use caution; I've done it that way too and it's a tricky scramble.) Suffice it to say there are several routes down, all steep.

Once at Bowerman Meadows (elevation 6,600 feet), you find yourself in an idyllic oasis of green grass and summer wildflowers. In fact, some visitors choose to approach Lake Anna from this direction, base camp in Bowerman Meadows, and day-hike to the lakes and surrounding areas from here. This is a good option, but it requires that you haul yourself up—instead of down—that steep hillside if you want to complete the loop through Long Canyon. (I've also tried it that way and can attest that it's only for confirmed masochists.)

From the meadow, pick up traces of use trail that lead downcanyon (southeast). Light use can leave the Bowerman Trail overgrown in the upper valley, but it's generally not hard to follow. Descend through Sound of Music meadows to the East Fork of Stuart Fork; then follow the river's north bank 2 miles to the junction with the Long Canyon Trail. The trail passes through open meadows, thick stands of alder, and shady groves of incense cedar, cottonwood, pine, and fir. Crossing Long Canyon's creek can be difficult in high water. If you're concerned, it's easy to come down and take a look at the water level when you pass the junction on the way in (the creek crossing is less than 100 yards from the junction). From here it's an easy stroll back to the trailhead, 1.3 miles away.

MILES AND DIRECTIONS

- **0.0** Start at the Long Canyon Trailhead.
- **1.3** Arrive at the Bowerman Meadows Trail junction. Stay right on Long Canyon Trail.
- **4.0** Follow the off-trail route to Lake Anna. Climb steeply.
- **4.5** Arrive at Lake Anna.
- **5.5** Reach Bowerman Meadows after a steep descent.
- **8.0** Reach the Long Canyon Trail junction. Turn right and retrace your steps to the trailhead.
- **9.3** Arrive back at the trailhead.

OPTIONS

The Four Lakes Loop is close to Lake Anna. Access it by following Long Canyon to Deer Creek Pass and then the beginning of the loop. The 5.2-mile roller coaster of a path boasts more views per mile than just about any other trail in the Trinity Alps, with many good swimming, fishing, and camping opportunities along the way.

20 SWIFT CREEK TO HORSESHOE AND WARD LAKES

This gentle hike makes a great introduction to the Trinity Alps—plenty of meadow camping along Swift Creek, thick wildflowers in summer, and good access to several high lakes and peaks for day trips or overnights.

Start: Swift Creek Trailhead
Type of hike: Backpack; out-and-back
Distance: 18.8 miles
Hiking time: About 2-6 days
Difficulty: Moderate
Elevation gain: 3,100 feet
Best season: Midsummer through early fall
Canine compatibility: Yes
Nearest town: Weaverville/Trinity Center
Fees and permits: Free wilderness permit required for overnight visitors; free campfire permits required for fires and camp stoves

Schedule: Trails in the Trinity Alps are always open; however, most trailhead access roads are closed or impassable during winter.
Maps: USGS Siligo Peak, Covington Mill, Ycatapom Peak, and Caribou Lake; USDAFS Trinity Alps Wilderness
Trail contact: Weaverville Ranger Station: (530) 623-2121; www.fs.usda .gov/stnf
Parking and trailhead facilities: Ample parking at the trailhead and an outhouse. The closest campground is Preacher Meadow, on CA 3 near Trinity Center.

FINDING THE TRAILHEAD

 From Weaverville drive 30 miles north on CA 3, past Trinity Center, to the signed Swift Creek Trail turnoff on FR 36N25 (just after crossing the Swift Creek bridge and just prior to Wyntoon Resort Trinity Lake KOA). Turn left (west) and proceed 6 miles to the trailhead (bearing left at the signed fork for Swift Creek) at the end of the road. GPS: N40 58.412' / W 122 48.009'

THE HIKE

Swift Creek is the main way to reach Horseshoe, Ward, and Granite Lakes—all of which attract a fair number of visitors with the lure of good swimming and great scenery (especially Granite). But the hike up Swift Creek is worth doing even if you never make it to the lakes. Parker and Mumford Meadows, situated along the banks of the river, together form one of the most enchanting chains of greenery in the Trinity Alps. The lush meadows extend for more than 3 miles along the north bank of Swift Creek and offer such an inviting array of wildflowers in summer that you may decide the lakes can wait. The forest fringes around Mumford Meadow are popular base-camping sites from which to explore the surrounding area. You can day-hike easily up to the lakes, as well as into the more remote meadows hanging above Swift Creek (Bear Basin, Mumford Basin, and meadows along Landers, Sunrise, and Parker Creeks).

At the Swift Creek Trailhead, don't be discouraged if the parking lot is full of cars and horse trailers. The trailhead serves a number of destinations, and people tend to spread out fairly evenly—except at perpetually crowded Granite Lake.

Horseshoe Lake is perched in a basin above Swift Creek.

Look back down the Swift Creek Valley shortly before arriving at Horseshoe Lake.

The Swift Creek Trail (8W15) descends briefly from the trailhead and then levels out, heading northwest through a shady mix of ponderosa pine, Douglas fir, and incense cedar, and soon leads to a shelf along Swift Creek. The trail generally parallels Swift Creek from here all the way to the Landers Lake Trail junction. The path ascends gradually for the first mile, passing a number of incense cedar and fir trees with old license plates nailed to them about 15 feet off the ground. (They are not remnants from some historic, catastrophic car accident. Rather, they help snow survey parties follow this route during the winter.) You also pass a small meadow on the right choked with California pitcher plants most of the summer. The rare insectivorous plants thrive in the Trinity Alps' wet meadows.

Soon the trail ascends moderately to a narrow ledge high above Swift Creek. Watch your step here—it's a long drop—but take the time to peer over the side, where Swift Creek cuts a dramatic gorge through solid rock. Waterfalls, deep pools, and sheer cliffs await adventurers who want to explore the depths of the gorge. You can get down to river level both upstream and downstream from the ravine.

Just past the overlook, 1.2 miles from the trailhead, arrive at the junction with the Granite Lake Trail. The left fork at the signed junction leads to a steel bridge crossing Swift Creek and then 4.1 miles up to Granite Lake. To continue on the Swift Creek Trail, stay right at the fork. The trail soon crosses an impressive swath of avalanche debris. Just under 1 mile from the Granite Lake junction, you cross the outlet stream from tiny Twin Lakes, a steep and brushy 0.5 mile up the hill on your right. Like some other generously named lakes in the Alps, these two are just a couple of lily pad–choked puddles.

Steer Creek is the next major tributary you cross, but a number of smaller unnamed creeks cross the trail in numerous places, providing plentiful water. After climbing more steeply on moderate switchbacks, the trail veers away from Swift Creek to cross a pretty little stream and skirt a lush meadow decorated with gaudy orange leopard lilies in midsummer.

Easy walking brings you to Parker Creek and the only significant stream crossing on the entire route. A bridge was built across Parker Creek in 1967, but only the concrete foundations remain. Early-season high water could make this a difficult crossing, but usually it's just a matter of boulder-hopping across. Shortly after crossing the creek, reach a three-way trail junction. Signs point southwest to Bear Basin, northwest to Fosters Cabin–Swift Creek, and north to Parker Creek–Deer Flat (Landers Lake Loop). Continue on the Swift Creek Trail toward Fosters Cabin.

The path hugs the southern edge of Parker Meadow from here, serving up a leisurely stroll along lush fields of meadow grasses and summer wildflowers. Parker is the first in a remarkable series of meadows from here to the head of the valley. At the top of Parker Meadow, you come to Fosters Cabin, 4.7 miles from the trailhead.

The forest service restored Fosters Cabin in 1989, but the original structure dates from 1946. The ruins of an older horse barn remain across the trail from the restored structure. The site is named for Bill Foster, who built a cabin here for his cowhands sometime in the late 1800s. The cabin's wooden porch is a fine place to lean your pack if you want to get some water from the nearby spring, duck out of the rain, or just daydream about the old-timers who used to spend their summers in this beautiful place here (find good camping nearby).

Proceed up the trail as it follows Swift Creek on a gradual bend to the west. As you enter the lower reaches of Mumford Meadow, pass the signed junction with the Landers Lake Trail (shortly before crossing Landers Creek) and continue west through wet, sometimes boggy terrain. As the path skirts the south side of Mumford Meadow, it passes a couple of well-used horse camps and a number of less visible campsites hidden in the stands of incense cedar, fir, and pine between the trail and Swift Creek. (There's also good camping just up the trail toward Landers Lake.)

From here to the head of the canyon, the trail alternates between shady forest cover and lush pockets of meadow. Flower gardens blooming in a rainbow of colors adorn the route, and sparkling little streams cross the path frequently. All the while, the trail ascends at a barely perceptible grade. Across Swift Creek lies a largely untraveled wilderness where solitude is nearly guaranteed. Less than 1 mile before reaching the head of the canyon, you pass an unmaintained route leading up to Mumford Basin and eventually over the ridge to Deer Creek. Compared to Swift Creek, this trail is seldom used—a wonderful place to explore if you have the inclination.

Of course, there's a price for all that easy strolling. The last section of the trail climbs more than 1,000 feet on rocky, exposed switchbacks. Leave the meadows behind at the head of the drainage, where you enter a stand of fir and cross the outlet coming

Salmon Lake is a steep, off-trail hike over the ridge from Horseshoe.

down from Horseshoe Lake. This stream and one more crossing midway up are the only sources of water on the steep climb (purify all water). In mid-July, the leopard lilies, shooting stars, and scarlet gilia at this second crossing are simply amazing.

HORSESHOE LAKE

At the top of the switchbacks, arrive at the signed junction for Horseshoe and Ward Lakes in a shady flat. Go left (south) to reach Horseshoe Lake, just 0.3 mile up the hill through granite ledges and scattered firs and a small waterfall that affords a nice shower. As the

Find this rarely seen view of Sawtooth Ridge at Salmon Lake.

name implies, 6-acre Horseshoe Lake (elevation 6,850 feet) is wrapped neatly around an island of rock. The clear water and sun-splashed slabs of granite look especially inviting after you've climbed those switchbacks on a summer afternoon. And on the far side, a large granite shelf offers the perfect staging area for swimming, jumping, and lounging. Campsites at Horseshoe are small and close to the water; consider camping in the meadows below and day hiking to the lake to minimize impact.

Ready for more exploring? On the northwest side of the lake, you can scout an off-trail route up the barren, rocky slope to the divide between Horseshoe and Salmon Lakes, on the ridgeline just north of Tri-Forest Peak. The 7,670-foot peak, the ridge beneath it, and Salmon Lake are all good bets for ambitious hikers. From the saddle, the view of Sawtooth Ridge and Caribou Mountain is breathtaking; about 500 feet beneath your feet, little 1.5-acre Salmon Lake beckons when you want solitude. No trails lead to the shallow lake, and very few people make the effort to reach it. The off-trail route from Horseshoe to Salmon is steep but not technically demanding. Just aim for the saddle and start climbing.

WARD LAKE

Back at the junction on the Swift Creek Trail (below Horseshoe Lake), turn right (north) to reach Ward Lake. The trail crosses a stream and then traverses the mountainside on a long contour to the northeast, across mostly open slopes. Finally, ascend a couple of steep switchbacks that lead around a prominent bulge guarding the entrance to Ward Lake. Follow the outlet stream, which tumbles down a narrow green corridor at the southeast side of the basin, for the last few minutes. It's almost a surprise when you finally emerge at the lip of 5.5-acre Ward Lake. Ward sits at an elevation of 7,100 feet, 9.4 miles from the trailhead. There are large campsites on both sides of the lake.

Red and gray cliffs hang over the basin, and an emerald meadow slopes steeply in from the north like a river of green grass. Like its neighbor, Ward also has a horseshoe shape that curves around a large prow of rocky terrain and stunted trees. For an excellent sunrise view, head for the ridge east of the lake. Use the Ward Lake Trail, which climbs to the saddle northeast of the lake, to reach the ridge. (Follow the trail nearly to the saddle; then head for the ridge when the angle seems right.)

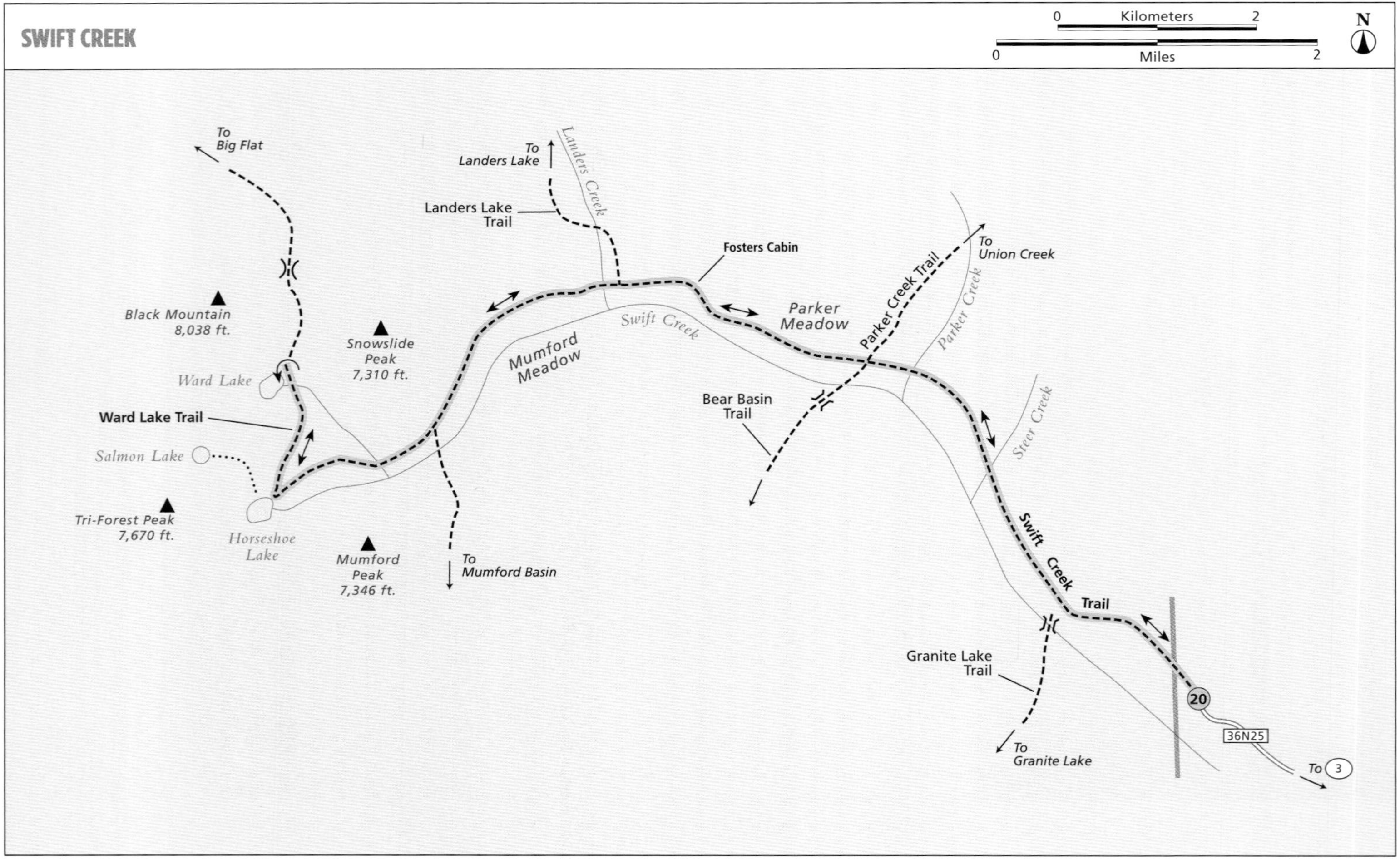

SWIFT CREEK

N

Kilometers
0   2

Miles
0   2

To Union Creek

Steer Creek

Swift Creek Trail

Parker Creek

Parker Creek Trail

Fosters Cabin

Parker Meadow

Bear Basin Trail

Granite Lake Trail

To Granite Lake

36N25

20

To 3

Landers Creek

Swift Creek

Landers Lake Trail

To Landers Lake

Mumford Meadow

To Mumford Basin

Snowslide Peak
7,310 ft.

Mumford Peak
7,346 ft.

To Big Flat

Black Mountain
8,038 ft.

Ward Lake

Ward Lake Trail

Salmon Lake

Horseshoe Lake

Tri-Forest Peak
7,670 ft.

The Ward Lake Trail originates at Big Flat and can be used as an alternate route to reach this area. It's typically less crowded than Swift Creek and is shorter by a few miles, but the trailhead is an hour's drive farther, and you miss out on Mumford Meadow.

MILES AND DIRECTIONS

0.0   Start at the Swift Creek Trailhead.

1.2   Reach the Granite Lake Trail junction. Stay right.

2.3   Cross Steer Creek.

3.4   Cross Parker Creek.

3.5   Arrive at the Bear Basin–Parker Creek Trail junction. Stay on the Swift Creek Trail.

3.6   Arrive at Parker Meadow, the first of many good camping areas.

4.7   Reach historic Fosters Cabin.

5.5   Arrive at the Mumford Meadow–Landers Lake Trail (a good side trip and more great camping).

8.0   Pass the spur trail to Horseshoe Lake. Stay right to continue to Ward Lake. Go left to reach Horseshoe Lake.

8.3   Reach Horseshoe Lake.

9.4   Arrive at Ward Lake. Return the way you came.

18.8 Arrive back at the trailhead.

OPTIONS

The Swift Creek Trail passes numerous paths with a bewitching array of options. Check out Bear Basin or Landers Lake, or use the map to create your own adventure.

Ambitious hikers can scramble up to the bridge above Horseshoe Lake for great views.

21 BEAR BASIN-GRANITE LAKE LOOP

While Granite Lake—easy access, spectacular setting—gets plenty of traffic, Bear Basin gets very little. Combine the two with a scenic loop that skirts 8,134-foot Seven Up Peak, and you get this sweet route. Bonus: There's good access to Four Lakes Loop.

Start: Swift Creek Trailhead
Type of hike: Backpack; loop
Distance: 16.4 miles
Hiking time: About 2–5 days
Difficulty: Moderate
Elevation gain: 3,500 feet
Best season: Midsummer through early fall
Canine compatibility: Yes
Nearest town: Weaverville/Trinity Center
Fees and permits: Free wilderness permit required for overnight visitors; free campfire permits required for fires and camp stoves

Schedule: Trails in the Trinity Alps are always open; however, most trailhead access roads are closed or impassable during winter.
Maps: USGS Covington Mill, Siligo Peak, and Ycatapom Peak; USDAFS Trinity Alps Wilderness
Trail contact: Weaverville Ranger Station: (530) 623-2121; www.fs.usda .gov/stnf
Parking and trailhead facilities: Ample parking (a good indication of the amount of use Swift Creek gets) and an outhouse. The closest campground is at Preacher Meadow, on CA 3 near Trinity Center.

FINDING THE TRAILHEAD

From Weaverville drive 30 miles north on CA 3, past Trinity Center, to the signed Swift Creek Trail turnoff on FR 36N25 (just after crossing the Swift Creek bridge, and just prior to Trinity Lake KOA). Turn left (west) and proceed 6 miles to the trailhead (bearing left at the signed fork for Swift Creek) at the end of the road. GPS: N40 58.412' / W122 48.009'

THE HIKE

This loop takes the scenic route to Granite Lake, a popular destination just 5.3 miles from the Swift Creek Trailhead. The lake sits in a dramatic granite cirque below Gibson Peak, and the easy effort-to-scenery ratio draws the predictable weekend crowds. By taking this route around Seven Up Peak, you'll travel through the comparative solitude of Bear Basin and then drop into the Granite Lake basin from above. The loop can be done in either direction but hiking it this way allows you to hike down (instead of up) the steep trail between Seven Up Pass and Granite Lake. Either way you go, you also have the option of taking a side trip to Deer Creek and the Four Lakes Loop.

The Swift Creek Trail (8W15) descends briefly from the trailhead and then levels out, heading northwest through a shady mix of ponderosa pine, Douglas fir, and incense cedar, and soon leads to a shelf along Swift Creek. The trail generally parallels Swift Creek from here all the way to the Landers Lake Trail junction. The path ascends gradually for the first mile. Look for California pitcher plants in a small meadow on the right. The rare insectivorous plants thrive in the Trinity Alps' wet meadows.

Soon the trail ascends moderately to a narrow ledge high above Swift Creek. Watch your step here—it's a long drop—but take the time to peer over the side, where Swift Creek cuts a dramatic gorge through solid rock. Just past the overlook, 1.2 miles from the trailhead, arrive at the junction with the Granite Lake Trail. (**Option:** If you have your heart set on swimming in Granite Lake and want to get there the quickest way, just hang a left here onto the Granite Lake Trail; you'll be doing the backstroke in a couple of hours. Then continue on the Bear Basin loop, in the opposite direction described here.) To continue on the Swift Creek Trail, stay right at the fork and start climbing gradually on the shady path. The trail soon crosses an impressive swath of avalanche debris. Just under 1 mile from the Granite Lake junction, you cross the outlet stream from tiny Twin Lakes, a steep and brushy 0.5 mile up the hill on your right. Like some other generously named lakes in the Alps, these two are just a couple of lily pad–choked puddles.

Steer Creek is the next major tributary you cross, but a number of smaller unnamed creeks with accompanying flower gardens cross the trail in numerous places. After climbing more steeply on moderate switchbacks, the trail veers away from Swift Creek to cross a pretty little stream and skirt a lush meadow decorated with gaudy orange leopard lilies in midsummer.

Easy walking brings you to Parker Creek and the only significant stream crossing on the entire route. A bridge was built across Parker Creek in 1967, but only the concrete foundations remain. Early-season high water could make this a difficult crossing, but usually it's just a matter of boulder-hopping across. Across the creek a level path leads quickly to a three-way trail junction.

To hike the loop, turn left (southwest) on the Bear Basin Trail (9W10). The path quickly descends to a bridge crossing of Swift Creek, just upstream from the confluence of Swift and Bear Creeks. After crossing the bridge begin a steady ascent into Bear Basin. The route into the thickly forested drainage is steep at first. The rocky trail passes several seeps and small tributaries as it climbs the west side of Bear Creek.

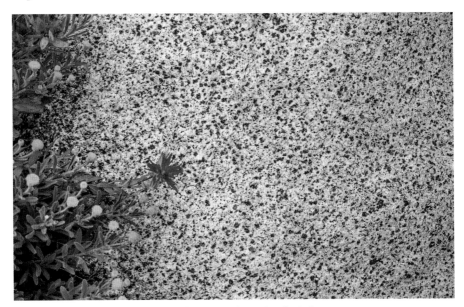

A rainbow of wildflowers blooms on the slopes above Granite Lake.

Slightly more than 2 miles from Swift Creek, the trail arrives at Bear Basin proper, where you skirt one of the prettiest meadows in all of the Trinity Alps. Mature incense cedars and ponderosa pines fringe the idyllic setting. The trail passes on the west side of the meadow. California pitcher plants and a variety of wildflowers thrive in the lush environment. The wet meadow is a rare and fragile ecosystem—please observe Zero Impact practices, and don't make new trails or campsites in the area. (Established campsites exist along the creek.)

Traveling southwest from the meadow, the trail continues to climb toward the ridge separating the Swift and Deer Creek drainages. The ascent is gentler now, as the path traverses several smaller meadows in the upper basin. You cross and recross Bear Creek as you climb higher, so access to drinking water is never a worry (purify all water here and elsewhere on the hike).

The trail reaches the headwaters of Bear Creek about 7.5 miles from the trailhead. Here the trail turns right (west) and climbs a steep set of switchbacks to gain the ridgeline above. If you have time and inclination, leave the trail here and follow Bear Creek to its source. Most years you'll find a late-summer snowbank in upper Bear Basin—a great place to poke around. (Cross to the east side of the valley for a nice view of Mount Shasta.)

The trail climbs 0.3 mile up a rocky hillside smothered in wildflowers in July and August. Once you gain the ridgeline you arrive at a fork in the trail. A right (west) turn leads to a junction with the Black Basin Trail and routes to Deer Creek and Mumford Basin. To continue the loop, turn left (southeast) on the Seven Up Peak Trail (9W67). This path leads across the ridge and after 100 yards passes another trail junction. This short spur trail (on the right) also leads down to the Black Basin Trail and is a slightly quicker route (by mere minutes) than the first fork if your destination is Deer Creek.

The Seven Up Peak Trail continues south and east, climbing a short set of switchbacks to the ridgeline above Deer Creek drainage. En route, the trail passes an old mine shaft, then contours gently along through sparse tree cover and open terrain. The entire Deer Creek drainage drops away beneath your feet, with drop-dead views across the valley to Siligo Peak, Luella Lake, and the Deer Lake basin. If you're still on the fence about whether to drop down to Deer Creek and the Four Lakes Loop, this vista might help make up your mind.

After passing beneath the shoulder of 8,134-foot Seven Up Peak (named for a card game played by a couple of cowhands long ago), the trail soon reaches a saddle where you run into the Granite Lake Trail (8W14). The gap in the knife-edge ridge commands an unbroken vista of the Granite Creek and Deer Creek drainages, both of which drop steeply away. Adding the Four Lakes Loop to the itinerary? Turn right (west) to descend to Deer Creek on a set of switchbacks that zigzag down to the meadow 2 miles below.

Turn left (east) to descend into the headwaters of Granite Creek. The next 1.8 miles is a delightful descent through open meadows, with endless views up and down the wild canyon. After dropping down to meet Granite Creek, the trail passes through a jungle-like profusion of corn lilies, leopard lilies, and monkshood. In late July this short section of trail can be head-high with wildflowers.

After crossing the creek a couple of times, the trail descends steeply again through forest cover to Granite Lake. Just before the second crossing, you traverse a rocky bench with excellent views of the lake below. The bench is just above a waterfall and marks a

BEAR BASIN—GRANITE LAKE LOOP

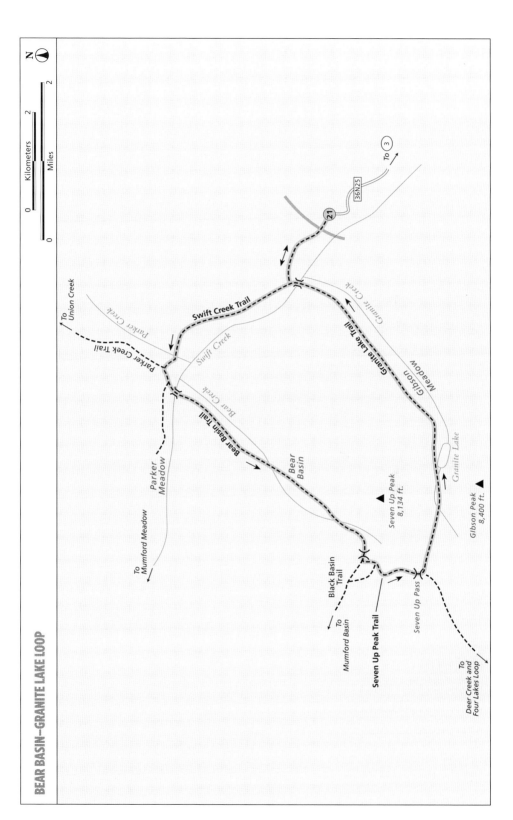

good point for off-trail scramblers to set off for the ridge on the south side of the creek (great sunrises, but you'll have to rise early—there are no good campsites here).

Granite Lake, tucked in a deep basin below 8,400-foot Gibson Peak, is a swimming and fishing haven. The basin is mostly forested on the east side, while the north side is lined with smooth slabs of gray granite and jumbled piles of rock. Like other beautiful wilderness destinations too close to the road for their own good, Granite Lake gets a high number of visitors on summer weekends. It also gets a lot of horsepacker traffic; the best campsites for backpackers are on the lake's southeast side. (Cross the outlet stream on a fallen log, if it's still there.) Or target the campsite where inlet stream enters the lake—you'll have a white-sand beach all to yourself.

To finish the loop, hike east on the Granite Lake Trail. The path traverses a rocky bench immediately east of the lake and then descends a short set of switchbacks to skirt the north side of Gibson Meadow. The route follows the course of Granite Creek the rest of the way, heading northeast on a gently descending grade in mostly shady forest cover. A number of small tributaries cross the path, so it's not necessary to fight your way through the brush along Granite Creek to get water. Arrive at a wood-and-steel footbridge that crosses Swift Creek 4.1 miles from Granite Lake and just upstream from the Swift–Granite Creek confluence. Climb about 100 yards up the opposite bank and rejoin the Swift Creek Trail. Turn right and retrace your steps 1.2 miles to the trailhead.

MILES AND DIRECTIONS

0.0   Start at the Swift Creek Trailhead.

1.2   Arrive at the Granite Lake Trail junction. Stay straight (right) to hike the loop in the recommended direction.

2.3   Cross Steer Creek.

3.4   Cross Parker Creek.

3.5   Reach the Parker Creek–Bear Basin Trail junction. Turn left on the Bear Basin Trail.

6.6   Arrive at Bear Basin.

8.3   Reach the Seven Up Peak–Black Basin Trail junction. Stay left.

9.3   Arrive at Seven Up Pass. Descend toward Granite Lake.

11.1   Reach Granite Lake.

11.6   Arrive at Gibson Meadow. Continue the descent.

15.2   Reach the Swift Creek Trail junction. Turn right.

16.4   Arrive back at the trailhead.

OPTIONS

The best side trip off this route is the Four Lakes Loop. Access the loop by turning right (west) at Seven Up Pass and descending to Deer Creek. From the trail junction at the bottom, you can hike the Four Lakes Loop in either direction. The 5.2-mile roller coaster of a path boasts more views per mile than just about any other trail in the Trinity Alps. Another good option is to head down the Deer Creek Trail, which connects to the Stuart Fork Trail.

22 LANDERS LAKE LOOP

This low-traffic loop leads up Swift Creek and then down Parker Creek, with good camping in Mumford Meadow, Landers Lake, and along Union and Parker Creeks. Cool off in Landers Lake and climb Red Rock Mountain for spectacular views.

Start: Swift Creek Trailhead
Type of hike: Backpack; lollipop
Distance: 16.4 miles
Hiking time: About 2–5 days
Difficulty: Moderate
Elevation gain: 4,100 feet
Best season: Midsummer through early fall
Canine compatibility: Yes
Nearest town: Weaverville/Trinity Center
Fees and permits: Free wilderness permit required for overnight visitors; free campfire permits required for fires and camp stoves

Schedule: Trails in the Trinity Alps are always open; however, most trailhead access roads are closed or impassable during winter.
Maps: USGS Covington Mill, Ycatapom Peak, and Caribou Lake; USDAFS Trinity Alps Wilderness
Trail contact: Weaverville Ranger Station: (530) 623-2121; www.fs.usda .gov/stnf
Parking and trailhead facilities: Ample parking (a good indication of the amount of use Swift Creek gets) and an outhouse. The closest campground is at Preacher Meadow, on CA 3 near Trinity Center.

FINDING THE TRAILHEAD

From Weaverville drive 30 miles north on CA 3 to the signed Swift Creek Trail turnoff on FR 36N25 (just after crossing the Swift Creek bridge and just prior to Trinity Lake KOA). Turn left (west) and proceed 6 miles to the trailhead (bearing left at the signed fork) at the end of the road. GPS: N40 58.412' / W122 48.009'

THE HIKE

This route follows four different creeks on a loop through some of the Trinity Alps' most varied terrain—both in the physical and social sense. Shady forests, vast meadows, lush flower gardens, a secluded lake, and endless vistas come in rapid succession. On the social side you have plenty of company on the Swift Creek Trail, but fellow hikers are few and far between on the rest of the route—especially along Parker Creek, a seldom-used trail despite its proximity to a popular trailhead.

Landers Lake, midway around the loop, isn't as spectacular as some of the other lakes in the Trinity Alps Wilderness, but its clear water and peaceful red-rock basin offer a nice change of pace from the more crowded areas in the Alps. Red Rock Mountain (7,853 feet) is an easy scramble west of the lake and offers one of the best 360-degree views in all the Alps. Side trips to Union, Foster, and Lion Lakes, as well as Shimmy and Lilypad, are within striking distance.

At the Swift Creek Trailhead, don't be discouraged if the parking lot is full of cars. The trailhead serves a number of destinations, and people tend to spread out fairly evenly—except at perpetually crowded Granite Lake.

The Swift Creek Trail (8W15) descends briefly from the trailhead and then levels out, heading northwest through a shady mix of ponderosa pine, Douglas fir, and incense cedar,

Landers Lake is a great basecamp for climbing Red Rock Mountain.

and soon leads to a shelf along Swift Creek. The trail generally parallels Swift Creek from here all the way to the Landers Lake Trail junction. The path ascends gradually for the first mile.

Soon the trail ascends moderately to a narrow ledge high above Swift Creek. Watch your step here—it's a long drop—but take the time to peer over the side, where Swift Creek cuts a dramatic gorge through solid rock. Just past the overlook, 1.2 miles from the trailhead, arrive at the junction with the Granite Lake Trail. Stay straight (right) at the fork and start climbing gradually on the shady path. The trail soon crosses an impressive swath of avalanche debris. Just under 1 mile after passing the Granite Lake junction, you cross the outlet stream from tiny Twin Lakes, a steep and brushy 0.5 mile up the hill on your right. Like some other generously named lakes in the Alps, these two are just a couple of lily pad–choked puddles.

Steer Creek is the next major tributary you cross, but a number of smaller unnamed creeks cross the trail in numerous places. After climbing more steeply on moderate switchbacks, the trail veers away from Swift Creek and skirts a lush meadow decorated with gaudy orange leopard lilies in midsummer.

The trail crosses a gentle, forested flat after climbing above the meadow. Easy walking brings you to Parker Creek and the only significant stream crossing on the entire route. A bridge was built across Parker Creek in 1967, but only the concrete foundations remain. Early-season high water could make this a difficult crossing, but usually it's just a matter of boulder-hopping across. Across the creek a level path leads quickly to a three-way trail junction. Signs point southwest to Bear Basin, northwest to Fosters Cabin–Swift Creek, and north to Parker Creek–Deer Flat. Continue on the Swift Creek Trail toward Fosters Cabin. (The Parker Creek Trail is your return route.)

The path hugs the southern edge of Parker Meadow from here, serving up a leisurely stroll along lush fields of meadow grasses and summer wildflowers. Parker is the first in a remarkable series of meadows that dot the Swift Creek drainage from here to the head of the valley. At the top of Parker Meadow, arrive at Fosters Cabin, 4.7 miles from the trailhead (good camping nearby).

The forest service restored Fosters Cabin in 1989, but the original structure dates from 1946. The ruins of an older horse barn remain across the trail from the restored structure. The site is named for Bill Foster, who built a cabin here for his cowhands sometime in the late 1800s. The cabin's wooden porch is a fine place to lean your pack if you want to get some water from the nearby spring, duck out of the rain, or just daydream about the old-timers who used to spend their summers in this beautiful place.

Proceed up the trail as it follows Swift Creek on a gradual bend to the west toward Mumford Meadow.

In the lower reaches of Mumford Meadow, look for the signed junction with the Landers Lake Trail at 5.5 miles (shortly before crossing Landers Creek). Pick your way north along the eastern edge of the meadow and pass a campsite just before heading steeply uphill on a well-defined trail.

Rough tread on steep switchbacks leads uphill 0.5 mile to the junction with the Sunrise Creek Trail, at the confluence of Sunrise and Landers Creeks. Bear right at the junction and descend to a crossing of Landers Creek; then continue uphill (north) as the trail hugs the east bank of Landers Creek.

Ascend to a meadow punctuated by sparkling ponds and a field of pitcher plants. The trail levels out to skirt the east side of the meadow, giving you a chance to catch your breath and enjoy the garden-like setting.

A mile from the Sunrise Creek junction, you arrive at another signed junction, this one with a spur trail that leads over the ridge to the Union Creek Trail (which you'll take on the way out). Bear left to continue up to Landers Lake. The trail again hugs the east side of a meadow and then starts the last steep climb up to the lake. Trees become more sparse and rocks more plentiful as you ascend the final 0.7 mile to Landers Lake.

Landers Lake sits at 7,100 feet in a shallow basin of red metamorphic rock. The forest service pegs the lake at 6 acres, but with little water trickling in from above, the lake usually shrinks back quite a bit by the end of summer. Black, water-stained rocks surround the shoreline and give the lake an eerie, lunar look. The lake is shallow and clear, ideal for lounging when the water warms up. Grass-lined ponds and meadows northwest of the lake offer plenty of elbow room. The spacious camps here are well used by horsepackers.

Peak baggers will appreciate the hike up to the top of Red Rock Mountain. The incline is gentle enough that you can get there any number of ways. One good way: Cross the meadow at the lake's northwestern edge and then hike uphill to an obvious use trail that zigzags up the rocky slope to a gap on the basin's southern ridge. Once you gain the ridgeline, just follow it 0.5 mile to the peak. The rocky summit commands a view of just about everything there is to see in the heart of the Alps: To the west lie Sawtooth Mountain, Thompson Peak, and Caribou Mountain, while Mount Shasta dominates the horizon in the other direction. You'll also get a good view down into Sunrise Basin to the south.

To continue the loop, head back down the trail to the junction in the meadow 0.7 mile below Landers Lake (signed "Union Creek"). Turn left (northeast) and climb moderately to a saddle on the ridge dividing Landers and Union Creeks. From the gap it's a steep 1 mile down to the floor of the valley below. Descend east into the heart of a large meadow at the head of Union Creek. Cross the clear-running creek just before the path you're on dead-ends at the junction with the Union Creek Trail.

A left turn here (northwest) leads downstream to many good campsites along uncrowded Union Creek; a right turn (southeast) takes you up and over the divide to Parker Creek and eventually back to Swift Creek.

Fill up on water before heading uphill—it's a steep haul to the saddle. Enjoy pleasant going as you ascend moderately through the lush headwaters of Union Creek. Long, moderate switchbacks lead up to the saddle through sparse tree cover. The top of the Union–Parker Creek divide is just under 1 mile from the junction in the meadow below. There's not much on the nearly 7,000-foot saddle to impede your view down the two pristine drainages.

A signed trail junction on the saddle indicates the Thumb Rock–Poison Canyon Trail heading east along the ridgeline (accessing Lilypad and Shimmy Lakes). The Parker Creek Trail—the route back down to Swift Creek—plunges southeast down Parker Creek Canyon. This is one of the least-traveled trails in the region, so if you appreciate backcountry solitude, you'll enjoy the hike along Parker Creek. The upper canyon is distinguished by sloping, wide-open meadows and intermittent stands of fir and pine, while the lower canyon becomes more densely forested and rocky. In late summer you walk through fields of knee-high grass that all but hide the little-used trail. The path crosses

Follow Landers Creek through a chain of lush meadows.

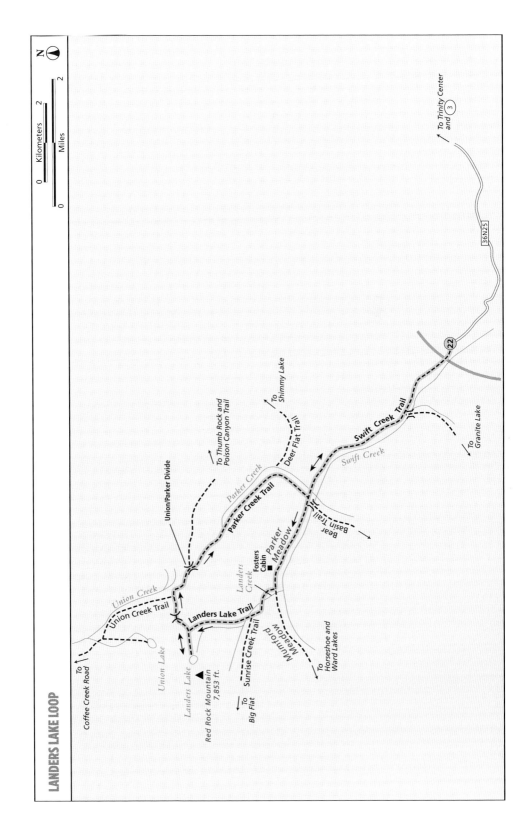

LANDERS LAKE LOOP

N

Kilometers
0   2

Miles
0   2

To Coffee Creek Road

Union Creek

Union Creek Trail

Union Lake

Landers Lake

Red Rock Mountain
7,853 ft.

To Big Flat

Landers Lake Trail

Sunrise Creek Trail

Landers Creek

Mumford Meadow

To Horseshoe and Ward Lakes

Fosters Cabin

Parker Meadow

Union/Parker Divide

Parker Creek

Parker Creek Trail

To Thumb Rock and Poison Canyon Trail

Deer Flat Trail

To Shimmy Lake

Bear Basin Trail

Swift Creek

Swift Creek Trail

To Granite Lake

22

36N25

To Trinity Center and 3

the headwaters of Parker Creek from east to west after passing the last big meadow and then descends the rest of the way on the creek's west bank. Stay right (south) at the junction with the Deer Flat Trail, which crosses Parker Creek and heads east. Rocky tread on a steep bank above the creek leads the rest of the way down to the junction with the Swift Creek Trail, 2.5 miles from the saddle. The path levels out next to the campsite at the three-way junction at Swift Creek. Turn left (southeast) on the Swift Creek Trail and retrace your steps 3.5 easy miles to the trailhead.

MILES AND DIRECTIONS

0.0   Start at the Swift Creek Trailhead.

1.2   Pass the Granite Lake Trail. Stay straight (right).

3.4   Cross Parker Creek.

3.5   Reach the Bear Basin–Parker Creek Trail junction. Stay straight on the Swift Creek Trail.

4.7   Arrive at historic Fosters Cabin.

5.5   Reach Mumford Meadow and the Landers Lake Trail. Turn right toward Landers Lake.

6.0   Pass Sunrise Creek Trail. Stay right.

7.0   Reach the Landers Lake spur trail. Turn left for the lake.

7.7   Arrive at Landers Lake.

9.6   Reach the Union Creek Trail. Turn right.

10.5   Arrive at the Union–Parker Creek divide. Descend along Parker Creek on the Parker Creek Trail.

13.0   Reach the Swift Creek Trail junction; turn left.

16.4   Arrive back at the trailhead.

OPTIONS

You can make forays into the Swift Creek, Sunrise Creek, Union Creek, and Poison Canyon drainages while on the Landers Lake Loop. Your best bet is to spend a night in Mumford Meadow or along Union Creek and then day-hike to one of the nearby lakes.

23 POISON CANYON

Don't be fooled by the name. This secluded hike slices through one of the Trinity Alps' pristine corners. The trade-off? No big, alpine lakes. The reward? Big solitude.

Start: North Fork Swift Creek Trailhead
Type of hike: Day hike or backpack; lollipop
Distance: 11.2 miles
Hiking time: About 1–3 days
Difficulty: Moderate
Elevation gain: 4,000 feet
Best season: Midsummer through early fall
Canine compatibility: Yes
Nearest town: Weaverville/Trinity Center
Fees and permits: Free wilderness permit required for overnight visitors; free campfire permits required for fires and camp stoves

Schedule: Trails in the Trinity Alps are always open; however, most trailhead access roads are closed or impassable during winter.
Maps: USGS Ycatapom Peak; USDAFS Trinity Alps Wilderness
Trail contact: Weaverville Ranger Station: (530) 623-2121; www.fs.usda.gov/stnf
Parking and trailhead facilities: Ample roadside parking, but no water or other facilities. The closest forest service campground is at Preacher Meadow, 2 miles south of Trinity Center on CA 3.

FINDING THE TRAILHEAD

From Weaverville drive 30 miles north on CA 3, past Trinity Center, to the signed Swift Creek Trailhead turnoff on FR 36N25 (just after crossing the Swift Creek bridge, and just prior to Trinity Lake KOA). Turn left (west) and proceed 1.4 miles to the signed right turn (north) for the Poison Canyon and Lake Eleanor Trails. Immediately take the next right (signed Poison Canyon) on FR 37N55, which heads west and then north as it climbs 8 miles to the trailhead. Stay right at an unmarked junction at 5.1 miles. GPS: N41 1.961' / W122 45.349'

THE HIKE

Maybe it's the ominous sounding name, or maybe it's the fact that the only lake here is covered with lily pads by midsummer, but Poison Canyon gets very few visitors. Though it's just one ridge away from Boulder Lake—one of the most popular day-hiking destinations in the Trinity Alps—Poison Canyon exists in its own quiet solitude. As they say, one person's loss is another's gain.

Poison Canyon is one of those hidden backcountry corners where wilderness with a capital W still reigns. Unlike most such places, however, you don't need to work all that hard to get here. The canyon is just 3 miles from the trailhead, but Poison Canyon remains off the radar of most Trinity Alps visitors. Those who do make it here will find beautiful hanging meadows, perfect views of Mount Shasta, and a chance to scramble up 7,596-foot Ycatapom Peak.

From the trailhead the Poison Canyon Trail (8W10) follows the North Fork Swift Creek in a westerly direction, with the first mile zigging and zagging steeply uphill. The route is mostly shaded, with the cascading North Fork and a number of sparkling tributaries feeding the canyon's lush undergrowth.

Greenery thrives around and in Lilypad Lake and its nearby ponds.

POISON CANYON

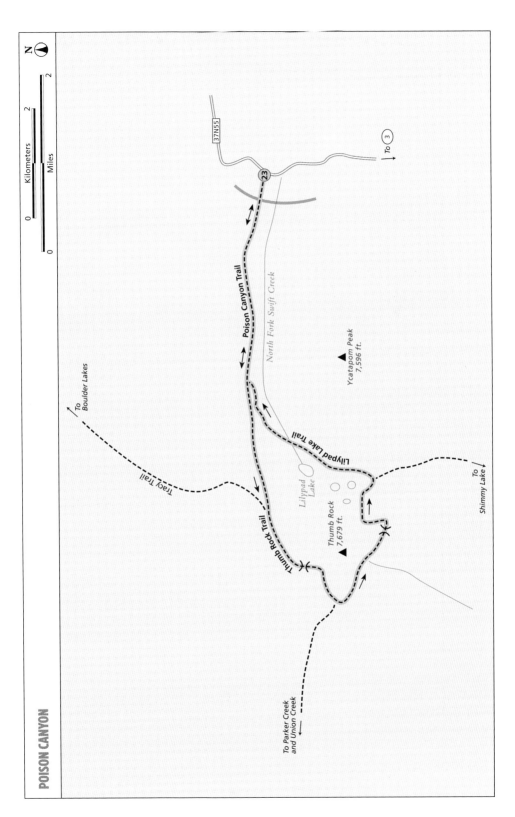

To Boulder Lakes

Tracy Trail

Poison Canyon Trail

North Fork Swift Creek

37N55

23

To 3

Thumb Rock Trail

Lilypad Lake Trail

Lilypad Lake

Thumb Rock
7,679 ft.

Ycatapom Peak
7,596 ft.

To Shimmy Lake

To Parker Creek
and Union Creek

N

Kilometers
0   2

Miles
0   2

Carnivorous pitcher plants often grow on the fringes of wet meadows.

A 2.7-mile ascent brings you to the junction with the Lilypad Lake Trail (8W21) in a flat on the north side of the North Fork. Look for cairns or a sign on a tree at the trail junction, as the path itself is often overgrown. Go left (southwest) to reach Lilypad Lake. The Poison Canyon Trail continues straight (west), climbing along the canyon's north wall. From here you can make a 5.8-mile loop around Thumb Rock. If you're day hiking, I recommend staying right and making the loop in a counterclockwise direction. If you're backpacking, you may want to hike 1 mile into the Lilypad Lake drainage to set up camp and then make your loop from there.

A mile up the Poison Canyon Trail, pass the junction with the Tracy Trail (8W26) on an open bench. The Tracy Trail leads north over the ridge to Boulder Lakes, less than 2 miles away. Continue west past the junction, climbing higher above Poison Canyon and gaining ever more spectacular views across the drainage—views of Mount Shasta to the east, Ycatapom Peak to the southeast, and Thumb Rock directly south. After gaining the ridgeline, the trail winds around the back side of Thumb Rock, skirting the head of the canyon above Cub Wallow (if you ever want to disappear from the world, head down there), and then descends slightly to the junction with the Thumb Rock Trail (8W16). The unsigned junction, on an exposed, rocky ridge on the west side of Thumb Rock, is easy to miss. Look for the trail soon after you round the base of Thumb Rock and start descending the spine of the ridge; turn left (southeast).

The Thumb Rock Trail doubles back to the southeast, leading down into wild, overgrown Sandy Canyon, then up to the forested ridgeline on the south side of Thumb Rock. Dip down to a junction with the Lilypad Lake Trail; go left (north) to head back into Poison Canyon and descend to Lilypad Lake. A right (south) turn here leads downhill to Deer Flat and Shimmy Lake, slightly over a mile away.

The descent from ridgeline to canyon bottom on the Lilypad Lake Trail is one of the most beautiful hikes in the Trinity Alps. The path leads down across hanging terraces of emerald-green grass, sparkling snowmelt tarns, clear -running streams, and view upon vista upon overlook. Amazingly, you could probably spend a week here in the middle of summer and not see a soul. Experienced mountaineers planning to climb Ycatapom Peak (the name is generally attributed to the Wintu word that means "mountain that leans") should start their climb before getting too comfortable on one of these idyllic terraces.

Due to lack of use, the route down to Lilypad Lake is not obvious. Cairns are sometimes visible, but you may have to use some common sense to pick your way down and across the rocky ledges between you and the lake. (Note: There are no established campsites at the lake.)

From the junction with the Thumb Rock Trail, the Lilypad Lake Trail descends north into the upper reaches of Poison Canyon. The path soon crosses a hanging meadow that holds two shallow, unnamed ponds surrounded by lush fields of grasses, corn lilies, and asters. The trail zigzags from west to east across the meadow and then descends steeply along the east side of the ponds' outlet stream. The short but steep descent brings you to another, smaller bench hanging above the canyon. Cross the rocky shelf and look for good views of Mount Shasta in the east and Lilypad Lake at your feet. Follow the last set of switchbacks down to the lake, 1.2 miles from the last trail junction.

From the lily pad–covered lake, the last mile of trail meanders through a parklike setting of mixed conifers and grassy glades. The mostly level path is easy to follow as it heads northeast to the junction with the Poison Canyon Trail. From here retrace your steps 2.7 miles to the trailhead.

MILES AND DIRECTIONS

0.0 Start at the Poison Canyon–Lake Eleanor Trailhead.

2.7 Arrive at the Lilypad Lake Trail junction. Stay straight to begin the loop.

3.5 Pass the Tracy Trail junction. Stay on the Poison Canyon Trail.

4.7 Reach the Thumb Rock Trail junction and take the Thumb Rock Trail (easy to miss).

6.5 Go left on the Lilypad Lake Trail.

7.7 Arrive at Lilypad Lake.

8.5 Turn right and take the Poison Canyon Trail back toward the trailhead.

11.2 Arrive back at the trailhead.

OPTIONS

Nearby destinations include Boulder Lakes and Shimmy Lake. You can make a longer foray into the Union Creek drainage by following the Poison Canyon Trail down to the Parker Creek–Union Creek divide. You can add a 20-mile loop to this hike by linking Union Creek, Foster Lake, Boulder Creek, and Boulder Lakes.

24 LAKE ELEANOR AND SHIMMY LAKE

This short hike leads to small and scenic Shimmy Lake, with lily pad–covered Lake Eleanor thrown in for good measure. It's a good hike when you want solitude without working hard or want a low-elevation hike in early or late season.

Start: Lake Eleanor Trailhead
Type of hike: Day hike or backpack; out-and-back
Distance: 7.2 miles
Hiking time: About 1–3 days
Difficulty: Easy
Elevation gain: 1,550 feet
Best season: Summer through early fall
Canine compatibility: Yes
Nearest town: Weaverville/Trinity Center
Fees and permits: Free wilderness permit required for overnight visitors; free campfire permits required for fires and camp stoves
Schedule: Trails in the Trinity Alps are always open; however, most trailhead access roads are closed or impassable during winter.
Maps: USGS Covington Mill and Ycatapom Peak; USDAFS Trinity Alps Wilderness
Trail contact: Weaverville Ranger Station: (530) 623-2121; www.fs.usda .gov/stnf
Parking and trailhead facilities: Parking for a few cars; more parking is available a few hundred yards farther up the road (if the forest service gate is open) and in pullouts along the road. No facilities. The closest developed campground is at Preacher Meadow (CA 3 near Trinity Center).

FINDING THE TRAILHEAD

From Weaverville drive 30 miles north on CA 3, past Trinity Center, to the signed Swift Creek Trail turnoff on FR 36N25 (just after crossing the Swift Creek bridge and just prior to Trinity Lake KOA). Turn left (west) and proceed 1.4 miles to the signed turn (north) for the Lake Eleanor–Poison Canyon Trails. Continue on FR 36N24, following the main route (stay straight at 1.9 miles, left at 3.4 miles, right at 4.6 miles, left at 6.3 miles, and right at 7.6 miles). The trailhead is 7.8 miles from the highway. GPS: N40 59.023' / W122 46.378'

THE HIKE

The route to Shimmy Lake rises moderately through mixed conifers and open slopes of ceanothus bushes, with sweeping views east over Trinity Lake. The trail skirts marshy, lily pad–covered Lake Eleanor almost immediately (a good destination for families with small children) and then climbs to little Shimmy Lake, a lightly visited pond at the base of a rocky ridge.

From the trailhead the path (8W13) jogs west and then heads north through incense cedars, ponderosa pines, and other conifers. In a few minutes you cross the access road, FR 36N24. (It's possible to drive this far if the gate is open, but it saves very little walking.) The trail continues north on the other side of the road, climbing gently through rocky, sparsely forested terrain to a slight rise and then dropping to the shore of Lake Eleanor (0.3 mile from the trailhead). The shallow lake is in a forested basin with a wet

Shimmy Lake makes a great destination early and late in the year, when deep snow makes higher lakes hard to reach.

meadow sprinkled with insectivorous pitcher plants near the inlet and grassy margins along most of the shoreline. The lake supports a lush supply of lily pads, but pay a visit to nearby Lilypad Lake if that's what you're after.

Lake Eleanor is visited mostly by day-trippers and anglers looking for a short hike. The lake's low elevation (4,950 feet) and easy access also make it a good destination in early and late season.

To continue to Shimmy Lake, follow the trail around the east side of Lake Eleanor and then head north-northwest away from the lake. The next 3 miles are a straightforward, moderate ascent through mixed forest, with some sunny, open sections that command good views of Trinity Lake. The trail is marked with red ribbons and/or cairns where it crosses old logging roads in the first mile after Lake Eleanor.

The trail follows a northwest route through gentle terrain, passing a tiny pond, then crosses Lick Creek 3.1 miles from the trailhead. A meadow slopes uphill from the easy creek crossing. The trail enters the forest again and then climbs the final short ascent to the eastern edge of Shimmy Lake. The little lake (1.5 acres, 10 feet deep) sits in a grassy bowl at the base of a jagged rock outcropping. If you want a lake with low-effort solitude, Shimmy is a good place to start.

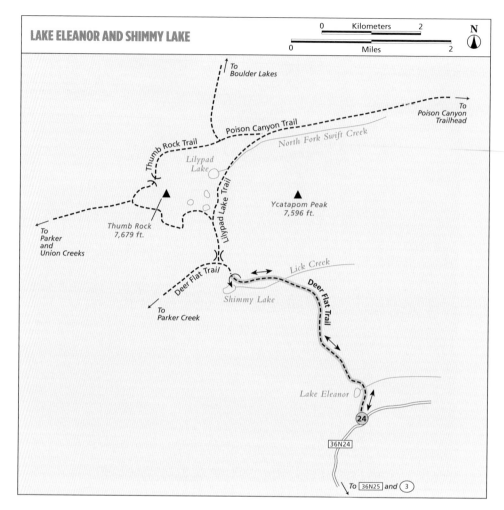

MILES AND DIRECTIONS

0.0   Start at the Lake Eleanor Trailhead.

0.3   Arrive at Lake Eleanor.

3.1   Cross Lick Creek.

3.6   Reach Shimmy Lake. Return the way you came.

7.2   Arrive back at the trailhead.

OPTIONS

From Shimmy Lake you can easily access Poison Canyon and Parker Creek, with extended journeys possible.

25 **BOULDER LAKES**

This short hike to two big, deep lakes delivers maximum scenery for minimum effort, making it a busy trail with both day hikers and backpackers. It's a great route for families with young children and other hikers who want an easy outing.

Start: Boulder Lakes Trailhead
Type of hike: Day hike or backpack; out-and-back
Distance: 3.8 miles
Hiking time: About 3–6 hours (day hike); 2–3 days (backpack)
Difficulty: Easy
Elevation gain: 800 feet
Best season: Midsummer through early fall
Canine compatibility: Yes
Nearest town: Weaverville/Trinity Center
Fees and permits: Free wilderness permit required for overnight

visitors; free campfire permits required for fires and camp stoves
Schedule: Trails in the Trinity Alps are always open; however, most trailhead access roads are closed or impassable during winter.
Maps: USGS Ycatapom Peak; USDAFS Trinity Alps Wilderness
Trail contact: Weaverville Ranger Station: (530) 623-2121; www.fs.usda .gov/stnf
Parking and trailhead facilities: Ample parking at the dead-end trailhead. No facilities, but several forest service campgrounds are located on nearby CA 3.

FINDING THE TRAILHEAD

The road to Boulder Lake Trailhead is located 0.3 mile south of Coffee Creek. From Weaverville drive 40 miles north on CA 3 and turn left (west) at the signed junction for Boulder Lakes Trailhead. Proceed 11 miles up the well-signed dirt road to the trailhead. (Follow FR 37N52 for 3.5 miles to a right turn on FR 37N53, stay left at 4.7 and 9.7 miles, and continue to the trailhead.) Ignore the logging roads that diverge from the main track. GPS: N41 3.883' / W122 47.422'

THE HIKE

It should come as no surprise that this trail gets busy in the summer. The hike is short, the lakes are great, and there's plenty of camping. If that's what you're looking for, you won't be disappointed. And if you're looking for solitude, you actually can find it here; just keep on walking past Boulder Lake, where you'll find small and uncrowded Found and Tapie Lakes and, farther still, the lonely meadows of Poison Canyon.

Boulder Lake didn't always draw such large numbers. The original route to the lake started on Coffee Creek Road and climbed 7 quad-burning miles up Boulder Creek and over the ridge to Boulder Lake. But that was decades ago. Now it's an easy 1.9-mile hop, skip, and jump from the new Boulder Lakes Trailhead. The "new" trail really isn't new anymore, but it has caught some Trinity old-timers off guard. A couple of hikers I know (okay, my parents) unwittingly slogged up the Boulder Creek Trail one time, thinking it was the only way in. They didn't see any other cars at the trailhead or other people on the trail, so they became rather smug with the knowledge they'd have Boulder Lake all to themselves. Imagine their surprise when they found themselves sharing the lake with families with little kids, big ice chests, and loud dogs.

The disclaimer about crowds aside, I must admit I've spent a delightful summer night at Boulder Lake with plenty of elbow room, awoke to a peaceful morning mist blanketing the basin, and never would have guessed I was a mere 45 minutes from the trailhead. The lake boasts lily pad–lined shores, good fishing, shady campsites, granite cliffs, and numerous opportunities for day hikes.

The trailhead itself is a parking lot–sized clearing at an elevation of nearly 6,000 feet, which means you only have to climb about 600 feet over a ridge and down the other side to reach the lake's 6,070-foot level.

The trail starts on a wide track heading south up the ridgeline. Fir and sugar pine are scattered to either side, but the first 0.25 mile is mostly open and exposed. While the ridgeline is still open, look back for your first of many Mount Shasta views.

After a small, level landing, the wide track gives way to trail and you start climbing more steeply through forest cover. The walking is pleasant and shady on soft duff. Continue the gradual ascent to the crest of the ridge, just over 1 mile from the trailhead.

After gaining the crest, the trail continues south at a nearly level grade. Good views of the drainages ahead and to the west open up. Arrive at the signed junction to Little Boulder Lake a few minutes after hiking along the ridge crest. A left (southeast) turn here leads to Little Boulder Lake; stay right (south) for Boulder Lake.

The Boulder Lakes Trailhead is relatively high, so you reach great views quickly.

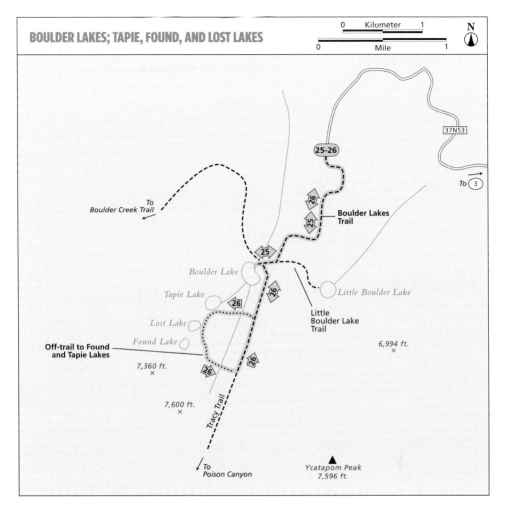

0 — Kilometer — 1

0 — Mile — 1

N

37N53

To 3

25-26

26

25

Boulder Lakes Trail

To
Boulder Creek Trail

25

Boulder Lake

Tapie Lake

26

26

Little Boulder Lake

Lost Lake

Little
Boulder Lake
Trail

Found Lake

**Off-trail to Found
and Tapie Lakes**

6,994 ft.
×

7,360 ft.
×

26

26

7,600 ft.
×

Tracy Trail

To
Poison Canyon

Ycatapom Peak
7,596 ft.

BOULDER LAKE

Start descending into the Boulder Lake basin on moderate switchbacks. Before dropping into the firs, get a glimpse of the upper reaches of the basin, where Found, Lost, and Tapie Lakes are tucked away out of sight. The trail is rocky but well worn.

Don't worry if it feels as though you're walking past the lake. The trail traverses nearly all the way across the basin before spitting you out on the north side of the lake, just before the outlet (1.9 miles from the trailhead). Arrive at a three-way trail junction next to a large campsite. The junction is signed "Boulder Lake Trail," "Poison Canyon–Tracy Trail," and "Foster–Lion Lake Trail." A right turn (north) here leads across the outlet stream and eventually to the Boulder Creek Trail and options of going up to Foster and Lion Lakes or down to Coffee Creek Road. A left turn (south) leads around Boulder Lake and climbs up and over the ridge to Poison Canyon. The Tracy Trail is also the way to start a cross-country hike to Found, Lost, and Tapie Lakes.

One of the reasons the 8-acre lake is so popular (besides the easy hike in) is the pleasing mixture of terrain: forest, meadow, water, lily pads, and granite seem to be in perfect harmony. The basin is more forested than many of the higher lakes, but there's also a lush wet meadow on the south side at the inlet, which likely accounts for the plentiful mosquitoes. A ring of lily pads hugs much of the water's edge, and a jumble of craggy granite hangs over the upper basin. The water is tinged slightly green with algae, and the bottom is a bit mucky, so it's not the best swimming lake (nearby Little Boulder is better). Using the Tracy Trail and an obvious use path on the west shore, it's possible to circumnavigate the entire lake.

Boulder Lake is an ideal base camp for staging hikes into the surrounding areas or a good destination for families with young children.

SIDE TRIP TO LITTLE BOULDER LAKE

Though only 0.5 mile (as the bird flies) and a few hundred feet in elevation separate Boulder and Little Boulder Lakes, the neighbors are surprisingly different in nature. Little Boulder is gouged into the flank of Peak 6994, with not much room for more than the lake itself and a few campsites.

A steep granite slope plunges into Little Boulder Lake's south shore. Except for the forested shelf where a few campsites are tucked away in the trees, the north shore falls away steeply as well, so there are fewer opportunities for exploring than at Boulder Lake. Still, the pretty little lake makes a fine destination as either a day hike or an overnight; target the far east shore for the best camp. Early-season azaleas decorate the perimeter of the north shore.

To reach Little Boulder Lake from the junction, take the left fork and head uphill (southeast) along the crest of the ridge between the two lakes. Climb gradually through fir and manzanita for 0.25 mile, and then start an easy descent (east) toward the lake. The trail emerges from tree cover onto a rocky, exposed slope before arriving at the southwest corner of the basin, still high above the lake. Look for great views of Mount Shasta as you descend rocky tread along the west side of the lake. The path bends right (east) at the bottom of the basin and traverses the shelf along the north shore. The elevation is 6,350 feet.

MILES AND DIRECTIONS

- 0.0   Start at the Boulder Lakes Trailhead.
- 1.4   Arrive at Little Boulder Lake Trail Junction. Stay right for Boulder Lake.
- 1.9   Reach Boulder Lake. (Reach Little Boulder Lake if you took a left at the junction.) Return the way you came.
- 3.8   Arrive back at the trailhead.

OPTIONS

Explore the upper reaches of the Boulder Lakes drainage, where you can hike to Found, Lost, and Tapie Lakes (Hike 26) via a moderate cross-country route. Or use the Tracy Trail to reach nearby Poison Canyon, a secluded drainage with good opportunities for solitude.

26 TAPIE, FOUND, AND LOST LAKES

Take this short cross-country trek to reach three little lakes in the rugged basin above Boulder Lake. Some easy route finding and minor scrambling over granite and talus slopes are required. Though these lakes are just a stone's throw from busy Boulder Lake, few visitors venture up here.

(See map on page 123.)
Start: Boulder Lakes Trailhead
Type of hike: Day hike or backpack; out-and-back
Distance: 6.6 miles
Hiking time: About 1–2 days
Difficulty: Strenuous (off-trail scrambling, route-finding skills required)
Elevation gain: 1,600 feet
Best season: Midsummer through early fall
Canine compatibility: Yes
Nearest town: Weaverville/Trinity Center
Fees and permits: Free wilderness permit required for overnight

visitors; free campfire permits required for fires and camp stoves
Schedule: Trails in the Trinity Alps are always open; however, most trailhead access roads are closed or impassable during winter.
Maps: USGS Ycatapom Peak; USDAFS Trinity Alps Wilderness
Trail contact: Weaverville Ranger Station: (530) 623-2121; www.fs.usda .gov/stnf
Parking and trailhead facilities: Ample parking but no facilities at the dead-end trailhead. The closest developed campground is Trinity River on CA 3.

FINDING THE TRAILHEAD

The road to Boulder Lakes Trailhead is located 0.3 mile south of Coffee Creek. From Weaverville drive 40 miles north on CA 3 and turn left (west) at the signed junction for Boulder Lakes Trailhead. Proceed 11 miles up the well-signed dirt road to the trailhead. (Follow FR 37N52 for 3.5 miles to a right turn onto FR 37N53, stay left at 4.7 and 9.7 miles, and continue to the trailhead.) Ignore the logging roads that diverge from the main track. GPS: N41 3.883' / W122 47.422'

THE HIKE

Reaching these tiny lakes requires a cross-country scramble that deters most visitors, leaving the lakes in relative obscurity next to one of the Trinity Alps' most-traveled trails.

The three little bodies of water tucked into the rugged upper basin challenge the notion of what, exactly, constitutes a lake in the Trinity Alps. Obviously, mapmakers can't agree. My preferred definition of a lake is anything that's big enough for skipping rocks. By my standards then, the little beauties above Boulder qualify as lakes.

There are several options for reaching these lakes. One is to scramble up the granite above the southwest corner of Boulder Lake. Though possible, it's not the recommended route. A better way is to hike up the Tracy Trail along Boulder's inlet and then contour northwest to the lakes after ascending above the brushy slopes and gullies that present a formidable barrier around the headwall of the upper basin.

It's hard to believe deserted Found Lake is so close to perpetually busy Boulder Lake.

The trail starts on a wide track heading south up the ridgeline. Fir and sugar pine are scattered to either side, but the first 0.25 mile is mostly open and exposed. While the ridgeline is still open, look back for your first of many Mount Shasta views on this hike.

After a small, level landing, the wide track gives way to single track trail and you start climbing more steeply through forest cover. The walking is pleasant and shady on soft duff. Continue the gradual ascent to the crest of the ridge, just over 1 mile from the trailhead.

After gaining the crest, the trail continues south at a nearly level grade. Good views of the drainages ahead and to the west open up. Arrive at the signed junction to Little Boulder Lake a few minutes after hiking along the ridge crest. A left (southeast) turn here leads to Little Boulder Lake; stay right (south) for Boulder Lake and the trio of lakes you're heading for.

Start descending into the Boulder Lake basin on moderate switchbacks. Before dropping into the firs, get a glimpse of the upper reaches of the basin, where Found, Tapie, and Lost Lakes are tucked away out of sight. The trail is rocky but well worn.

Don't worry if it feels as though you're walking past the lake. The trail traverses nearly all the way across the basin before spitting you out on the north side of the lake, just before the outlet (1.9 miles from the trailhead). Arrive at a three-way trail junction next to a large campsite. The junction is signed "Boulder Lake Trail; Poison Canyon–Tracy Trail; and Foster–Lion Lake Trail."

Head south on the Tracy Trail (toward Poison Canyon) along the lake's east shore; then start climbing as the path parallels the inlet. The trail crosses several small meadows as it ascends. These isolated flower gardens are spectacular in July and August.

On the way up, you pass an obscure use trail that leads up a gully to the west. Be patient and stay on the Tracy Trail as it switchbacks steeply up toward the ridgeline. Save the bushwhacking for the descent, if you want to try that route.

The path crosses the creek several times on the way up. The refreshing stream runs even in late summer. Near the headwaters of the stream, a couple of hundred feet below the Poison-Boulder divide, the trail bends east and climbs the last few steep switchbacks to the ridgeline. Jump off the trail here and pick your way west across the creek; the easiest crossing is near the bottom of a small meadow. (This point is just over 0.5 mile from Boulder Lake.)

After leaving the trail, contour northwest around Tapie Peak and work your way over to the upper basin. You should end up below Lost Lake and above Tapie. If you want a good look at the route before setting off, climb up to the divide and look back toward Boulder Lake. A slice of Tapie Lake is visible beyond a shoulder of granite and gives you a good view of the route across sunny, treeless slopes of granite and talus. (The climb to the ridgeline is only a few minutes' extra hiking and, as a bonus, you get yet another great view of Mount Shasta.)

From the west side of the inlet creek, pick your way through the bushes and out onto the open slopes. A few rock ducks are scattered here and there, but the route is fairly straightforward: Stay as high as you can (a sheer cliff band prevents you from going too high, and steep brushy slopes await below) and make your way northwest across the granite and talus. The rock-hopping is fun, but watch your footing—the sharp-edged granite can cut like a knife.

Once you make it around to the middle of the drainage on the northwest side of Tapie Peak, you have the option of going up 0.25 mile to Lost Lake or down the same distance to Tapie. Found Lake lies 100 yards beyond Lost.

Found Lake is hidden in the uppermost reaches of the basin—nearly invisible until you're practically swimming in it. It's a small, charming lake with a spectacular backdrop of granite and truly wild country. The shoreline is rocky, with just a few stunted trees and grass fringes.

A short walk up the ridge northwest of Found Lake leads to a ridgetop with a magnificent view. It commands an unbroken vista of upper Boulder Canyon and Cub Wallow. If you want a private slice of paradise in the Trinity Alps without going on a long trek, it's hard to find a better place than Found Lake.

To reach Tapie Lake, head back downhill (northeast) and skirt the edge of Lost Lake, which dries up to a puddle in late summer. (All three lakes in the basin are fed by snow-melt only, so they tend to shrink over the course of the summer.)

Continue down the slope above Tapie by staying left (northwest) of the main gully below Lost. Zigzag down a series of granite benches to reach the south end of the narrow 2-acre lake. Thick stands of pine and fir crowd the west shore of Tapie, and a rocky bluff hems in the east side, enfolding the quiet little lake in an isolated cleft.

MILES AND DIRECTIONS

0.0   Start at the Boulder Lakes Trailhead.

1.4   Stay right at the Little Boulder Lake Trail Junction.

1.9   Pass Boulder Lake and turn left at the three-way trail junction onto the Tracy Trail; follow it upward.

2.8   Reach Tapie Lake after leaving the Tracy Trail and hiking cross-country.

3.3   Reach Found Lake. Return the way you came.

6.6   Arrive back at the trailhead.

OPTIONS

Options for the return trip include going back the way you came; following a rough route down Tapie's outlet to Boulder Lake (steep); and picking your way down the gully southeast of the lake (also steep, but rock cairns show that most people prefer this route). The outlet route deposits you on Boulder's west shore; the gully route returns you to the Tracy Trail.

Another good side trip from here includes Poison Canyon (Hike 23), which lies just over the ridge to the south, along the Tracy Trail.

27 **FOSTER LAKE LOOP**

Sample a bit of everything on this loop. You'll visit classic lakes, dive deep into uncrowded canyons, and gain spectacular ridgetop views. Bonus: a sweet sunset view at Foster Lake.

Start: Boulder Lakes Trailhead
Type of hike: Backpack; loop
Distance: 22.0 miles
Hiking time: About 3–6 days
Difficulty: Strenuous
Elevation gain: 5,600 feet
Best season: Midsummer through early fall
Canine compatibility: Yes
Nearest town: Weaverville/Trinity Center
Fees and permits: Free wilderness permit required for overnight visitors; free campfire permits required for fires and camp stoves

Schedule: Trails in the Trinity Alps are always open; however, most trailhead access roads are closed or impassable during winter.
Maps: USGS Ycatapom Peak; USDAFS Trinity Alps Wilderness
Trail contact: Weaverville Ranger Station: (530) 623-2121; www.fs.usda .gov/stnf
Parking and trailhead facilities: Ample parking but no facilities at the dead-end trailhead. The closest campground is Trinity River on CA 3.

FINDING THE TRAILHEAD

The road to Boulder Lakes Trailhead is located 0.3 mile south of Coffee Creek. From Weaverville drive 40 miles north on CA 3 and turn left (west) at the signed junction for Boulder Lakes Trailhead. Proceed 11 miles up the well-signed dirt road to the trailhead. (Follow FR 37N52 for 3.5 miles to a right turn on FR 37N53, stay left at 4.7 and 9.7 miles, and continue to the trailhead.) Ignore the logging roads that diverge from the main track. GPS: N41 3.883' / W122 47.422'

THE HIKE

This loop combines spectacular scenery (Foster Lake) with spectacular solitude (Poison Canyon). It's an up-and-down journey with three deep canyons en route, but there's ample compensation for your effort. **Note:** If you only want to go to Foster Lake, just retrace your steps instead of completing the loop, or better yet, consider one of the other routes mentioned below.

The two alternate ways to approach Foster Lake are both good options, but the route from Boulder Lake offers the most variety and the best loop. The alternative trailheads are Boulder Creek and Union Creek. Using one of these other routes is more direct, but you get less variety and miss out on the satisfaction of doing a loop that's mostly off the beaten track (except for the first 2 miles to Boulder Lake).

The Boulder Lakes Trail starts on a wide track heading south up the ridgeline. Fir and sugar pine are scattered to either side, but the first 0.25 mile is mostly open and exposed. While the ridgeline is still open, look back for your first of many Mount Shasta views on this hike.

After a small, level landing, the wide track gives way to trail and you start climbing more steeply through forest cover (mostly fir). The walking is pleasant and shady on soft

Look for great camping on Foster Lake's western shore.

duff. Continue the gradual ascent to an obvious switchback; then climb northwest to the crest of the ridge, just over 1 mile from the trailhead.

After gaining the crest, the trail continues south at a nearly level grade. Good views of the drainages ahead and to the west open up. Arrive at the signed junction to Little Boulder Lake a few minutes after hiking along the ridge crest. A left (southeast) turn here leads to Little Boulder Lake; stay right (south) for Boulder Lake.

Start descending into the Boulder Lake basin on moderate switchbacks. Before dropping into the firs, get a glimpse of the upper reaches of the basin, where Found, Tapie, and Lost Lakes are tucked away out of sight.

Don't worry if it feels as though you're walking past the lake. The trail traverses nearly all the way across the basin before spitting you out on the north side of the lake, just before the outlet (1.9 miles from the trailhead). Arrive at a three-way trail junction next to a large campsite. **Note:** Boulder or Little Boulder makes a nice stopover if you need an extra night coming or going; though keep in mind that both lakes are likely to be crowded on summer weekends.

The junction at the north end of Boulder Lake is signed "8W20 Coffee Creek Road" to the north (this is the trail to Foster and Lion Lakes) and "8W26 Poison Canyon–Lilypad Lake" to the south. The route to Foster Lake is north, and if you're contemplating the loop via Thumb Rock, you'll return on the other trail.

Head north and descend slightly to cross the outlet of Boulder Lake. Fill up here if you need water; the next available water is just over 2 miles away in Boulder Creek. Purify water here and at all other sources on the hike.

After crossing the outlet the trail descends gradually to round the shoulder of the ridge between you and the Boulder Creek drainage. The descent is shady under a canopy of mixed fir and pine. This trail is not shown on the 1986 USGS quadrangle, which instead displays an older path that dipped down to an out-of-use jeep road before climbing steeply to the ridgeline. Look for a good view of Mount Shasta just before crossing the crest of the ridge.

The trail nearly doubles back on itself after crossing the ridgeline. Head southwest now on a long but gradual descent to Boulder Creek. Mixed conifers shade the path all the way down to the bottom of the canyon—a drop of nearly 1,000 feet. Despite the elevation change, the traverse strikes the perfect grade and is gentle on your knees.

At the bottom of the drainage, cross a small meadow splashed with bright purple monkshood in summer, then arrive at Boulder Creek. Alders and willows line the banks in most places, but the sparkling clear stream is generally easy to cross (except very early in the year), and plenty of large, smooth boulders are strewn about if you want to put your feet up. The creek crossing is slightly more than halfway to Foster Lake—and much of the remainder is uphill—so it's a logical place to take a break. In any case, be sure to replenish your water supplies before heading off. The rest of the way is steep and hot on a summer afternoon. A few small tributaries do cross the trail farther up, but it's wise to carry plenty of water on the steep ascent.

The trail proceeds downstream (southeast) less than 0.25 mile to the junction with the Lion Lake Trail. The junction is marked by cairns and a sign. The Boulder Creek Trail (8W08) continues downstream (northeast) to Goldfield Campground and Coffee Creek Road; the Lion Lake Trail (8W12) turns sharply uphill (west) and climbs out of the drainage on a rocky path.

The first leg out of the drainage is as steep as any trail in the Trinity Alps. It's the exact opposite of the trail you just descended—so if you didn't appreciate the gentle grade on the way down, you will now. Climb through mixed fir, pine, and incense cedar, occasionally crossing small meadows. The trail ascends a series of benches on the canyon wall,

Most people on the way to Foster Lake hike right by little Conway Lake.

Lion Lake is an easy detour off the Foster Lake Loop.

heading southwest toward the pass between Lion and Foster Lakes. As you gain elevation, look for good views up the Boulder Creek drainage. The headwaters of the creek are in a trail-less, seldom-visited wilderness called Cub Wallow. If you plan on returning via Thumb Rock, your path traverses the divide just south of Cub Wallow, above Parker Creek.

SIDE TRIP TO CONWAY AND LION LAKES

Almost 2.5 miles from the Boulder Creek crossing, arrive at the junction with the Lion–Conway Lakes Trail. A left turn at this fork brings you first to Conway Lake, a pretty but small, lily pad–choked puddle. Conway is surrounded by lush, wet meadows on a shelf high above Boulder Creek.

To reach Lion Lake, merely follow Conway Lake's inlet creek uphill to its source. The water tumbling down the granite slope west of Conway leads directly to spectacular and deep Lion Lake (elevation 7,000 feet). Scramble up the south side of the creek for the easiest path to the lake. The 3-acre lake sits in a glacier-gouged basin behind a granite dike. The water is clear, blue, and incredibly refreshing on a summer afternoon. A sheer granite wall rises on Lion's north shore, where a rockslide has deposited a pile of debris that reaches nearly to the water's surface. The other sides of the lake aren't much less steep, creating a dramatic setting. A few stunted firs grow on the lake's west side. The contrast between sheer-sided Lion and meadow-lined Conway makes the two-lake basin a nice place to spend a day exploring—look for the lake's single campsite on the south shore.

FOSTER LAKE

To continue on the main trail to Foster Lake, take the right fork at the junction with the Lion–Conway Lakes Trail and keep climbing. The path zigzags up the canyon wall to a rocky, exposed shelf above Lion Lake. The route traverses the steep hillside directly above the lake, offering great views of Lion's brilliant blue water—and a few narrow sections where it's wise to watch your step. The trail reaches the divide between Lion and Foster Lakes in 0.5 mile, on a rocky pass with a good vantage point down both drainages and a perfect view of Mount Shasta.

From the saddle above Foster Lake, you can look down and see the 5.5-acre body of water in an oblong basin. The north-facing lake stays fairly cold through the summer, with snow often remaining on the south side of the cirque in August. The trail descends through boulders on the lake's northeast side and then switchbacks down to cross the

Foster Lake has one of the best sunset views in the Trinity Alps.

Find lush ponds in the Foster Lake basin.

outlet. The west shore has plenty of room to spread out, even for groups with several tents. There you'll find shady firs and mountain hemlocks and a couple of lily pad–lined ponds. The north shore has the best site for a solo camper or a single tent for two.

A rounded, rocky bluff west of the lake commands an awesome view of the western horizon and, far below, the Union Creek drainage. Get an early seat here for one of the best sunset shows in the Trinity Alps. Golden light fills the basin behind you as the sun sinks into a sea of mountains on the horizon. You also get a good look at the endless switchbacks leading down to Union Creek. Foster's elevation is 7,245 feet.

To continue on the loop, descend those formidable switchbacks to Union Creek, 1.5 miles and nearly 1,500 feet below, passing a seldom-used trail to Sugar Pine Lake just before reaching the bottom of the drainage. There's a large campsite along Union Creek here. Cross the stream and turn left (southeast) at the trail junction 100 yards up the slope on the other side, at the lower end of a wide meadow. Follow the Union Creek Trail (9W07) southeast, toward the Union–Parker Creek divide.

A pleasant 2.5-mile climb leads through the upper end of the canyon (passing the spur trail to Landers Lake) and then brings you, more steeply on the final push, to the saddle between Union and Parker Creeks. Be sure to replenish water before leaving Union Creek. From the divide, turn left (east) on the Poison Canyon Trail. (If you continue along Parker Creek, you'll descend to Swift Creek.) From here you're on a trail that sees very few boot prints. Enjoy great views of Swift Creek drainage and Cub Wallow as you climb the ridgeline toward Thumb Rock. Just before reaching the base of Thumb Rock, bear right on the Thumb Rock Trail (8W16) at an unsigned junction in an open, rocky area on the ridgeline. The trail descends southeast toward Shimmy Lake and the Lilypad Lake Trail. The left fork contours around Thumb Rock, to the east and then north, before descending into the head of Poison Canyon and arriving at the Tracy Trail, which leads back to Boulder Lake. (Take the left fork if you're in a hurry; otherwise stay on the recommended route.)

FOSTER LAKE LOOP

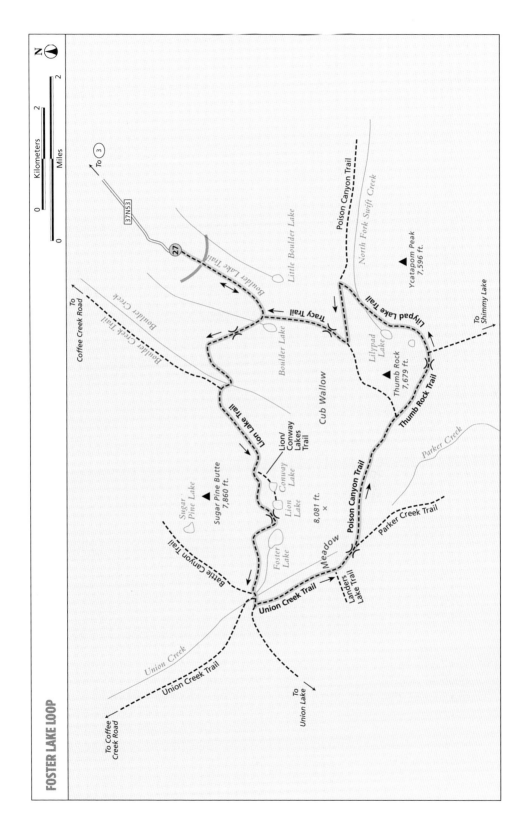

To 3

37N53

27

To Coffee Creek Road

Coffee Creek Road

Sugar Pine Lake

Sugar Pine Butte 7,860 ft.

Boulder Creek

Boulder Creek Trail

Boulder Lake Trail

Little Boulder Lake

Boulder Lake

Tracy Trail

Lion Lake Trail

Conway Lake

Lion/Conway Lakes Trail

Lion Lake

Foster Lake

Battle Canyon Trail

Meadow

8,081 ft.

Cub Wallow

Union Creek

Union Creek Trail

To Coffee Creek Road

Union Creek Trail

To Union Lake

Union Creek Trail

Landers Lake Trail

Poison Canyon Trail

Parker Creek Trail

Parker Creek

Poison Canyon Trail

North Fork Swift Creek

Ycatapom Peak 7,596 ft.

Lilypad Lake Trail

Lilypad Lake

Thumb Rock 7,679 ft.

Thumb Rock Trail

To Shimmy Lake

N

Kilometers

0   2   2

Miles

0   2

For my preferred route, take the Lilypad Lake Trail (8W21) at mile 15.7 and descend north across a series of gorgeous hanging meadows with great views of Ycatapom Peak and Mount Shasta (lots of good camping through here). Skirt Lilypad Lake and continue northeast to the Poison Canyon Trail; then turn left (west) and ascend 1 mile to the Tracy Trail (8W26). Turn right (north) on the Tracy Trail and proceed over the ridge to the Boulder Lake basin. From here it's an easy 1-mile descent to the three-way junction at Boulder Lake, where you started the loop. Retrace your steps 1.9 miles to the trailhead.

MILES AND DIRECTIONS

0.0   Start at the Boulder Lakes Trailhead.

1.9   Pass Boulder Lake.

2.0   Cross a Boulder Lake outlet.

4.4   Cross Boulder Creek.

4.6   Go left at the Lion Lake Trail junction.

6.5   Stay straight at the Conway Lake Trail and Lion Lake Trail junction.

8.0   Reach Foster Lake (great camp option).

9.5   Cross Union Creek and soon turn left on the Union Creek Trail.

12.0   Take the Poison Canyon Trail.

13.8   Stay right on the Thumb Rock Trail. (**Option:** Go left for a shorter return.)

15.7   Take the Lilypad Lake Trail.

16.8   Reach Lilypad Lake.

17.7   Go left on the Poison Canyon Trail.

18.7   Go right on the Tracy Trail.

20.1   Reach Boulder Lake and turn right on the Boulder Creek Trail.

22.0   Arrive back at the trailhead.

OPTIONS

From Union Creek, take side trips to Union Lake or Landers Lake, or tackle the steep climb up Battle Canyon Trail and visit Sugar Pine Lake. The Foster Lake Loop passes numerous trail junctions, allowing you to create custom side trips. Red Rock Mountain, above Landers Lake, makes for a great day trip from a basecamp along Union Creek.

This lightly used trail connects with trails to Foster and Lion Lakes and Boulder Lakes. It can be used to create a longer loop using the Sugar Pine Lake Trail or a loop using most of the route for the Foster Lake Loop. It also makes a fine day hike, especially if you're car camping at Goldfield Campground.

Start: Boulder Creek Trailhead
Type of hike: Day hike or backpack; out-and-back
Distance: 8.6 miles
Hiking time: About 4–6 hours (day hike); 2 days (backpack)
Difficulty: Moderate
Elevation gain: 2,150 feet
Best season: Midsummer through early fall
Canine compatibility: Yes
Nearest town: Weaverville/Trinity Center
Fees and permits: Free wilderness permit required for overnight visitors; free campfire permits required for fires and camp stoves

Schedule: Trails in the Trinity Alps are always open; however, most trailhead access roads are closed or impassable during winter.
Maps: USGS Ycatapom Peak; USDAFS Trinity Alps Wilderness
Trail contact: Weaverville Ranger Station: (530) 623-2121; www.fs.usda.gov/stnf
Parking and trailhead facilities: Limited parking at the trailhead; more is available at the creek crossing and back at Goldfield Campground. The campground has an outhouse but no potable water.

FINDING THE TRAILHEAD

From Weaverville drive 40 miles north on CA 3 and turn left (west) on Coffee Creek Road. Proceed 5 miles up the paved road to the signed turnoff for Goldfield Campground/Boulder Creek Trailhead. Turn left and continue 0.5 mile on the dirt road to the trailhead, on the right, just before the road crosses Boulder Creek. GPS: N41 5.983' / W 122 47.218'

THE HIKE

The Boulder Creek Trail ascends gradually along its namesake creek, climbing steadily but not steeply through oak, madrone, incense cedar, and fir. The path can be used a number of ways: an uncrowded day hike; a good place to start a trip to Foster or Lion Lake (less crowded and more direct than starting at Boulder Lake, but less scenic variety); or used with the Sugar Pine Lake Trail to create a spectacular 20-mile loop (requires a 3-mile walk on Coffee Creek Road). Unless you're a glutton for punishment, don't use the Boulder Creek Trail to reach Boulder Lakes. It's more than twice as far as the route from the Boulder Lakes Trailhead, quite a bit steeper, and your reward is cooler-carrying crowds at Boulder Lake.

The first part of the route is on an old track blocked by a metal gate. Go around the gate and head uphill on the Boulder Creek Trail (8W08). The wide dirt track gives way to trail soon after the initial ascent and continues climbing southwest at a moderate grade. Forest on both sides of the trail consists mostly of incense cedar, oak, fir, and madrone.

Look for fall colors in valley bottoms throughout the Trinity Alps.

BOULDER CREEK

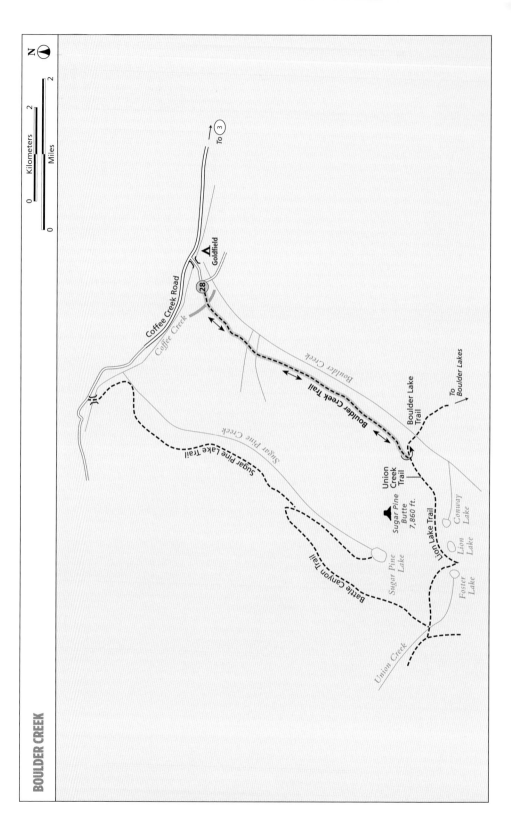

The path ascends gradually up the side of Boulder Creek Canyon. Soon enough you find yourself high on the canyon wall, the creek now tumbling quietly far below.

Madrones give way to oaks and firs as the trail contours higher and higher. Cross two strong tributaries of Boulder Creek in quick succession 1.5 miles from the trailhead. The water is clear, cold, and dependable, but it still should be purified, like all water in the wilderness. Plentiful water along the trail alleviates the need to fill water bottles at every tributary. Look for good views of Billys Peak behind you as the canyon opens up a short distance after the creek crossings.

The first (and only) switchback appears after 3 miles as the trail continues its moderate ascent, dipping occasionally to run alongside Boulder Creek, through a couple of small, lush meadows. Just before the trail reaches Boulder Creek, arrive at the junction with the Lion Lake Trail. The signed junction is 4.1 miles from the trailhead. A wooden sign indicates trails 8W08 (back to Coffee Creek Road), 8W20 (to Boulder Lakes), and Foster-Lion Lakes. The trail to Foster and Lion Lakes (and little Conway) heads steeply uphill to the west. The trail to Boulder Lakes continues upstream for less than 0.25 mile and then crosses the creek before climbing the opposite side of the canyon and heading east over the ridge. An obvious use trail at the creek crossing leads west a short distance to a small, pleasant campsite. Even if you're not spending the night here, it's a fine lunch stop coming or going.

If you're heading on up to Lion or Foster Lake, take a break and replenish water supplies before tackling the steep route. From the junction with the Boulder Creek Trail, it's a long haul uphill. If you want to make a loop using the Sugar Pine Trail, continue past Foster Lake toward Union Creek; then use the Battle Canyon Trail to reach the Sugar Pine Lake Trail and Coffee Creek Road.

MILES AND DIRECTIONS

0.0   Start at the Boulder Creek Trailhead.

4.1   Reach the junction with the Foster Lake–Lion Lakes Trail. Go left to Boulder Creek.

4.3   Reach Boulder Creek. The Boulder Lakes Trail crosses the water here and climbs to Boulder Lakes. Return the way you came.

8.6   Arrive back at the trailhead.

OPTIONS

Most people on this trail are heading for Lion or Foster Lake, just over 7 miles from the trailhead. You could also make a long loop connecting the Union Creek, Poison Canyon, and Boulder Lakes Trails (see the Foster Lake Loop hike).

29 SUGAR PINE LAKE

Hike to an isolated granite cirque sheltering Sugar Pine Lake. Got more time? An optional loop through Battle Canyon (with off-trail sections) delivers incredible views and solitude.

Start: Sugar Pine Lake Trailhead
Type of hike: Backpack; out-and-back with optional loop
Distance: 12.4 miles (Sugar Pine Lake only); 21.7 miles (loop)
Hiking time: About 2–5 days
Difficulty: Moderate (to Sugar Pine Lake only); strenuous (loop)
Elevation gain: 3,400 feet (lake only); 6,500 feet (loop)
Best season: Midsummer through early fall
Canine compatibility: Yes
Nearest town: Weaverville/Trinity Center
Fees and permits: Free wilderness permit required for overnight visitors; free campfire permits required for fires and camp stoves
Schedule: Trails in the Trinity Alps are always open; however, most trailhead access roads are closed or impassable during winter.
Maps: USGS Ycatapom Peak and Caribou Lake; USDAFS Trinity Alps Wilderness
Trail contact: Weaverville Ranger Station: (530) 623-2121; www.fs.usda .gov/stnf
Parking and trailhead facilities: Ample parking both here and across the road at East Fork Coffee Creek Trailhead; no facilities. The closest campground is Goldfield, 3.5 miles east on Coffee Creek Road.

FINDING THE TRAILHEAD

From Weaverville drive 40 miles north on CA 3 to Coffee Creek Road and go left (west). Follow this road 8 miles to the trailhead on the left (Coffee Creek Road is unpaved after the first 5 miles), just before the East Fork Coffee Creek Trailhead. GPS: N41 7.304' / W122 48.976'

THE HIKE

Despite being at the head of a beautiful drainage and surrounded by impressive granite cliffs, Sugar Pine Lake doesn't get as many visitors as one might expect. The lake isn't really on the way from or to anywhere and the scenery is not as dramatic as some other spots, so it tends to get less hike-by traffic than some other Trinity Alps destinations. Add a steep approach (the trail climbs more than 3,500 feet, most of it in the first 4 miles) and more steep hiking to go anywhere beyond the lake, and you get a rather lonely outpost.

A bridge across Coffee Creek leads to the start of the Sugar Pine Lake Trail. (Old maps will show the bridge downstream, but it was washed away in 1996 and was replaced by this one, which adds about 1.1 miles to the original route.) The "new" section is mostly an easy contour along Coffee Creek, then you meet the old trail and it's uphill to Cabin Flat. The last 2.2 miles to Sugar Pine Lake are a walk in the park.

You have several options on the Sugar Pine Lake Trail. You can simply hike up to the lake and back, which makes a pleasant route by itself. Ambitious hikers can use the Battle Canyon Trail to create a spectacular loop through Union Creek and past Foster and Lion Lakes. Complete the loop by returning via Sugar Pine Lake, which requires a short but steep off-trail hike, or by using the Boulder Creek Trail to reach Coffee Creek Road at

Hike to the ridge between Sugar Pine Lake and Foster Lake for this view down the Sugar Pine drainage.

Goldfield Campground. (This alternative lands you about 3.5 road miles east of the Sugar Pine Trailhead.) The route described here is the off-trail version.

From Sugar Pine Trailhead, cross Coffee Creek on the steel bridge and climb gently southeast. The low-elevation forest consists mostly of oak, madrone, and Douglas fir. As you gain altitude, white fir, incense cedar, and several varieties of pine begin to appear. In midsummer expect hot hiking on this initial ascent. And though the map shows Sugar Pine Creek near the trail, it's really too far away to be useful. Refill water at tributaries.

Sugar Pine Lake Trail, though steep, doesn't employ many switchbacks—just a long southward climb. The ascent eases at Cabin Flat, 4 miles from the trailhead. There, amid a welcome meadow of lush grass and corn lilies, you find the junction with the Battle Canyon Trail (9W59). A sign indicates that's the way to Union Creek. To reach Sugar Pine Lake, continue southwest on the Sugar Pine Lake Trail. The 9-acre lake lies 2.2 miles away in a granite cirque at the head of the drainage. This last section of trail crosses lush meadows before ending abruptly at the shore of Sugar Pine Lake. There's good camping in the basin.

If you're not hiking the loop beyond Sugar Pine Lake, just retrace your steps back to the trailhead from here. If you want to make the 9.3-mile loop by way of Battle Canyon, Union Creek, and Foster Lake, you have the choice of starting at Sugar Pine Lake and going clockwise or returning to Cabin Flat and hiking counterclockwise. The description here is counterclockwise, so hikers who prefer not to do the off-trail portion can follow the described route to Lion Lake and then keep going on maintained trails.

Back at Cabin Flat, go left (west) on the Battle Canyon Trail (signed "Union Creek"). The little-used trail is not obvious until you start climbing away from the meadow. Veer

Trail signs come and go in the backcountry; this one at Cabin Flat has been there a while.

right (northwest) from the trail sign. You pick up the path as you leave the meadow's western edge. Once you clear the lower canyon, the trail becomes distinct again as it climbs steeply west and south (gaining 1,000 feet in 1 mile). Then enjoy a more moderate grade as the trail winds along the open ridge separating Battle and Sugar Pine Creeks. This portion of the route is blessed with beautiful views and wildflower gardens of aster, angelica, monkshood, lupine, and other blooms. It also passes an interesting array of knob-like rock formations called the Battleship.

Amid open terrain and great views, the trail dips down into the head of Battle Canyon before making yet another steep climb (about 700 feet) up to the saddle between Battle and Union Creeks. The trail may be overgrown and indistinct at times as you traverse the head of Battle Canyon. Set your sights on that low gap to the south and you should have no problem. The view from the saddle is a nearly 360-degree jaw-dropper that encompasses Mount Shasta, Caribou Mountain, Sawtooth Mountain, and a number of lesser peaks.

The way down to Union Creek, 1,500 feet below, is literally at your feet. The trail plummets the whole way in about 1.2 miles. Midway down, the trail appears to peter out in a grassy bench. It's there; just look for it on the meadow's southwest side. The rest of the descent is straightforward, leading to a three-way junction with the Lion Lake Trail (8W12) and Union Creek Trail (9W07). A right (west) turn leads to Union Creek, with numerous exploring and camping options.

To continue the loop, turn left (east) and follow the Lion Lake Trail. The path makes a steep, nearly 1,500-foot, 1.5-mile ascent to Foster Lake. The deep-blue lake is tucked into a granite shelf with one of the most beautiful sunset views in the Trinity Alps. The approach to Foster is a straightforward climb up the north side of the drainage, alongside an impressive avalanche gully and with ever-better views as you climb out of the forest cover. Traverse a series of smooth granite slabs just before arriving at lake level. Find great camping near the outlet.

SUGAR PINE LAKE

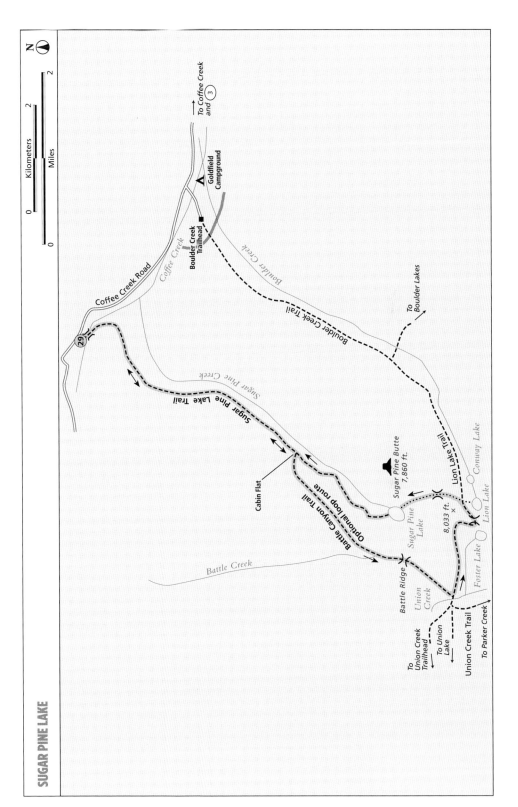

The trail climbs above the lake on rocky tread to an obvious saddle between Foster and Lion Lakes (and another great view of Mount Shasta). Once over the saddle, descend northeast on a rocky path that literally hangs over the west edge of Lion Lake. After passing the lake, look for the low gap on the ridge to the northwest. That's the off-trail route back to Sugar Pine Lake. The 1.2-mile hike is not exceptionally difficult, but it does require some rough scrambling and good route-finding skills. To return via established trails, continue down to the Boulder Creek Trail and hike out to Coffee Creek Road; then walk 3.5 miles back to Sugar Pine Lake Trailhead on Coffee Creek Road. From this point, it's about 10 miles back to the trailhead on this route.

The most difficult part of the off-trail hike to Sugar Pine Lake is picking your way through fields of manzanita when you first leave the trail. It's a trade-off between staying high (more manzanita) and dropping lower before leaving the trail (less manzanita but more elevation gain). Choose your poison and shoot for the saddle south of Sugar Pine Butte.

Once on the saddle it's a simple matter of picking your way down to Sugar Pine Lake. Granite benches lead down into the basin like a series of huge stone steps. Proceed carefully and use caution to avoid any hazardous sections with dangerously steep drops. Once at the lake, make your way over to the outlet and resume hiking on the Sugar Pine Lake Trail. Retrace your steps to the trailhead.

MILES AND DIRECTIONS

0.0 Start at the Sugar Pine Lake Trailhead.

1.1 Pass the junction with Old Sugar Pine Trail (unmarked).

4.0 Arrive at the Cabin Flat–Battle Canyon Trail junction. Stay straight (left) to reach Sugar Pine Lake.

6.2 Reach Sugar Pine Lake. Turn around here and retrace your steps for a moderate 12.4-mile hike. If you're doing the loop, retrace your steps as far as Cabin Flat and then turn left onto Battle Canyon Trail.

10.9 Top out on Battle Ridge.

12.1 Arrive at Union Creek after a long descent. At the three-way junction, turn left onto Lion Lake Trail and begin climbing toward Foster Lake.

13.5 Reach Foster Lake; continue climbing.

14.3 Turn left and start the off-trail route to Sugar Pine Lake.

15.5 Arrive back at Sugar Pine Lake; continue the descent on-trail.

17.7 Pass the Cabin Flat–Battle Canyon Trail junction.

21.7 Arrive back at the trailhead.

OPTIONS

Use the Union Creek Trail to connect with the Landers Lake Loop and Bullards Basin. See Hike 30 for details on exploring downstream on Union Creek.

30 **UNION CREEK**

This often-overlooked trail leads to one of the Trinity Alps' most underrated valleys. Union Creek drainage has wonderful camping, accesses lakes like Foster and Landers, and provides a good base camp for bagging Red Rock Mountain. But none of these highlights are on the Trinity Alps "A-list," so traffic remains relatively low.

Start: Union Creek Trailhead
Type of hike: Day hike or backpack; out-and-back
Distance: 12.4 miles
Hiking time: About 1–4 days
Difficulty: Easy
Elevation gain: 1,700 feet
Best season: Mid-summer through early fall
Canine compatibility: Yes
Nearest town: Weaverville/Trinity Center
Fees and permits: Free wilderness permit required for overnight visitors; free campfire permits required for fires and camp stoves

Schedule: Trails in the Trinity Alps are always open; however, most trailhead access roads are closed or impassable during winter.
Maps: USGS Caribou Lake and Ycatapom Peak; USDAFS Trinity Alps Wilderness
Trail contact: Weaverville Ranger Station: (530) 623-2121; www.fs.usda .gov/stnf
Parking and trailhead facilities: Adequate parking, but horse trailers sometimes take up a lot of room; no facilities. The closest campgrounds are Goldfield and Big Flat.

FINDING THE TRAILHEAD

From Weaverville drive 40 miles north on CA 3 to Coffee Creek Road and go left (west). Continue 11 miles to the signed trailhead; the trail is on the left, parking on the right. Coffee Creek Road is unpaved after the first 5 miles. GPS: N41 6.790' / W122 52.736'

THE HIKE

Other destinations in the Trinity Alps are more spectacular. Other creeks are bigger, other valleys more dramatic. But if you want quiet wilderness with lots of high country to explore, and you want to avoid the busier corners of Trinity, it's hard to beat Union Creek. The approach is more like a walk in the park than an alpine hike. After 6 gently ascending miles, you find yourself in a sprawling meadow at the heart of a perfectly proportioned valley—a sparkling creek here, a sweet-smelling forest of Jeffrey pines there, a field of wildflowers over here.

There's plenty of elbowroom along Union Creek and its secluded little glades, but what makes this hike truly attractive is the variety of side trips available. From an 0.5-mile stroll to shallow Union Lake to a leg-burning 1,500-foot climb to Foster Lake, there's something for everyone. Connecting trails make it possible to extend this hike by several days, and you'll find plenty of base-camping sites along Union Creek and at Union Lake. **Note:** If Foster Lake is your primary goal, this hike and the Boulder Creek hike are the most direct routes and about the same distance, but I prefer Union Creek for the stream side walking and access to side trips.

Come to Union Lake for solitude (swimming is better at the higher lakes).

At the trailhead start hiking south up the old roadbed (signed "Union Creek"). The Union Creek Trail (9W07) follows this wide track for the first 1.5 miles. Immediately pass a locked forest service gate; then head east until a sharp switchback sends you on a long traverse to the southwest. Don't be alarmed by the initial climb, which rises steadily above a boulder field on an exposed slope. The path levels out as soon as you round the nose of the ridge above Union Creek proper. From there it's an easy hike, downhill at times, to a bridge crossing at 2.5 miles. There's plenty of water along the way, and mature stands of Douglas fir, white fir, and mixed pines shade the trail. In early summer look for a lush and fragrant stand of azalea bushes at about 1 mile, near a small pond beside the trail.

After crossing Union Creek the trail follows the west side of the drainage, climbing gently through alternating thickets of mixed conifers and pretty green glades of meadow grass, alders, and wildflowers. At 3 miles the trail crosses Pin Creek on a cement-lined creek bed. Use caution if the water is high in early season.

More gentle hiking leads to the next creek crossing, a wide braid of water that flows out of Bullards Basin. The ford, upstream from the creek's confluence with Union Creek, can be difficult in early season. A log across the water (if it's still there) provides a dry crossing upstream from the trail. (Pick your way through a stand of alders to find the log.)

The next mile climbs more earnestly as the trail winds around to the southeast, following the bending course of the drainage. At 4.8 miles, just before the junction with the Dorleska Mine Trail, you skirt the lower end of an emerald meadow filled with corn lilies. A sparkling little stream flows across the west side of the meadow, nourishing a small field of California pitcher plants that thrive in the wet environment.

At the east end of the meadow, continue on the Union Creek Trail and soon arrive at the junction with the Dorleska Mine Trail (9W65). To the right (west), 2 miles away,

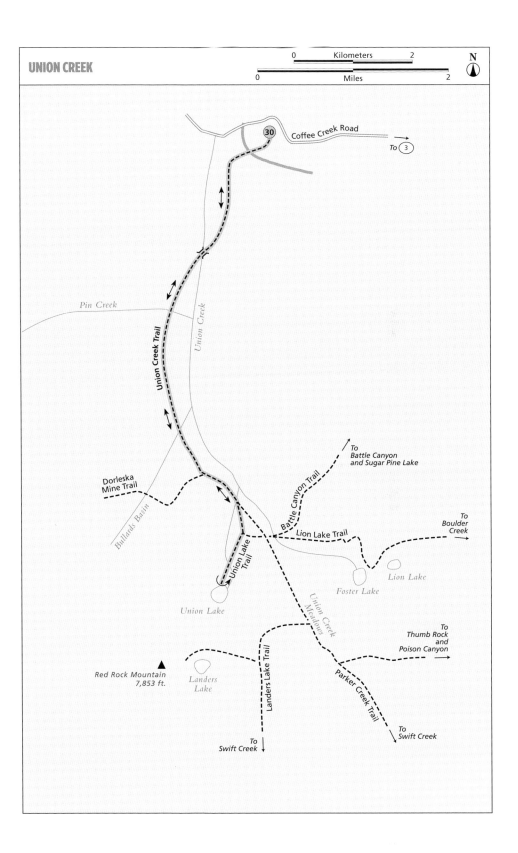

UNION CREEK

0 Kilometers 2
0 Miles 2

N

Coffee Creek Road
To 3

Pin Creek

Union Creek

Union Creek Trail

Dorleska Mine Trail

Bullards Basin

Union Lake Trail

Union Lake

To Battle Canyon and Sugar Pine Lake

Battle Canyon Trail

Lion Lake Trail

To Boulder Creek

Foster Lake

Lion Lake

Union Creek Meadows

To Thumb Rock and Poison Canyon

Landers Lake Trail

Landers Lake

Red Rock Mountain 7,853 ft.

Parker Creek Trail

To Swift Creek

To Swift Creek

To Swift Creek

lie the remains of the Dorleska Mine, tucked away on a bench overlooking rarely visited Bullards Basin. The Dorleska Mine Trail can also be used to connect with Big Flat, the campground and trailhead located at the upper end of Coffee Creek Road. The Union Creek Trail continues southeast. After another jaunt through easygoing terrain, cross Union Lake's outlet stream and arrive at the junction with the Union Lake Trail (9W64). This junction marks the northwest corner of a triangle formed by three trail segments that intersect in the Union Creek drainage. A glance at the map will show that these short segments (about 0.5 mile each) are the two spur trails to Union Lake, along with the main Union Creek Trail. In the past, poor or missing trail signs at the southeast corner of the triangle have made the junction confusing.

From this first junction to the head of the Union Creek drainage, 2 miles upstream, you find expansive meadows, views of the surrounding peaks, towering ponderosa and white pines, and plenty of places to pitch a tent in perfect solitude.

Turn right (south) on the Union Lake Trail to reach the shallow, low-lying (6,200 feet) lake. Go straight, then left (northeast) on the Lion Lake Trail (8W12) to reach Foster Lake. This direction also connects, quickly, with Battle Mountain Trail and the route to Sugar Pine Lake. Continue southeast on the Union Creek Trail to reach the junctions for Landers Lake and Parker Creek. Use the Landers Lake Trail to reach the base of Red Rock Mountain. The off-trail hike to the summit is a relatively straightforward scramble, and the view from the top is one of the best in Trinity (see the Landers Lake Loop hike).

Either use Union Creek as a base camp and explore the surrounding area by day; or, if you have more time, consider making a longer loop (see "Options" below). Retrace your steps to the trailhead.

MILES AND DIRECTIONS

0.0   Start at the Union Creek Trailhead.

2.5   Cross the bridge across Union Creek.

3.0   Cross Pin Creek.

5.0   Pass the Dorleska Mine Trail junction. Stay left.

5.5   Arrive at the Union Lake Trail junction. Turn right to reach the lake.

6.2   Reach Union Lake. Return the way you came.

12.4   Arrive back at the trailhead.

OPTIONS

Use Landers Lake, Sunrise Creek, and Bullards Basin to make a 10-mile loop around Red Rock Mountain ending at the Dorleska–Union Creek Trail junction, or use Parker Creek to make a loop through Swift Creek and ending at the Landers Lake–Union Creek trail junction. You can also do an out-and-back detour to Sugar Pine Lake via the Battle Canyon Trail. And climbing to Foster Lake from a base camp on Union Creek is a must.

31 BULLARDS BASIN-SUNRISE CREEK LOOP

This lightly used route passes through lush meadows and broad valleys, affording access to several lakes and an easily climbed peak. Bonus for history buffs: The trail skirts some of the area's best mining relics at the Yellow Rose and Dorleska Mines.

Start: Big Flat Trailhead
Type of hike: Backpack; loop
Distance: 15.5 miles
Hiking time: About 2–4 days
Difficulty: Moderate
Elevation gain: 4,600 feet
Best season: Midsummer through early fall
Canine compatibility: Yes
Nearest town: Weaverville/Trinity Center
Fees and permits: Free wilderness permit required for overnight visitors; free campfire permits required for fires and camp stoves

Schedule: Trails in the Trinity Alps are always open; however, most trailhead access roads are closed or impassable during winter.
Maps: USGS Caribou Lake and Ycatapom Peak; USDAFS Trinity Alps Wilderness
Trail contact: Weaverville Ranger Station: (530) 623-2121; www.fs.usda.gov/stnf
Parking and trailhead facilities: Ample parking at Big Flat Trailhead. The campground (no fee) is a popular creek-side camp. An outhouse is available but no potable water.

FINDING THE TRAILHEAD

From Weaverville drive 40 miles north on CA 3 to Coffee Creek Road and go left (west). Continue 20 miles to an obvious fork (Coffee Creek Road is unpaved after the first 5 miles). Go left (east) at the signed fork. The signed entrance to Big Flat Trailhead and campground is located 0.8 mile beyond the fork, on the right. GPS: N41 4.062' / W122 56.058'

THE HIKE

This mellow loop is ideal for hikers who place solitude above check lists. Expect lots of meadows, sparkling streams, and idyllic creek-side camps. The trail passes within casting distance of several lakes, and Red Rock Mountain is within easy reach for anyone who wants to score one of the best 360-degree views across the Trinity high country. You also pass three historic mine sites on the way.

The trailhead is directly across the road (east) from the parking area at Big Flat. A sign on the left, just beyond the locked gate, indicates that Yellow Rose Mine is 3 miles away (the distance is slightly exaggerated). Start ascending steadily but moderately to the southeast on a well-defined track. Forest cover provides plenty of shade, and outstanding views of Caribou Mountain appear when you break out of the trees. Plenty of water is available in creeks along the way.

Scattered debris and a decrepit old shack signal your arrival at Yellow Rose Mine, 2 miles from the trailhead. Just beyond the mine, arrive at the junction with the Dorleska Mine Trail (9W65). The path ahead continues to Sunrise Creek Trail (the way you return). To hike the loop in the direction described, turn left (east) on the Dorleska

Mine Trail and continue uphill to the northeast. Half a mile later you top out on the ridge, with panoramic views of the Union Creek drainage spread out beneath your feet.

Descend through open, grassy terrain sprinkled with yarrow and asters. Half a mile below the ridgeline, arrive at a bench littered with ancient, rusted machinery—the first signs of Dorleska Mine. The mine was a bustling operation during the first thirty years of the twentieth century. Dorleska was the name of the mine owner's wife.

A quarter of a mile downhill from the first mine relics, look for a faint trail leading off to the right (south). This unmarked, unmaintained path leads a few hundred yards over a rise to a little gem of a pond perched on a knoll above Bullards Basin. The nameless pond is well worth the detour.

The Dorleska Mine Trail continues a steep descent into the bottom of the canyon, descending into a dense forest distinguished by enormous incense cedars and then crossing the creek at the heart of the canyon. Upstream lies Bullards Basin, one of those rarely visited drainages—with neither lake nor trail to attract crowds—that's guaranteed to delight lovers of true wilderness. Anyone looking for an adventure can follow the basin south, up a steep headwall of unstable talus and onto the northern shoulder of Red Rock Mountain. A little snowmelt pond up there probably sees only a handful of visitors each year. Above the pond, a gap in the ridgeline allows access to the summit of Red Rock Mountain, as well as the entire Landers Lake basin. Only experienced hikers should attempt this off-trail route.

After crossing the stream in Bullards Basin, descend northeast, contouring along the base of a spur ridge. Skirt the top of a corn lily–filled meadow just before dropping down to the junction with the Union Creek Trail (9W07), 4.4 miles from the trailhead.

Turn right (southeast) on the Union Creek Trail (a left turn leads back to a trailhead on Coffee Creek Road). Half a mile up Union Creek, cross the outlet stream from Union Lake and enter the wide, welcoming valley of Union Creek proper. The broad

Gold miners hauled heavy equipment into the deepest backcountry claims.

Follow Sunrise Creek on the return leg of this loop.

valley ahead offers a number of trail junctions, plus a wealth of inviting meadows if you don't want to go anywhere at all.

Union Lake lies 1 mile south of the first junction (signed "Union Lake" to the right). The low-elevation, shallow lake warms up considerably by midsummer, but a mucky bottom puts off most swimmers. The lake sits on the east side of a wide basin, with extensive meadows that make the site popular with horsepackers. As in Bullards Basin, a steep off-trail scramble up the cirque's southern headwall will land you on the shores of an idyllic pond high on the shoulder of Red Rock Mountain. A grassy slope as smooth as a putting green and steep as a waterfall leads over the divide to Landers Lake. Experienced hikers will enjoy exploring this area, but the terrain is steep and there are plenty of loose rocks, so use caution. The easier way to Landers Lake (and an optional trip up Red Rock Mountain) follows the recommended loop route, below.

Back along Union Creek, a three-way junction lies 0.5 mile southeast of the last one. Arriving along Union Creek Trail, to the right (west) is a connecting path to Union Lake (a spur trail, 9W64A); to the left (east) is Lion Lake Trail (8W12), which also connects to Battle Canyon Trail–Sugar Pine Lake Trail (9W59); and straight (southeast), the Union Creek Trail continues up the drainage.

Foster Lake lies 1.5 miles and 1,500 feet up the Lion Lake Trail. It's higher, deeper, colder, and much clearer than Union Lake. It's a steep climb but well worth it on a hot summer day.

To continue the loop, hike southeast from the three-way junction on the Union Creek Trail and make your way 1.3 miles up the gently rising valley to the head of the canyon. In a treeless, flower-sprinkled meadow, arrive at the Landers Lake Trail junction. Turn right (west) to reach Landers Lake and Sunrise Creek. The Union Creek Trail continues southeast, ascending to a saddle on the ridge ahead and connecting with the Parker Creek and Thumb Rock Trails.

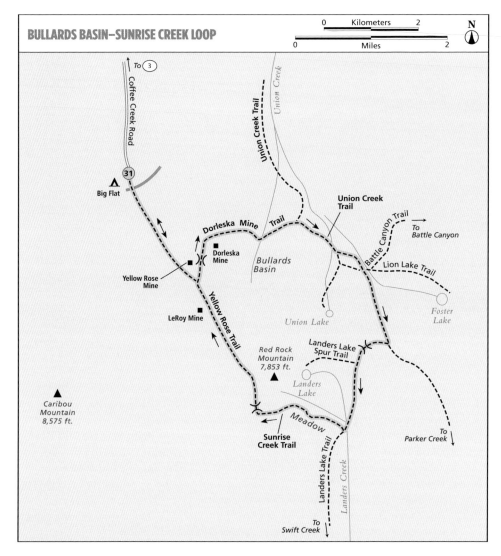

0   Kilometers   2

0   Miles   2

N

To (3)

Coffee Creek Road

Union Creek Trail

Union Creek

31

Big Flat

Union Creek Trail

Battle Canyon Trail

To Battle Canyon

Dorleska Mine Trail

Dorleska Mine

Bullards Basin

Lion Lake Trail

Yellow Rose Mine

Yellow Rose Trail

LeRoy Mine

Union Lake

Foster Lake

Red Rock Mountain 7,853 ft.

Landers Lake Spur Trail

Landers Lake

Caribou Mountain 8,575 ft.

Meadow

Sunrise Creek Trail

Landers Lake Trail

Landers Creek

To Parker Creek

To Swift Creek

The Landers Lake Trail (9W09) crosses the high meadow and then climbs west and south through open forest to a saddle on the ridge above Landers Creek. An easy descent, accompanied by superlative views of Red Rock Mountain, the Swift Creek drainage, and Snowslide Peak, brings you to the Landers Lake Spur Trail (9W09A), 1.2 miles from Union Creek. The junction is at the bottom of a wet meadow dotted with incredibly clear pools of water.

Turn right (north) to reach Landers Lake, just under 1 mile farther up the canyon. That's also the way to go for the easiest ascent of Red Rock Mountain, with one of the best views in the Trinity Alps. (See the Landers Lake Loop hike for more detail on Landers Lake and climbing Red Rock Mountain.)

Turn left (south) to descend to the junction with the Sunrise Creek Trail (9W15), 1.1 miles away. The hike down to the junction is a pleasant stroll along the east side of

Landers Creek, with more wet meadows thick with California pitcher plants and flower-lined borders.

Cross Landers Creek just below the confluence of Landers and Sunrise Creeks and just before the trail junction. Turn right (west) on Sunrise Creek Trail. The Landers Lake Trail continues down to Mumford Meadow and Swift Creek.

Heading west on Sunrise Creek Trail, climb moderately along the south side of the creek. Mixed forest of white fir, pine, and incense cedar provides shade for the first push, but you soon break into open terrain as the valley widens and the trail levels out. Look for colorful fields of Indian paintbrush, yarrow, and asters when you cross to the north side of the creek. The drainage gets relatively few visitors and is well worth some extra exploring time.

After crossing the stream, the trail climbs steeply again as you tackle the canyon's headwall. Water may not be available above the lower canyon, so be sure to refill while you can. The path is faint at times, but the route sticks dependably to the center of the drainage—just hike up to the saddle if you lose the trail. Blue gentians, yellow lupine, and lilies grow along the way.

Once you gain the saddle, the red meta-igneous rocks of Red Rock Mountain are off to the north (the summit can be easily reached from here). Caribou Mountain in all its glory is directly across the valley to the west.

The view hardly changes as you descend into the open basin, contouring northwest along the canyon wall. The hike from here is a pleasant downhill stroll on the Yellow Rose Trail, the path on which you started. Pass the LeRoy Mine, then the Yellow Rose Mine; then arrive at the trailhead, 5 miles from the saddle above Sunrise Creek.

MILES AND DIRECTIONS

0.0   Start at the Big Flat Trailhead.

2.0   Pass the Yellow Rose Mine.

2.1   Reach the Dorleska Trail junction; turn left.

3.4   Pass the Dorleska Mine.

4.4   Turn right at the Union Creek Trail junction.

5.1   Pass the Union Lake Trail junction; stay straight.

5.5   Pass the Lion Lake Trail–Battle Canyon Trail junction.

6.6   Turn right at the Landers Lake Trail junction.

7.8   Pass the Landers Lake Spur Trail junction.

8.6   Turn right at the Sunrise Creek Trail junction.

10.4 Turn right onto the Yellow Rose Trail.

13.3 Turn left at the junction and head back toward the trailhead.

13.5 Pass the Yellow Rose Mine.

15.5 Arrive back at the trailhead.

OPTIONS

Besides making jaunts to various lakes (Union, Foster, Lion, Sugar Pine, Landers), you can make the loop longer by using the Swift Creek Trail to return to Big Flat via Ward Lake.

32 WARD LAKE LOOP

Score great views of Caribou Mountain, enjoy good swimming in Ward and Horseshoe Lakes, and stroll through more meadows than you can shake a corn lily at. Bonus: This "backdoor" route to Ward Lake sees far less traffic than the popular Swift Creek approach due to the longer drive to the trailhead.

Start: Big Flat Trailhead
Type of hike: Backpack; loop
Distance: 18.7 miles
Hiking time: About 3–5 days
Difficulty: Moderate
Elevation gain: 4,600 feet
Best season: Midsummer through early fall
Canine compatibility: Yes
Nearest town: Weaverville/Trinity Center
Fees and permits: Free wilderness permit required for overnight visitors; free campfire permits required for fires and camp stoves

Schedule: Trails in the Trinity Alps are always open; however, most trailhead access roads are closed or impassable during winter.
Maps: USGS Caribou Lake, Siligo Peak, and Ycatapom Peak; USDAFS Trinity Alps Wilderness
Trail contact: Weaverville Ranger Station: (530) 623-2121; www.fs.usda .gov/stnf
Parking and trailhead facilities: Ample parking at Big Flat Trailhead. The campground (no fee) is a popular, pleasant, creek-side camp. An outhouse is available but no potable water.

FINDING THE TRAILHEAD

From Weaverville drive 40 miles north on CA 3 to Coffee Creek Road and go left (west). Continue 20 miles to an obvious fork (Coffee Creek Road is unpaved after the first 5 miles). Go left (east) at the signed fork. The signed entrance to Big Flat Trailhead and campground is located 0.8 mile beyond the fork, on the right. GPS: N41 4.062' / W122 56.058'

THE HIKE

If Goldilocks were a hiker, she'd pronounce this loop just right: just the right amount of steeps (great views without killing yourself); just the right amount of lakes (three, with remarkably different settings); and just the right amount of easy meadow walking (lots). Traffic can be high along Swift Creek, but the other drainages offer an excellent chance for solitude. This is also the shortest way to reach Ward Lake, so a lot of people just go there and turn around. There's no compelling reason to hike this loop in either direction, but I like counterclockwise because you go down instead of up the steep, exposed hill at the head of Swift Creek.

Start at the Big Flat Trailhead and follow signs to the Kidd Creek and Caribou Lake Trailheads. A sign by the trailhead parking area indicates a path leading south through a shady stand of firs to the wilderness boundary and then to a crossing of the South Fork Salmon River. Just before the creek, the Valley Loop Trail diverges to the south. Crossing the South Fork Salmon River shouldn't pose any problem (other than wet feet), but like any stream crossing, use caution in early-season high water. Or avoid the crossing (and what amounts to a scenic but unnecessary detour) altogether by walking south on the

Kidd Creek Divide overlooks a sea of granite.

dirt road you drove in on. This gated road leads to Josephine Creek Resort, a private inholding at the head of the drainage. The Tri-Forest Peak Trail, your ticket to Kidd Creek, actually recrosses South Fork Salmon River and crosses the road 2.7 miles south.

If you're taking the scenic route along the trail, once across the creek you find two trails on your right climbing the opposite bank. The first (heading northwest) is the Old Caribou Trail. You want the "new" trail (actually decades old) to the southwest. Take this path out of the streambed and head west across a parklike meadow to the junction with the Tri-Forest Peak Trail (9W11). Turn left (south) and proceed along the level, forested course of South Fork Salmon River. The pleasant streamside walk makes a nice excursion in its own right, meandering along the west side of the creek through ferny glades and shady glens before crossing back to the east bank and crossing the road, 2.7 miles from the trailhead. (Stay right at the signed fork 1.5 miles in, or you'll make a loop and end up back where you started.)

At the road crossing, a trail sign indicates mileages to Kidd Creek, Ward Lake, and Swift Creek (all fairly accurate). Still on the Tri-Forest Peak Trail, head southeast through dense fir forest, past some private cabins, and climb very gradually to cross Kidd Creek and arrive at the Ward Lake Trail junction. Turn left (east) to continue up the Kidd Creek drainage. (The Tri-Forest Peak Trail continues south to cross Sawtooth Ridge.)

The going gets steeper as you ascend along the side of Kidd Creek. As you climb, tree cover thins and you get glimpses of the view behind you (nice shot of Caribou Mountain) and the view ahead (sheer walls of the upper basin). Just over 5 miles from the trailhead, leave the trees behind and cross the meadows at the head of the drainage, where you'll find crystal-clear snowmelt pools and gardens of summer wildflowers. Cows may occasionally graze here—you can check with rangers to see if cattle are present when you plan to go—but in any case they don't cross the divide to Ward Lake.

Find a private campsite near the meadow on Ward's north shore.

The trail may fade in the meadow, but don't lose hope. It soon becomes distinct again on the west side of the rockslide above the meadows. If all else fails, just aim for the notch in the ridgeline directly south. You're sure to pick up the well-defined path on the west side of the narrowing gully. The final going is steep but short.

At 6.5 miles top out on the saddle above Kidd Creek, just east of 8,038-foot Black Mountain. Take a rest and enjoy the view. To the south lies an array of peaks, including Gibson, Siligo, and Seven Up, plus all of the Swift Creek drainage at your feet. Should you find yourself here at sunrise someday, head out on the rocky ridgeline east of the saddle for a fine show.

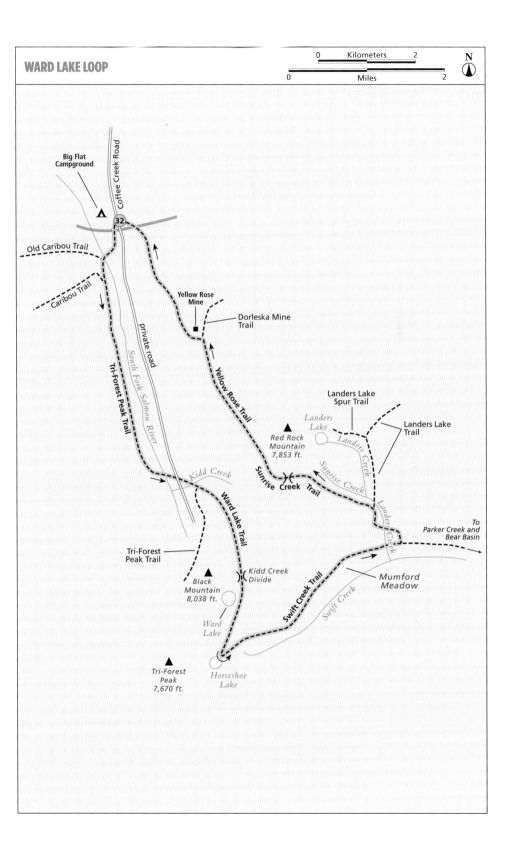

Kilometers

Miles

N

Big Flat
Campground

Coffee Creek Road

32

Old Caribou Trail

Caribou Trail

private road

South Fork Salmon River

Tri-Forest Peak Trail

Yellow Rose
Mine

Dorleska Mine
Trail

Yellow Rose Trail

Landers Lake
Spur Trail

Landers Lake
Trail

Landers
Lake

Landers Creek

Red Rock
Mountain
7,853 ft.

Sunrise Creek Trail

Sunrise Creek

Creek

Kidd Creek

Ward Lake Trail

Landers Creek

To
Parker Creek and
Bear Basin

Tri-Forest
Peak Trail

Black
Mountain
8,038 ft.

Kidd Creek
Divide

Swift Creek Trail

Mumford
Meadow

Swift Creek

Ward
Lake

Tri-Forest
Peak
7,670 ft.

Horseshoe
Lake

South of the saddle the trail descends steeply on switchbacks to cross a small glade and then drops to the north shore of Ward Lake. For campsite planning: Ward has better sites than Horseshoe, and there's also good camping in the valley along Swift Creek.

The route down to Swift Creek, then on to the Landers Lake Trail, is one of the prettiest sections of trail in the Trinity Alps. Descending from Ward Lake (pick up the path on the south side, at the outlet), the trail winds around to the southwest, traversing an open, ferny slope with expansive views of the valley below. It's all downhill—past the junction for Horseshoe Lake (the lake is 0.3 mile to the right; stay left for Swift Creek), down a rocky set of switchbacks, past flower gardens of columbines and shooting stars, then on down to the broad, level valley at the head of Swift Creek.

Proceed east along the Swift Creek Trail (8W15) through a chain of meadows with forests of corn lilies, yarrow, and cow parsnip. Consider spending a night at Mumford Meadow, just before leaving Swift Creek to continue the loop.

At the Landers Lake Trail junction, 11.2 miles from the trailhead, turn left (north) and proceed 0.8 mile to the Sunrise Creek Trail junction. To return to the trailhead, turn left on the Sunrise Creek Trail and continue 1.5 miles to the junction with the Yellow Rose Trail and turn right. Continue to a junction with the Dorleska Mine Trail, where you'll stay left, and pass the Yellow Rose Mine at 16.2 miles. Proceed downhill to the trailhead.

MILES AND DIRECTIONS

- 0.0   Start at the Big Flat Trailhead.
- 0.3   Pass the Old Caribou Trail junction and cross Salmon Creek.
- 0.4   Reach the Tri-Forest Peak Trail junction. Stay left.
- 2.7   Cross Carters Road.
- 3.6   Take the Ward Lake Trail.
- 6.5   Cross the Kidd Creek divide.
- 6.9   Arrive at Ward Lake.
- 8.9   Arrive at Horseshoe Lake. Continue the descent to Swift Creek on the Swift Creek Trail.
- 11.2   Go left on the Landers Lake Trail.
- 12.0   Go left on the Sunrise Creek Trail.
- 13.5   Turn right on the Yellow Rose Trail.
- 16.0   Stay left at the junction with the Dorleska Mine Trail.
- 16.2   Pass the Yellow Rose Mine.
- 18.7   Arrive back at the trailhead.

OPTIONS

You can extend this hike by using the Union Creek and Dorleska Mine Trails to return. This adds another valley, several more lakes, and about 4 more miles to the itinerary. You can also make an off-trail hike to Salmon Lake from Horseshoe Lake. It's possible to make an alternate loop by descending from Salmon Lake to Tri-Forest Peak Trail and returning to Big Flat, but it's steep with no trail. Only experienced hikers with good route-finding skills should attempt it.

33 TRI-FOREST PEAK–DEER CREEK LOOP

Put yourself right in the teeth of Sawtooth Ridge on this hike. It makes a great day hike if you're car camping at Big Flat and also serves as the start for a longer loop that passes through the low-traffic Deer Creek drainage.

Start: Big Flat Trailhead
Type of hike: Day hike or backpack; out-and-back (day hike) or loop (backpack)
Distance: 13.0 miles (to Tri-Forest Peak); 26.9 miles (loop)
Hiking time: About 8–10 hours (day hike to Tri-Forest Peak); 3–5 days (loop).
Difficulty: Moderate (Tri-Forest Peak); strenuous (loop)
Elevation gain: 2,200 feet (to Tri-Forest Peak); 6,600 feet (loop)
Best season: Midsummer through early fall
Canine compatibility: Yes
Nearest town: Weaverville/Trinity Center
Fees and permits: Free wilderness permit required for overnight visitors; free campfire permits required for fires and camp stoves
Schedule: Trails in the Trinity Alps are always open; however, most trailhead access roads are closed or impassable during winter.
Maps: USGS Caribou Lake, Covington Mill, Siligo Peak, and Ycatapom Peak; USDAFS Trinity Alps Wilderness
Trail contact: Weaverville Ranger Station: (530) 623-2121; www.fs.usda .gov/stnf
Parking and trailhead facilities: Ample parking at Big Flat Trailhead. The campground (no fee) is a popular but pleasant creek-side camp. An outhouse is available but no potable water.

FINDING THE TRAILHEAD

From Weaverville drive 40 miles north on CA 3 to Coffee Creek Road and go left (west). Continue 20 miles to an obvious fork (Coffee Creek Road is unpaved after the first 5 miles). Go left (east) at the signed fork. The signed entrance to the Big Flat Trailhead and campground is located 0.8 mile beyond the fork, on the right. GPS: N41 4.062' / W122 56.058'

THE HIKE

Of all the high places with a drop-dead view of the inner Trinity Alps, the jagged crest at the east end of Sawtooth Ridge may just be my favorite. Just 6.5 miles from the Big Flat Trailhead, you top out on a 7,200-foot saddle, stroll a few hundred yards through a beautiful meadow, and take a seat among the teeth of Sawtooth Ridge. At your feet are Sapphire and Emerald Lakes, as well as the entire Stuart Fork drainage, Sawtooth Mountain, and Thompson Peak.

The Tri-Forest Peak Trail (9W11) makes a fine day hike if you turn around at Sawtooth Ridge. Except for the last steep mile (1,200-foot rise), the route is a pleasant, level walk along the South Fork Salmon River. (A brief section passes Josephine Creek Resort, a private inholding that actually encompasses Josephine Lake.) Hikers looking for a longer backpack through some of the most beautiful corners of the Trinities can continue

along Deer, Swift, and Sunrise Creeks to make a 26.9-mile loop back to Big Flat. Either way, you will not be disappointed.

The scenic route, first on the west side of South Fork Salmon River, then on the east, is a mostly level, shady streamside hike.

Start at the Big Flat Trailhead and follow signs to the Kidd Creek and Caribou Lake Trailheads. A sign by the trailhead parking area indicates a path leading south through a shady stand of firs to the wilderness boundary and then to a crossing of the South Fork Salmon River. Just before the creek, the Valley Loop Trail diverges to the south. Crossing the South Fork Salmon River shouldn't pose any problem (other than wet feet), but like any stream crossing, use caution in early-season high water. Or avoid the crossing (and what amounts to a scenic but unnecessary detour) altogether by walking south on the dirt road you drove in on. This gated road leads to Josephine Creek Resort, a private inholding at the head of the drainage. The Tri-Forest Peak Trail actually recrosses South Fork Salmon River and crosses the road 2.7 miles south.

Once across the creek you find two trails on your right climbing the opposite bank. The first (heading northwest) is the Old Caribou Trail. You want the "new" trail (actually decades old) to the southwest. Take this path out of the streambed and head west across a parklike meadow to the junction with the Tri-Forest Peak Trail (9W11). Turn left (south) and proceed along the level, forested course of South Fork Salmon River. The streamside walk makes a nice excursion in its own right, meandering along the west side of the creek through ferny glades and shady glens before crossing back to the east bank and crossing the road, 2.7 miles from the trailhead. (Stay right at the signed fork 1.5 miles in, or you'll make a loop and end up back where you started.)

At the road crossing, a trail sign indicates mileages to Kidd Creek, Ward Lake, and Swift Creek (all fairly accurate). Still on the Tri-Forest Peak Trail, head southeast through dense fir forest, past some private cabins, and climb very gradually to cross Kidd Creek and arrive at the Kidd Creek Trail junction.

At this junction (marked "Ward Lake Trail" on the forest service map but signed "Kidd Creek"), stay straight (south) on the Tri-Forest Peak Trail. The next 1.5 miles skirts the eastern edge of the private property. The trail meanders through mixed forest on a level, well-defined track. Occasionally the path climbs a short way above the valley bottom in order to clear the private property. Ignore trails or cow paths coming in from the west.

Soon you emerge from the trees and start ascending the east side of the valley. Views of Caribou Mountain, directly to the west, start out big and get bigger. Look for a creek descending the east wall of the canyon 2 miles from the Ward Lake Trail junction. It's the last major tributary you encounter before starting up the steep switchbacks at the head of the drainage. Be sure to fill water bottles (purify all water).

The creek also marks the starting point for hikers looking to tackle the off-trail route to Salmon Lake. The pretty little lake, perched on a bench about 1,200 feet above the valley, is a worthwhile goal for ambitious hikers who like a tough scramble. The route is brushy and steep (detour north of the waterfall) but follows a gorgeous, flower-filled gully. Use a map and common sense.

Past Salmon's outlet creek, the Tri-Forest Peak Trail starts climbing more earnestly. Gradually at first, then more steeply, the trail ascends a well-defined track up the south wall of the drainage. Well-designed switchbacks lead up the last steep mile, making the climb much easier than it appears to be from below.

Just over 6 miles from the trailhead, top out on the saddle directly west of 7,671-foot Tri-Forest Peak. The trail continues south, crossing the crest and plunging downhill along the headwaters of Willow Creek. But don't do that right away. First hike up that meadow to the right (west) to aptly named Horse Heaven Peak and take your well-earned seat atop Sawtooth Ridge. Get out your map and see how many peaks you can identify. Or just picture yourself diving into Emerald Lake.

When you've had enough of the view, either retrace your steps to the trailhead or continue on the loop by heading southwest, into the Willow Creek drainage. Beyond the saddle, the trail is much less distinct, fading in and out of rocky slopes and meadows. Occasional cairns mark the path, but you don't have to work too hard to find it. The trail bends to the southwest, descending steeply into the canyon, and then curves back to the southeast to follow the west bank of Willow Creek. This is wild, rarely visited terrain. Great views of the Deer Creek drainage open up as you cross a meadow 1 mile below the saddle.

Descend through a dense forest after the meadow, making your way down to Willow Creek, where you cross the stream and continue on the east bank. The final steep descent brings you to a junction with the Deer Creek Trail (9W17). A right (west) turn here leads to Morris Meadow and the Stuart Fork Trail. It's possible to make a loop back to Big Flat by going that way and returning via Caribou Lake. That route, however, requires a tough, waterless, shadeless climb out of Stuart Fork, and is also bound to be more crowded than the recommended loop.

To continue on this route, turn left (east) and head up the Deer Creek drainage. The forested valley is popular among deer hunters, who descend on Deer Creek Camp in the fall. The trail follows the north bank of Deer Creek, arriving at Deer Creek Camp and the Black Basin Trail junction in 2 gradually ascending miles (great camping through here).

The loop back to Big Flat goes up Black Basin Trail, but allow time (at least a day) for the Four Lakes Loop, a spectacular route that circles Siligo Peak and four beautiful lakes. It starts at the end of Deer Creek Trail, 1 mile to the southeast.

To continue this loop, head east from Deer Creek Camp on the Black Basin Trail, which climbs northwest then southeast through mixed conifers on a steep, switchbacking ascent of Deer Creek canyon's east ridge. Nearly 1,000 feet up, after passing the ruins of Longs Cabin and a small pond, come to the first of two poorly marked junctions. The first path, on the right, is the Seven Up Trail (9W67), which connects with the Granite Lake Trail after a jaw-dropping traverse of the ridge beneath Seven Up Peak. The second path, also on the right, leads to the Bear Basin Trail (9W10).

Stay left at both junctions, heading northwest on a long, gradual contour that brings you to a saddle on the ridge between Deer and Swift Creeks. Manzanita gets higher and trees more sparse as you climb. This section of trail is one of the least-traveled paths in the Trinity Alps Wilderness, with signs that come and go and portions that have all but faded from view. (If you prefer a well-maintained trail with dependable signage, you can use the Bear Basin or Granite Lake Trail to connect to Swift Creek and the rest of this loop.)

Once you gain the saddle, the route down into Mumford Basin becomes more distinct. A steep descent on a well-defined trail leads to a high, wildflower-dotted meadow at the heart of Mumford Basin, a secluded and wild canyon that hangs above Swift Creek.

The final 2.5-mile descent to Swift Creek, through green glades then forests of white fir, ponderosa pine, and incense cedar, is easy to follow. The trail stays on the west bank of the creek flowing out of Mumford Basin. It fades away again at the bottom, but cross Swift Creek and you run into the Swift Creek Trail (8W15). It's a regular highway compared with the trail you've been on. Turn right (northeast) to complete the loop; turn left (southwest) to reach Horseshoe and Ward Lakes (2 and 3 miles away, respectively). You can shorten the loop by returning to Big Flat via the Ward Lake Trail.

To complete the longer loop, proceed east along the Swift Creek Trail through a chain of meadows with forests of corn lilies, yarrow, and cow parsnip (find good camping along Swift Creek). Continue 1.7 miles to the junction with the Landers Lake Trail and turn left. The wet meadow can become a mud bog here after numerous hikers and horses have stomped through it. Pick your way north along the eastern edge of the meadow and pass a campsite on your right, just before heading steeply uphill on a well-defined trail marked by cairns and a conspicuous blaze on a huge pine.

Rough tread on steep switchbacks leads uphill 0.5 mile to the junction with the Sunrise Creek Trail, at the confluence of Sunrise and Landers Creeks. Turn left and head west on Sunrise Creek Trail, climbing moderately along the south side of the creek. Mixed forest provides shade for the first push, but you soon break into open terrain as the valley widens and the trail levels out. Look for colorful fields of Indian paintbrush, yarrow, and asters when you cross to the north side of the creek. The drainage gets relatively few visitors and is well worth some extra exploring time.

After crossing the stream the trail climbs steeply again as you tackle the canyon's headwall. Water may not be available above the lower canyon, so be sure to refill while you can. The path is faint at times, but the route sticks dependably to the center of the drainage—just hike up to the saddle if you lose the trail. Look for blue gentians, yellow lupine, and lilies along the way.

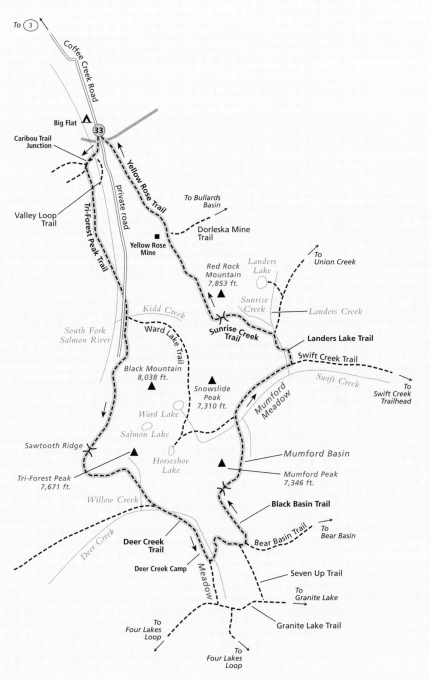

0 Kilometers 2

0 Miles 2

N

To 3

Coffee Creek Road

Big Flat

33

Caribou Trail Junction

Valley Loop Trail

Yellow Rose Trail

private road

Tri-Forest Peak Trail

To Bullards Basin

Dorleska Mine Trail

Yellow Rose Mine

Red Rock Mountain 7,853 ft.

Landers Lake

To Union Creek

Sunrise Creek

Landers Creek

Kidd Creek

Ward Lake Trail

Sunrise Creek Trail

Landers Lake Trail

South Fork Salmon River

Swift Creek Trail

Black Mountain 8,038 ft.

Snowslide Peak 7,310 ft.

Mumford Meadow

Swift Creek

To Swift Creek Trailhead

Ward Lake

Salmon Lake

Sawtooth Ridge

Horseshoe Lake

Mumford Basin

Tri-Forest Peak 7,671 ft.

Mumford Peak 7,346 ft.

Willow Creek

Black Basin Trail

Deer Creek

Deer Creek Trail

Bear Basin Trail

To Bear Basin

Deer Creek Camp

Meadow

Seven Up Trail

To Granite Lake

To Four Lakes Loop

Granite Lake Trail

To Four Lakes Loop

Once you gain the saddle, the red meta-igneous rocks of Red Rock Mountain are off to the north (the summit can be easily reached from here). Caribou Mountain in all its glory is directly across the valley to the west.

The view hardly changes as you descend into the open basin, contouring northwest along the canyon wall. The hike from here is a downhill stroll on the Yellow Rose Trail. Pass the Le Roy Mine, the Dorleska Mine Trail (stay left), then the Yellow Rose Mine; then arrive at the trailhead, 5 miles from the saddle above Sunrise Creek.

MILES AND DIRECTIONS

0.0   Start at the Big Flat Trailhead and bear right.

0.3   Pass the Old Caribou Trail junction.

0.4   Continue on the Tri-Forest Peak Trail.

1.5   Arrive at the Valley Loop junction; continue on the Tri-Forest Peak Trail.

2.7   Cross a private road.

3.6   Reach the Kidd Creek–Tri-Forest Peak Trail junction; stay on the Tri-Forest Peak Trail.

6.5   Arrive at the Tri-Forest saddle after a steep climb. (Option: Turn around here for a moderate 13-mile out-and back hike.)

9.0   Turn left at the Deer Creek Trail junction.

10.5 Turn left onto the Black Basin Trail.

12.0 Turn left onto the Mumford Basin Trail.

17.0 Arrive at the Swift Creek Trail junction; go right.

18.7 Go left at the Landers Lake Trail junction.

19.5 Go left on the Sunrise Creek Trail.

24.7 Stay left at the Dorleska Mine Trail.

24.9 Pass the Yellow Rose Mine.

26.9 Arrive back at the trailhead.

OPTIONS

Choose an alternate route back to Big Flat by using the Ward Lake Trail from Ward Lake or the Union Creek Trail to Bullards Basin. Lakes within easy reach include Deer, Summit, Diamond, Luella, Granite, Horseshoe, Ward, and Landers. Good walk-up peaks are Siligo, Seven Up, and Red Rock Mountain.

34 CARIBOU LAKES

If you've heard of the Trinity Alps before, or seen pictures, odds are good you've heard of this hike. The Caribou Basin is a classic—big lakes tucked into a gorgeous cirque—and should be on every hiker's life list. Just remember: If you want solitude, plan a weekday trip or come in the fall.

Start: Big Flat Trailhead
Type of hike: Backpack; out-and-back (with optional figure eight on the Old Caribou Trail)
Distance: 19.0 miles
Hiking time: About 3–6 days
Difficulty: Moderate
Elevation gain: 2,500 feet (3,500 feet for optional loop)
Best season: Midsummer through early fall
Canine compatibility: Yes
Nearest town: Weaverville/Trinity Center
Fees and permits: Free wilderness permit required for overnight visitors; free campfire permits required for fires and camp stoves

Schedule: Trails in the Trinity Alps are always open; however, most trailhead access roads are closed or impassable during winter.
Maps: USGS Caribou Lake; USDAFS Trinity Alps Wilderness
Trail contact: Weaverville Ranger Station: (530) 623-2121; www.fs.usda .gov/stnf
Special considerations: No campfires are allowed in the Caribou Lakes Basin.
Parking and trailhead facilities: Ample parking at Big Flat Trailhead. The campground (no fee) is a popular, pleasant, creek-side camp. An outhouse is available but no potable water.

FINDING THE TRAILHEAD

From Weaverville drive 40 miles north on CA 3 to Coffee Creek Road and go left (west). Continue 20 miles to an obvious fork (Coffee Creek Road is unpaved after the first 5 miles). Go left (east) at the signed fork. The signed entrance to the Big Flat Trailhead and campground is located 0.8 mile beyond the fork, on the right. GPS: N41 4.062' / W122 56.058'

THE HIKE

The most spectacular place in the Trinity Alps is a matter of some debate among Alps aficionados. But no matter who's doing the talking, you can bet Caribou Basin will come up for consideration. At 72 acres, Caribou Lake (or Big Caribou, as old-timers often call it) is by far the biggest lake in the Trinity Alps. But size alone does not a beautiful basin make. Add sweeping cliffs and wide benches of white granite, stunning meadows, three more charming lakes, and endless views, and you begin to get a picture of Caribou Basin. Of course, such beauty has not gone unnoticed. Expect plenty of company here: In recent years, this spot, like other popular destinations in Trinity, has seen significant increases in visitors. For that reason and to minimize the risk of wildfires, no campfires are allowed in the Caribou Basin. An optional side trip (off-trail) to Little Caribou Lake is the best place to find solitude in this region.

Though not difficult, the 9.5-mile hike to Caribou Lake can seem long and hot on a midsummer day. There are actually two ways to get to Caribou: the new trail and the old trail (that's the way they're referred to, no matter that the "new" trail is more than

Caribou is the largest lake in the Trinity Alps.

Climb the switchbacks above Caribou Lake for this panoramic view.

fifty years old). The new trail is a couple miles longer but clearly better: It goes around Caribou Mountain, not up and over its shoulder as the old trail does, which makes it a lot easier. But that doesn't make the old trail obsolete. History buffs, peak baggers, masochists, and seekers of solitude can create an interesting figure-eight route by using the new trail on the way out and the old trail on the way back (see optional side trip to Little Caribou Lake). Either way, there's not a lot of water en route, so be sure to refill when you have the opportunity.

From the trailhead the path leads south through a shady stand of firs to the wilderness boundary and then to a crossing of the South Fork Salmon River. Just before the creek, the Valley Loop Trail diverges to the south. Crossing the South Fork Salmon River shouldn't pose any problem (other than wet feet) but use caution in early-season high water. Once across the creek, you find two trails climbing the opposite bank. The one to the right (northwest) is the Old Caribou Trail. This is the route you'll return on if you opt for the figure-eight loop. The new trail is on the left (southwest). Take this path out of the streambed and head west across a tree-dotted meadow.

After leaving the river the trail meanders through a parklike setting of mixed conifers; you soon pass the junction with the Tri-Forest Peak Trail. Stay right, continuing west past the junction and begin climbing... and climbing. You ascend the lion's share of this route's elevation gain on a series of long, gradual switchbacks that climb the lower reaches of Caribou Mountain. The trail is generally shady in mixed forest, but look for great views when the tree cover opens up. Red Rock and Black Mountains dominate the ridgeline on the opposite side of the South Fork drainage, and Caribou Mountain looms directly ahead.

Top out in Caribou Meadow, a small clearing nestled on the shoulder of the mountain 4 miles from the trailhead. This is also the site of a junction with the Old Caribou Trail. It crosses your path from north to south, heading steeply uphill. Little Caribou Lake lies about 1,000 feet (and a couple of miles) above you in a basin on the north side of the mountain. No trail leads to the secluded lake, but the easiest way to get there is to take the Old Caribou Trail to a point level with the basin and then strike off across the granite slopes. (The route to Little Caribou Lake is described in the optional side trip at the end of this chapter.)

To continue on the new trail, head west as the path contours around the shoulder of Caribou Mountain, passing through an area burned in a wildfire more than a decade ago. The trail is mostly level all the way around, traversing a sunny bench literally carved into the mountain's sweeping granite flank. You'll likely find the first water sources since the South Fork along this section of exposed granite, where little streams collect and drain into Big Conrad Gulch. All water along the route should be purified.

Look for big views to the west as you round the shoulder of Caribou Mountain and head slightly downhill to reach Browns Meadow, 6 miles from the trailhead. If you're going to spend a night along the trail, this is the only good place to do it. Browns Meadow is a wide, sloping meadow stocked with a few granite boulders, an alder-choked stream, a rusty wheelbarrow, and an assortment of summer wildflowers—pussytoes, corn lilies, Shasta daisies. A spring crosses the trail just after the meadow. (**Note:** Local hiker Leon Nelson says another good way to reach Little Caribou Lake, described in the section on the Old Caribou Trail below, is by going off-trail from Browns Meadow and heading up and over the ridge to the southeast.)

From Browns Meadow ascend moderate switchbacks to an obvious notch in the ridgeline. Here you emerge onto the west side of Caribou Mountain and get your first view of what all the fuss is about. Thompson Peak and its permanent snowfields dominate the skyline, and the whole of Caribou Basin soon comes into view as the trail contours along through the granite. Snowslide and Lower Caribou are the first lakes you see, with the huge bowl containing Caribou looming above them. Easy hiking, ever-expanding views, and a rainbow's worth of wildflowers dominate the last few miles of the trail.

Just past the second junction with the Old Caribou Trail, 8.5 miles from the trailhead, the path follows a series of moderate switchbacks downhill into the basin. Cross a small meadow before arriving at the granite dike separating Snowslide and Lower Caribou Lakes, then choose any one of the meandering trails that crisscross the heavily used area. More people choose to stay in this area than at Caribou proper, probably because the lower basin is more protected from wind and because these campsites are the first you encounter—hence the first place to put down that heavy pack. Avoid using campsites too close to the water.

To reach Caribou Lake, follow cairns on either side of the dike (both trails lead up to the lake). The path on the left (southeast) is the most direct; the path on the right, which goes around the northwest side of Middle Caribou Lake, meanders up the outlet stream. Middle Caribou Lake is really just a pond sandwiched between Snowslide and Lower Caribou Lakes.

At 72 acres and 72 feet deep, Caribou dwarfs all other lakes in the Trinity Alps, and the setting is equal to the size. Caribou simply sweeps you up in a smorgasbord of alpine delights: sparkling ponds and hanging gardens with late summer gentians, primroses, and monkey flowers cluster around the lake's southern shore. The western shore is steep and rocky, but a delightful series of meadows on the southwest side of the lake make for one of the most beautiful sights in the Alps. Look at but definitely don't camp in this fragile environment. Plenty of low-impact campsites are available on the granite slabs; campfires are prohibited anywhere in the basin.

The deep-blue water is ideal for long swims; the possibilities for exploration are endless. The only hike you should feel obligated to do while at Caribou is a short jaunt to the saddle between this basin and Stuart Fork. An obvious use trail leads up the south wall of the cirque to the low point on the ridgeline. The switchbacks get steeper and steeper as you rise 700 feet in just under 1 mile to the gap. Once on top, enjoy one of the most spectacular vistas in all the Alps. Sawtooth Ridge is so close on your left it seems as though you must be sitting right in the granite maw. In front and far below stretch Stuart Fork and Morris Meadow, and on your right are Emerald and Sapphire Lakes in their sheer-sided granite trough. You can also see every major peak in the Trinity Alps: Sawtooth, Siligo, Granite, Wedding Cake, and Thompson Peak. Caribou Basin is spread beneath your feet. For the best view of all this alpine finery, wander a short way west up the ridgeline for an unobstructed vista.

Of course, you might also consider hiking down to Stuart Fork, but think before you hike. The route down is called the Caribou Scramble; it plummets nearly 2,500 feet to the canyon bottom, and every foot is exposed to the sun. Endless switchbacks and no

Climb the switchbacks to the divide above Caribou Lake for this view of Emerald and Sapphire Lakes.

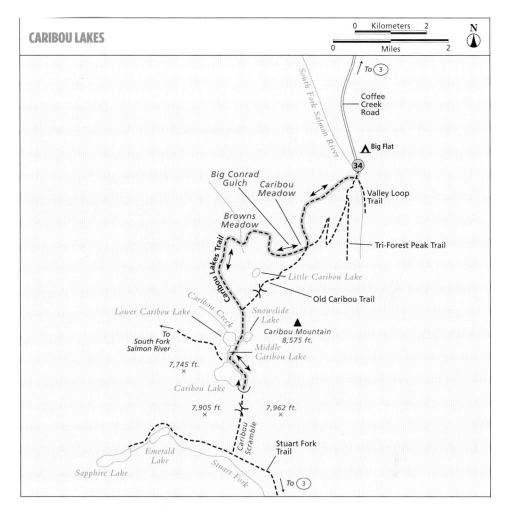

shade or water make this one of the most arduous sections of trail in the Alps. You can use this trail to make a longer loop back to Big Flat by connecting the Stuart Fork, Deer Creek, and Tri-Forest Trails.

For the return to the trailhead, you have two choices: Return the way you came or go up and over Peak 8118 on the Old Caribou Trail.

OLD CARIBOU TRAIL

To return via the Old Caribou Trail and make an elegant figure-eight loop, hike back to the junction in the trees 0.5 mile before Snowslide–Lower Caribou. Take the obvious trail going east up Caribou Mountain. It's a steep 1,200-foot haul to the top of Peak 8118. At the top a short ramble to the north of the saddle yields a view of Little Caribou Lake, tucked into a rocky bowl 1,000 feet below. Don't be tempted to head straight down to the lake from here. A much better route is to follow the trail down the northeast slope of the mountain. A mile below the saddle, take a line across the open granite slope and shoot for the obvious basin to the west. Rock cairns may lead the way.

Little Caribou Lake is a secluded body of water at 7,150 feet. The 10-acre lake gets very few visitors. Swimmers will appreciate the lake's small granite islands. Make it a lunch stop or a layover day— either way you won't regret this detour.

After returning to the trail from Little Caribou Lake, it's a steep descent to Caribou Meadow on rough tread, then more steep hiking down Caribou Gulch before finally winding back around to the crossing at the South Fork Salmon River near the trailhead. In Caribou Meadow you can pick up the new trail again if you want a quicker return.

MILES AND DIRECTIONS

0.0   Start at the Big Flat Trailhead.

0.2   Cross the creek.

0.3   Pass the Old Caribou Trail junction; stay left on the new trail.

0.4   Pass the Tri-Forest Peak Trail junction; stay right.

4.0   Reach the Caribou Meadow–Old Caribou Trail junction; stay on the new trail.

6.0   Arrive at Browns Meadow; continue on the Caribou Lakes Trail.

8.5   Pass the Old Caribou Trail junction; bear right to stay on the new trail.

9.0   Reach Lower Caribou, Snowslide, and Middle Caribou Lakes; continue on the Caribou Trail.

9.5   Arrive at Caribou Lake. Return the way you came. (**Option:** Make the steep climb to the saddle between Caribou Basin and Stuart Fork, adding 2 miles to the hike.)

19.0   Arrive back at the trailhead.

OPTIONS

Create a longer loop back to Big Flat by descending into Stuart Fork on the Caribou Scramble, then returning via the Tri-Forest Peak Trail, Ward Lake Trail, or Yellow Rose Trail.

35 ADAMS LAKE

This is an easy hike to a glorified frog pond, but it's well worth visiting as an easy day trip in early or late season, or as a backpack for families with young kids or beginners. Indeed, this is the first lake I camped at in the Trinity Alps Wilderness, when I was 4 years old.

Start: Adams Lake Trailhead
Type of hike: Day hike or backpack; out-and-back
Distance: 5.2 miles
Hiking time: About 3–6 hours (day hike); 2–3 days (backpack)
Difficulty: Easy
Elevation gain: 1,400 feet
Best season: Summer through early fall
Canine compatibility: Yes
Nearest town: Weaverville/Trinity Center
Fees and permits: Free wilderness permit required for overnight visitors; free campfire permits required for fires and camp stoves

Schedule: Trails in the Trinity Alps are always open; however, most trailhead access roads are closed or impassable during winter.
Maps: USGS Caribou Lake; USDAFS Trinity Alps Wilderness
Trail contact: Weaverville Ranger Station: (530) 623-2121; www.fs.usda .gov/stnf
Parking and trailhead facilities: A small pullout is the only parking. There's more parking available along Coffee Creek Road in both directions; no facilities. The closest campgrounds are Goldfield and Big Flat.

FINDING THE TRAILHEAD

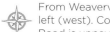

From Weaverville drive 40 miles north on CA 3 to Coffee Creek Road and go left (west). Continue 16 miles to the signed trailhead on the right (Coffee Creek Road is unpaved after the first 5 miles). The trailhead is small and easy to miss. Look for an old jeep track on the right, several feet higher than Coffee Creek Road. GPS: N41 7.039' / W 122 55.940'

THE HIKE

The short route to little Adams Lake makes for a pleasant and easy day trip. It's also a nice overnight destination for families with young children.

A forest service gate and information sign are located at the beginning of the trailhead, but there may or may not be a sign for Adams Lake (it comes and goes, usually goes). The old jeep road switchbacks uphill to the northeast and then turns on itself to climb moderately but steadily southwest up the ridgeline. Look for the remnants of an old mining ditch near the turn.

Continue up the ridgeline in a forest of large fir and pine, and don't be tempted to take any of the faint jeep tracks diverging from the main road. The trees thin out 0.5 mile up the ridgeline as the trail contours around the hill in front of you.

A brief downhill is followed by more moderate climbing through shady stands of fir, pine, incense cedar, and manzanita, then easy walking alongside Adams Creek. The rest of the hike follows the alder-choked creek, making for a gentle grade and plenty of greenery. A gap in the alders opens up about 2.1 miles in, and you cross the creek to finish the hike on the west bank. A few hundred yards uphill from the crossing, you pass

A marshy oasis thrives at Adams Lake.

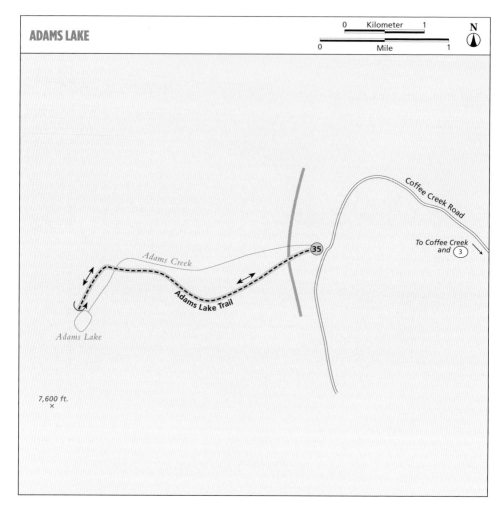

through a small meadow, skirt a few large granite outcroppings, and then arrive at the lake itself. Two modest campsites on the west side are sufficient for the few overnight visitors who typically come each season.

The 1-acre lake is bordered by talus slopes and a steep granite wall on the south; willows, alders, and grassy shores on the other sides. A cattail pond thrives at the outlet. The last time I visited Adams Lake was on a misty, drizzly day in late September. The scenic little pond was as quiet as any place I've ever been in the Alps—not a soul was around and even the frogs were silent—and I would have sworn I was 20 miles deep in the wilderness, not barely more than 2.

MILES AND DIRECTIONS

0.0   Start at the Adams Lake Trailhead.

2.1   Cross Adams Creek.

2.6   Reach Adams Lake. Return the way you came.

5.2   Arrive back at the trailhead.

36 SOUTH FORK COFFEE CREEK LOOP

Take a tour on an off-the-beaten-track route through several scenic drainages in the Coffee Creek drainage and visit a couple of on-the-beaten-track lakes en route. This is a good hike for people who have seen a lot of the Trinity Alps and want to explore some less-known corners.

Start: South Fork Coffee Creek Trailhead
Type of hike: Backpack; lollipop
Distance: 16.8 miles
Hiking time: About 3-4 days
Difficulty: Moderate
Elevation gain: 4,000 feet
Best season: Midsummer through early fall
Canine compatibility: Yes
Nearest town: Weaverville/Trinity Center
Fees and permits: Free wilderness permit required for overnight visitors; free campfire permits required for fires and camp stoves

Schedule: Trails in the Trinity Alps are always open; however, most trailhead access roads are closed or impassable during winter.
Maps: USGS Deadman Peak; USDAFS Trinity Alps Wilderness
Trail contact: Weaverville Ranger Station: (530) 623-2121; www.fs.usda.gov/stnf
Parking and trailhead facilities: The parking area is in a little clearing a few rough yards off the main road; no water or other facilities. The closest campgrounds are Goldfield and Big Flat.

FINDING THE TRAILHEAD

From Weaverville drive 40 miles north on CA 3 to Coffee Creek Road and go left (west). Continue 15 miles to the signed trailhead on the right (Coffee Creek Road is unpaved after the first 5 miles). The trailhead is 0.5 mile past the South Fork bridge. GPS: N41 7.593' / W122 55.363'

THE HIKE

Much has been made about South Fork Coffee Creek's location—it's entirely north of Coffee Creek. Still, the water flows south, so I suppose that's something (though so does the water in the North and East Forks). In any event, whoever named the tributaries sure wasn't holding a compass.

Directional problems aside, this is a splendid hike through little-traveled drainages with lush meadows, incredible views, and a couple of good swimming lakes. Solitude is always a good bet (except at the lakes), and peak baggers will pass within easy reach of 7,617-foot Deadman Peak.

Hiking north from the trailhead, you immediately pass a metal forest service gate (closed to keep vehicles off the old jeep track). Past the gate the track starts climbing up a gully and then switchbacks moderately up a hillside thick with Douglas fir and ponderosa pine. A gentler grade leads northeast to a point high above South Fork Coffee Creek, where you round the shoulder of the ridge and continue north along the course of the creek. The going is shady and the grade easy as you make your way up the drainage.

Just over 1 mile from the trailhead, pass an old, overgrown jeep track that veers to the right (east), toward the creek. Don't take it. A trail sign for the South Fork Trail points the way north on the path you're on. Pass a cabin site just after the trail sign. Debris indicates the cabin was of relatively recent vintage.

The trail bisects a couple of small meadows lined with mature incense cedar, some of the biggest cedar trees in the Trinity Alps. After the meadows, descend to a crossing of the South Fork, 2 miles from the trailhead. On the east bank now, climb moderately just under 0.5 mile to a junction with the Steveale Creek Trail (9W61). To the right (east) the sign indicates connections with the Chipmunk Meadow and North Fork Coffee Creek Trails. That's the way you return. To the left (northwest), the South Fork Coffee Creek Trail (9W04) continues up the drainage. A sign points the way to Taylor Creek (a rather obscure destination to get a sign all to itself).

Stay left on the South Fork Coffee Creek Trail and make your way northwest through the wide, very gently sloping valley. Forest and ferny meadows alternate for the next 2 miles, with only one thing to mar the scenery: occasional cow pies and cattle-trampled grass. (You can check with rangers on current grazing conditions, but this is one of the few drainages south of the Scott Mountains divide that has had grazing in recent years.) Cattle trails obscure the path somewhat in a few places, but cairns show the way.

Fill water bottles from the South Fork or one of its tributaries before starting the ascent at the head of the canyon. (Be sure to purify all water.) A 0.5-mile climb ends at a saddle on the Salmon–Scott Mountains divide, where a few battered and broken signs mark a three-way junction. The Poison Canyon Trail goes left (west), the Fish Lake Trail goes north, and the Long Gulch Trail goes right (northeast), plunging over the ridgeline and down to Long Gulch Lake. Both Long Gulch and Trail Gulch Lakes are accessible via relatively easy trails (3.5 and 2.5 miles, respectively) on the north side of the divide.

To continue the loop, head downhill on the Long Gulch Trail, switchbacking to the bottom of the drainage and another junction. A left (south) turn leads to the Long Gulch Trailhead on FR 39N08. Turn right (east) onto the Trail Gulch Trail and walk slightly uphill over rocky tread to Long Gulch Lake. The 12-acre, deep-blue lake is great for swimming. Repeatedly. You can do laps around the island. The best (and most secluded) campsite is on the west end of the lake. Horsepackers camp on the northeast side.

At the outlet on the northeast side of the lake, near a much-used campsite, pick up the trail as it crosses the creek to the east. Look up. Your challenge is to climb to the ridgeline on the east side of the cirque. It's a steep haul, so tank up on water before you start the ascent.

Less than 1 mile from the lake, top out on the crest and enjoy the view. It's fantastic—especially the granite-rimmed blue gem at your feet. Also at your feet is another trail junction. Ignore it. The trail going straight downhill is the old path, which descends

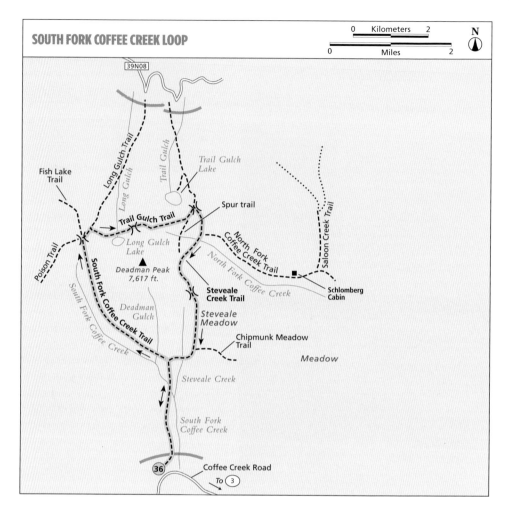

0   Kilometers   2

0   Miles   2

N

39N08

Fish Lake
Trail

Long Gulch Trail

Long Gulch

Trail Gulch

Trail Gulch
Lake

Trail Gulch Trail

Spur trail

Long Gulch
Lake

Poison Trail

South Fork Coffee Creek Trail

Deadman Peak
7,617 ft.

North Fork
Coffee Creek Trail

North Fork Coffee Creek

Saloon Creek Trail

Schlomberg
Cabin

Steveale
Creek Trail

Deadman
Gulch

South Fork Coffee Creek Trail

Steveale
Meadow

Chipmunk Meadow
Trail

Meadow

South Fork Coffee Creek

Steveale Creek

South Fork
Coffee Creek

36   Coffee Creek Road

To 3

steeply toward the North Fork Coffee Creek and then climbs back up toward Trail
Gulch Lake. A new trail, shown on the forest service Trinity Alps Wilderness map but
not on the USGS quad, avoids that elevation loss by cutting across the ridgeline to the
saddle above Trail Gulch Lake. (**Note:** The names of Long and Trail Gulch Lakes are
reversed on the USGS quad.) Go left (east) on the newer trail and arrive at the saddle in
an easy downhill mile. The stroll is shaded by mature firs and accompanied by excellent
views of the North Fork Coffee Creek drainage. (**Note:** If you're contemplating climbing Deadman Peak, this is as fine a place as any to leave the trail.)

At the saddle above Trail Gulch Lake, a trail junction provides several options. Turn
left (north) to descend 0.8 mile to the lake. The only camps are on the north shore, and
they're crowded together. The camping at Long Gulch is better.

To start the return portion of the loop, take either the North Fork Coffee Creek or
Steveale Creek Trail (you end up in the same place). They both lead downhill (south)
from the crest. Both paths can be difficult to follow as you descend into the forested
drainage. I recommend the North Fork Coffee Creek Trail, which is a bit more distinct
and a bit more scenic. Once you descend into the large, lush meadow at the head of

North Fork Coffee Creek, you should have no trouble identifying a signed junction at the bottom of the glade. (Even if you lose the trail on the way down, you're sure to end up in the meadow.)

At the junction the North Fork Coffee Creek Trail (9W02) continues east, across the creek, to Saloon Creek, Schlomberg Cabin, and the heart of the North Fork Coffee Creek drainage. To the right (southwest) a spur trail, signed "Steveale Creek," leads to the Steveale Creek Trail (9W61). Pass through a cool, lush thicket of alders as you cross the wet drainage bottom and then ascend moderately through shady fir forest to a junction with the Steveale Creek Trail proper (0.7 mile from the last junction). This is where you end up if you take the other trail from the saddle above Trail Gulch Lake. Trail Gulch is to the right (north) and Steveale Meadow is to the left (south). Go south.

The next stretch contours pleasantly along a slope high above the North Fork Coffee Creek drainage. Wildflowers appear in little bunches where granite gives way to grass. On the horizon, Mount Shasta's white summit pierces the sky above the distant ridges. The short traverse leads to the divide above Steveale Creek, where you descend to a saddle at the head of a steeply sloping meadow.

The path descends the east side of the meadow. Alder thickets line the canyon bottom, and Caribou Mountain looms directly ahead on the horizon. A 0.5-mile descent leads to an old cow camp at the bottom of Steveale Meadow ("Camp Siberia," says an old hand-carved sign). Just beyond the camp is an unmarked junction. The trail back to South Fork Coffee Creek crosses to the west bank of Steveale Creek. On the east bank the little-used Chipmunk Trail bends away from the creek and climbs east to wild and empty Chipmunk Meadow. An old mine is just a few hundred yards up the path.

On the west bank the Steveale Creek Trail enters the forest and veers southwest, away from the deepening canyon, and descends in less than 1 mile to a junction with South Fork Coffee Creek Trail. Turn left (south) and retrace your steps 2.3 miles to the trailhead.

MILES AND DIRECTIONS

0.0 Start at the South Fork Coffee Creek Trailhead.

2.3 Arrive at Steveale Creek Trail junction; go left on the South Fork Coffee Creek Trail.

5.4 Turn right on the Long Gulch Trail.

6.4 Arrive at Long Gulch Lake.

10.3 Reach Trail Gulch Lake. Climb to the ridge above the lake.

10.9 Take the North Fork Coffee Creek Trail downhill.

12.2 Go right at the Steveale Creek Trail junction.

14.5 Reach the South Fork Coffee Creek Trail junction. Go left.

16.8 Arrive back at the trailhead.

OPTIONS

Explore the upper North Fork Coffee Creek drainage down to Schlomberg Cabin, Saloon Creek, and Hodges Cabin.

This rugged canyon provides a private escape of cascading rivers and dense forest where you only need to wander 100 yards from the trail to feel as though you've gone off the map. Bonus: You'll also find some of the best historic cabins in the wilderness area.

Start: North Fork Coffee Creek Trailhead

Type of hike: Day hike or backpack; out-and-back

Distance: 13.0 miles

Hiking time: About 1–3 days

Difficulty: Easy to moderate; it's relatively short, but the trail can be rough.

Elevation gain: 1,750 feet (to Schlomberg Cabin)

Best season: Midsummer through early fall

Canine compatibility: Yes

Nearest town: Weaverville/Trinity Center

Fees and permits: Free wilderness permit required for overnight visitors; free campfire permits required for fires and camp stoves

Schedule: Trails in the Trinity Alps are always open; however, most trailhead access roads are closed or impassable during winter.

Maps: USGS Billys Peak and Deadman Peak; USDAFS Trinity Alps Wilderness

Trail contact: Weaverville Ranger Station: (530) 623-2121; www.fs.usda .gov/stnf

Parking and trailhead facilities: Adequate parking, but don't be surprised to find numerous cars here on summer weekends; no facilities. The closest campgrounds are Goldfield and Big Flat.

FINDING THE TRAILHEAD

From Weaverville drive 40 miles north on CA 3 to Coffee Creek Road and go left (west). Continue 9 miles to the signed trailhead on the right (Coffee Creek Road is unpaved after the first 5 miles). The trailhead is just before the North Fork bridge. GPS: N41 7.281' / W122 50.115'

THE HIKE

Most people use the North Fork Coffee Creek Trail (9W02) to stroll 3.5 miles to historic Hodges Cabin, spend the day poking around the idyllic site, eat a picnic lunch, sign the guest register, then skip back down the trail at the end of the day. It's a fine way to spend a day in the Trinity Alps. But to sample some of the most rugged, lonely wilderness in the Alps, don't stop at Hodges Cabin.

Beyond Hodges Cabin you can use the North Fork Coffee Creek Trail to reach Schlomberg Cabin, a dilapidated old miner's shelter in a green glade above the North Fork, as well as Wolford Cabin and the headwaters of North Fork Coffee Creek. **Note:** You'll see fire-scarred terrain on the hike to Hodges Cabin, and erosion along the North Fork Coffee Creek has caused trail damage in recent years.

The trail starts with a quick climb to gain a line high above the creek. After the initial ascent, the path assumes a more moderate grade as it contours northwest and then north, following the course of North Fork Coffee Creek. Oak, Douglas fir, and several varieties of pine provide some shade, but expect sunny and hot hiking in the first mile. At 1.5 miles the trail descends to creek level just before a bridge (and near an old cabin

Hodges Cabin was a deluxe outpost a century ago, with electricity and a telephone.

site, minus the cabin). Crossing to the west bank, you hike the rest of the way to Hodges Cabin on a meandering path that wanders up and down along the creek. **Fly fishermen take note:** You pass within casting distance of several sparkling holes guaranteed to contain trout.

At Hodges Cabin a makeshift bridge on a tree trunk permits a dry crossing of the now wide and placid river. The two-story structure, with assorted outbuildings, was restored by the USDA Forest Service in 1987 (firefighters saved it from sure destruction during the 2014 Coffee Fire). The original cabin was built by Walter Hodges in the early 1920s. The Southern California businessman wanted a vacation home in his beloved Trinity Alps and constructed a 2,000-square-foot house in the remote valley. It was once a bustling little outpost, with its own hydroelectric plant and telephone. Be sure to fill your water bottles at the cabin's sweet-tasting spring.

Another historic site, unknown to most visitors, lies 0.5 mile downstream above the confluence of the North Fork and Lick Creek. Though little remains at the site, a seasonal Native American village was once located in a meadow neatly hidden in the forest above the confluence. To reach it, follow an unmaintained path south of Hodges Cabin, on the east side of the North Fork, and make your way up to the hidden plateau, passing some old mining relics on the way.

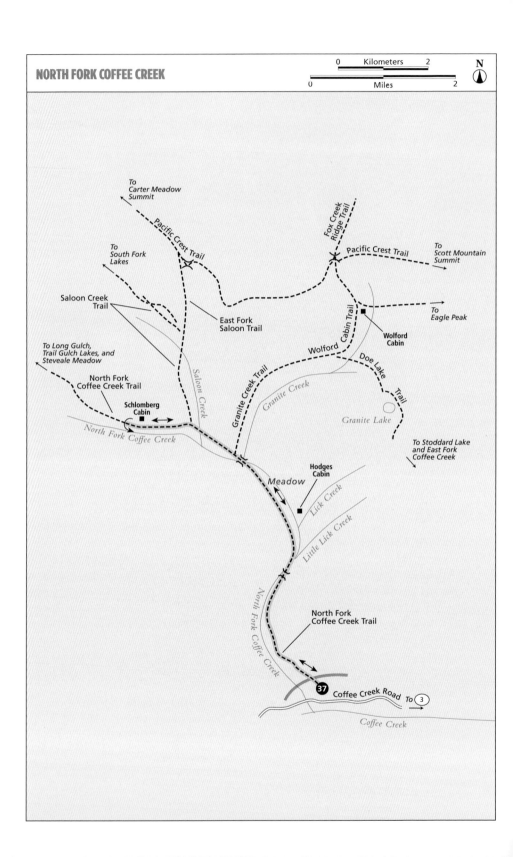

NORTH FORK COFFEE CREEK

0 Kilometers 2
0 Miles 2

N

To
Carter Meadow
Summit

Pacific Crest Trail

Fox Creek Ridge Trail

Pacific Crest Trail

To
Scott Mountain
Summit

To
South Fork
Lakes

Saloon Creek
Trail

East Fork
Saloon Trail

To
Eagle Peak

Wolford Cabin Trail

Wolford
Cabin

To Long Gulch,
Trail Gulch Lakes, and
Steveale Meadow

North Fork
Coffee Creek Trail

Schlomberg
Cabin

Saloon Creek

Granite Creek Trail

Wolford

Granite Creek

Doe Lake Trail

North Fork Coffee Creek

Granite Lake

To Stoddard Lake
and East Fork
Coffee Creek

Hodges
Cabin

Meadow

Lick Creek

Little Lick Creek

North Fork Coffee Creek

North Fork
Coffee Creek Trail

37

Coffee Creek Road To 3

Coffee Creek

North of Hodges Cabin, the canyon of the North Fork widens into a broad valley where forest and meadow alternate regularly along the drainage and sandy streamside beaches invite a lazy afternoon in the sun. An easy mile of near-level walking brings you to another steel bridge over the North Fork, where you cross back to the east side. Look (and sniff) for a remarkably fragrant stand of azaleas at the crossing (best in early summer). Just across the bridge, 4.5 miles from the trailhead, arrive at the Granite Creek Trail (8W09) junction. Signs indicate that Wolford Cabin, Granite Lake, and the Doe Lake Trail (8W05) lie to the right (northeast). Turn here if you want to reach Wolford Cabin in the most direct way.

To reach Schlomberg Cabin and the headwaters of North Fork Coffee Creek, continue northwest on the North Fork Trail. The path crosses Saloon Creek and ascends to a signed junction with the Saloon Creek Trail. Another historic cabin, this one unnamed, is located on a flat that you pass just after crossing the creek. It reportedly belonged to Hodges's carpenter.

At the Saloon Creek Trail junction, stay left (west) on the North Fork Trail to reach Schlomberg Cabin. (The junction is signed "South Fork Lakes" to the right, "Long Gulch Lake–Steveale Meadow" to the left.) A mile west of the junction you emerge into an open meadow; the historic cabin is located in a forest-fringed clearing just below. Schlomberg is the most deteriorated of the cabins still standing in this corner of the Trinity Alps.

MILES AND DIRECTIONS

0.0 Start at the North Fork Coffee Creek Trailhead. Hike upstream, along a gradually ascending trail.

3.5 Arrive at Hodges Cabin.

4.5 Continue upstream on the North Fork Coffee Creek Trail.

6.5 Reach Schlomberg Cabin. Return the way you came.

13.0 Arrive back at the trailhead.

OPTIONS

Two miles beyond Schlomberg Cabin, the trail connects with the Steveale Creek Trail and Trail Gulch and Long Gulch Lakes. For a scenic loop route, take the Saloon Creek and East Fork Saloon Trails to the Pacific Crest Trail; then make a loop back by way of Wolford Cabin and the Granite Creek Trail (adds about 10 miles). Small Granite and Doe Lakes are also within striking distance (not described here; check with rangers on current condition of the trail). The loop can also be extended by using the East Fork Coffee Creek Trail and walking back to the North Fork trailhead on Coffee Creek Road.

38 BILLYS PEAK LOOKOUT

Want a short hike with a big payoff? Take this steep route to an old fire lookout site and enjoy the 360-degree view—on a clear day, Mount Shasta dominates the horizon.

Start: Billys Peak Trailhead
Type of hike: Day hike; out-and-back
Distance: 6.0 miles
Hiking time: About 4–6 hours
Difficulty: Moderate to strenuous; it's steep, and the upper, exposed section can be hot on a sunny day.
Elevation gain: 2,900 feet
Best season: Midsummer through early fall
Canine compatibility: Yes
Nearest town: Weaverville/Trinity Center
Fees and permits: Free wilderness permit required for overnight visitors; free campfire permits required for fires and camp stoves

Schedule: Trails in the Trinity Alps are always open; however, most trailhead access roads are closed or impassable during winter.
Maps: USGS Carrville; USDAFS Trinity Alps Wilderness
Trail contact: Weaverville Ranger Station: (530) 623-2121; www.fs.usda.gov/stnf
Special considerations: The access road is closed Oct 30 to May 1.
Parking and trailhead facilities: No facilities or drinking water. The nearest forest service developed campground is Trinity River, 1 mile away on CA 3, immediately south of FR 38N34.

Get an unobstructed view of Mount Shasta from Billys Peak Lookout.

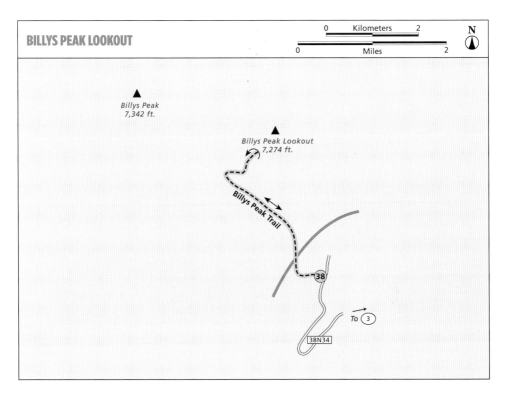

FINDING THE TRAILHEAD

From Weaverville drive 42 miles north on CA 3 (past Coffee Creek) and turn left (west) on FR 38N34. Trailhead signs may point the way where logging roads merge with the main road. At 4.6 miles park at a wide landing. Billys Peak Trail starts on the uphill (north) side of the clearing (it's hard to see from the parking area). GPS: N41 6.169' / W122 43.921'

THE HIKE

The Billys Peak Trail (7W08) is the path to take if you're a fan of big views and you want instant gratification. Well, nearly instant. It's a stairway hike straight to the top of a 7,000-foot granite perch on the very edge of the Trinity Alps Wilderness. The 360-degree view from the summit takes in Mount Shasta, Lassen Peak, the Coffee Creek drainage, and a host of peaks in the inner Alps. Despite the name, the summit reached by the trail is not really Billys Peak but an unnamed island of rock where the fire lookout was built. (The real Billys Peak is slightly higher and lies to the northwest.) **Note:** In recent years the trail has become overgrown in places.

The trail rises steeply at first but soon settles into a more moderate grade on shady switchbacks that lead northwest under a canopy of mixed fir and pine. In less than 1 mile you gain the ridgeline and continue to climb moderately, with ever better views of Coffee Creek as you ascend. The forest cover gets more sparse and the trail more rocky as you climb. The upper portion of this hike can be very hot and sunny in the summertime.

A long contour to the southwest leads to the final assault on the peak, where a series of steep, rocky, and exposed switchbacks leads to the summit. In the middle of this steep

Mullein thrives in meadows throughout the Trinity Alps.

section, which will certainly be strenuous on a hot day, someone has painted this message on a boulder: "The spirit indeed is willing, but the flesh is weak." While I can't condone the graffiti, it's an appropriate sentiment on a hot day.

The last few steps are in a rock gully; then you pop up on top—nothing but air and horizon in every direction. The only remains of the fire lookout are the foundation and a few rusted old cans, but it's enough to make you wonder about the fortunate few who used to spend their summers up here.

MILES AND DIRECTIONS

0.0 Start climbing at the Billys Peak Lookout Trailhead.

3.0 Reach Billys Peak Lookout. Return the way you came.

6.0 Arrive back at the trailhead.

39 STODDARD LAKE

This short, easy hike leads to a big lake surrounded by pretty meadows and thick forests. Sound tempting? Others agree. Expect plenty of company on summer weekends.

Start: Stoddard Lake Trailhead
Type of hike: Day hike or backpack; loop or out-and-back
Distance: 6.4 miles (loop); 7.0 miles (out-and-back)
Hiking time: About 1–3 days
Difficulty: Easy; relatively level and short
Elevation gain: 1,150 feet (loop); 750 feet (out-and-back)
Best season: Midsummer through early fall
Canine compatibility: Yes
Nearest town: Weaverville/Trinity Center
Fees and permits: Free wilderness permit required for overnight

visitors; free campfire permits required for fires and camp stoves
Schedule: Trails in the Trinity Alps are always open; however, most trailhead access roads are closed or impassable during winter.
Maps: USGS Billys Peak and Tangle Blue Lake; USDAFS Trinity Alps Wilderness
Trail contact: Weaverville Ranger Station: (530) 623-2121; www.fs.usda .gov/stnf
Parking and trailhead facilities: Ample parking but no facilities. Horse Flat, Eagle Creek, and Trinity River Campgrounds are within a few miles of the trailhead.

FINDING THE TRAILHEAD

From Weaverville drive 43 miles north on CA 3 to the signed turn for Eagle Creek–Horse Flat (3 miles north of Coffee Creek). Turn left (west) onto CR 135 and proceed 1.2 miles to the signed left turn for the Stoddard Lake Trailhead (on FR 38N22). The unpaved road is easy to follow (stay left at 5.4 miles) to the junction with FR 38N27 at 5.8 miles. Go left (west) and continue to the trailhead at 8.7 miles. GPS: N41 9.554' / W122 43.379'

THE HIKE

The Stoddard Lake basin's attractions are easy to list: good swimming, fishing, and camping 90 minutes from the trailhead, all of which draw hikers in summer. Add frequent horseback riders from nearby dude ranches, and you might want to give Stoddard Lake a wide berth if it's a quiet wilderness experience you're after.

Of course there's usually a good reason for a crowd, and Stoddard is no exception. At just under 6,000 feet elevation, the lake warms up early in the summer and offers a great base camp from which to explore the area. Stoddard and neighboring McDonald Lake are both deep-blue lakes in the protected shelter of a low-lying basin. Each lake is rimmed by thick forests of mixed conifers, with plenty of elbow room for campers to spread out and lots of opportunities for exploring the surrounding area.

The Stoddard Lake Trail (7W06) starts uphill, heading west on a wide path through a forest of Douglas fir, incense cedar, and ponderosa pine. The trail soon levels out and climbs gently to a meadow 0.4 mile from the trailhead. The main trail veers right (northwest) through the meadow; an unmarked and obscure path forks left (southwest). This unmarked path is the Old Stoddard Lake Trail, which climbs steeply over a ridgeline and

McDonald and Stoddard Lakes are separated by a thin strip of forest.

Stoddard Lake is surrounded by dense forest.

into the lake basin by the most direct route. While shorter than the new trail by about 1 mile, the old trail is considerably steeper and unmaintained (it's not even on the new forest service wilderness map). There's no good reason to take the abandoned trail, but it's a pretty route, and I recommend hiking it on the way back if you want to add a little spice to this tame outing.

To continue on the new trail, stay right and ascend moderately through the shady forest. Look for views of Mount Shasta to the east as you climb. The route is easy the rest of the way. Pass flower-filled meadows and a little creek that feeds a glade full of California pitcher plants.

After crossing aster-filled Stoddard Meadow, arrive at the junction with East Fork Coffee Creek Trail in a flat next to the old Stoddard Cabin site. (There's nothing left of the historic cabin, which, like the lake and meadow, was named for nineteenth-century rancher John Stoddard.) The junction is signed "Doe Flat" to the right (west), "Stoddard Lake" to the left (south). The junction is just over 2 miles from the trailhead.

The last mile to Stoddard rises moderately to the south, arriving abruptly at the shoreline in a shady stand of fir and lodgepole pine. You'll find a row of campsites where the main trail hits the lake. These are in open view of one another, with no seclusion. The best campsite here is located at the eastern tip of the lake, just past a creeklet. Find excellent fishing and swimming from the granite slab that slopes into the lake.

McDonald Lake is located immediately south of Stoddard, behind a screen of mixed conifers. McDonald is simply a smaller version of Stoddard. (It's a favorite destination of horsepackers.) Farther to the southwest and 450 feet higher is Upper Stoddard Lake, a little pond tucked into the granite shelf at the head of the basin. No trail leads to Upper Stoddard, but you can pick your way up the rocky outlet without much difficulty, staying north to avoid the steepest sections. The lake is a 0.5-mile scramble from McDonald Lake. Consider camping cowboy style on the flat-rock clifftop that rims the north side of McDonald Lake.

To return to the trailhead, you can either retrace your steps or create a loop by using the unmaintained Old Stoddard Trail. At the northeast side of Stoddard Lake, where the

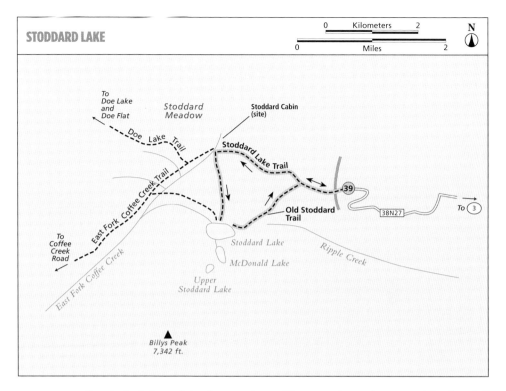

new trail ends, find the path leading northeast. The sometimes-obscure path leads uphill to the crest of a ridge and then plunges a mile to a junction with the new trail. Look for great views of Mount Shasta from the ridgetop. **Fair warning:** The route is steep and overgrown. Arrive at the junction in the first meadow you passed on the way in. Turn right (east) and proceed 0.4 mile to the trailhead.

MILES AND DIRECTIONS

- 0.0 Start at the Stoddard Lake Trailhead.
- 0.4 Stay right at the Old Stoddard Trail junction.
- 2.3 Reach the East Fork Coffee Creek Trail junction–Stoddard Cabin site; stay left.
- 3.5 Reach Stoddard Lake. Retrace your steps to the trailhead for a 7 -mile out-and-back hike or continue the loop.
- 3.6 Head steeply uphill on the Old Stoddard Trail.
- 6.0 Turn right onto the Stoddard Lake Trail and retrace your steps to the trailhead.
- 6.4 Arrive back at the trailhead.

OPTIONS

The East Fork Coffee Creek Trail (8W06) connects to Doe and Granite Lakes (Doe Lake Trail, 8W05) and Coffee Creek Road. The Stoddard spur trail (8W24), located on the northwest side of Stoddard Lake, also leads to the East Fork Trail.

40 BEAR LAKES

Score a classic Trinity Alps setting—granite cirques, great views, and sparkling lakes—with this short but steep hike. Bonus: plenty of off-trail options for explorers.

Start: Bear Lakes Trailhead
Type of hike: Day hike or overnight; out-and-back
Distance: 11.2 miles
Hiking time: About 1–3 days
Difficulty: Moderate
Elevation gain: 3,200 feet
Best season: Midsummer through early fall
Canine compatibility: Yes
Nearest town: Weaverville/Trinity Center
Fees and permits: Free wilderness permit required for overnight visitors; free campfire permits required for fires and camp stoves
Schedule: Trails in the Trinity Alps are always open; however, most trailhead access roads are closed or impassable during winter.
Maps: USGS Tangle Blue Lake; USDAFS Trinity Alps Wilderness
Trail contact: Weaverville Ranger Station: (530) 623-2121; www.fs.usda .gov/stnf
Parking and trailhead facilities: Limited parking and no facilities. (More than a few cars here is a good indication to go elsewhere—all the cars' occupants are most likely at Bear Lake.) A few undeveloped campsites are available, but the closest developed campgrounds are at Eagle Creek and Trinity River, a few miles south on CA 3.

FINDING THE TRAILHEAD

From Weaverville drive 48 miles north on CA 3 to the signed turn for Bear Lakes Trailhead on CR 137 (8 miles north of Coffee Creek). If the first Bear Lake Road access is closed (as it was in recent years), proceed another 2 miles to the second entrance (the road makes a loop with two ends on CA 3). Turn left (west) at either entrance and proceed just over 1 mile to the signed trailhead at Bear Creek. A bridge over the creek is closed to vehicles, so you'll have to park on the north side of the stream (if you come from that end) and walk across the bridge to the trailhead. GPS: N41 11.647' / W122 39.169'

THE HIKE

The Bear Lakes basin presents the classic problem caused by too much beautiful scenery too close to the trailhead. Here the problem is exacerbated by the basin's limited camping opportunities and lack of alternative trail systems. (The hike is a dead end, so if you arrive at the trailhead and there are more than a few cars, consider going elsewhere.) The Bear Lakes basin is still not as heavily used as many other easy-to-reach destinations in the Alps, and it's not uncommon to find solitude here on weekdays and out of season. There are enough campsites for several parties to spread out.

The Trinity Alps' easternmost lakes (if you examine the map, you'll see it took a creative eastward jog of the wilderness boundary to include the Bear Lakes basin) are set in a northeast-facing cirque at a relatively low elevation of 6,000 feet. But the northern exposure, granite surroundings, and impressive view of Mount Shasta create a slice of alpine wonder equal to many higher, more remote settings. Good swimming, fishing, and exploring abound.

The Bear Lakes Trail (7W03) starts at a signed trailhead on the south side of Bear Creek and climbs steeply up a set of switchbacks through mixed forest of fir, cedar, and scattered oaks. After the initial ascent, the trail contours more moderately up the drainage. A mile from the trailhead, cross Bear Creek on a wood-and-steel bridge; continue climbing on the north side of the creek.

The trail ascends through open hillsides of oak and manzanita on the ridgeline high above Bear Creek. Over the next couple of miles, continue to climb in a westerly direction, steeply at times, up the drainage. Pine, fir, and incense cedar dominate the forest as you ascend. Look for an emerald fern meadow just over halfway to Big Bear Lake and an obvious avalanche path shortly after that. The broken trees and other winter wreckage are an impressive sight.

Just over 4 miles in, the trail breaks out into the open, rocky upper drainage, where cairns lead the way up beautiful granite slabs. Across Bear Creek, the notch in the ridge to the south marks the entrance to Little and Wee Bear Lakes. (There's no trail to the gap, but you can get there from Big Bear without much difficulty.) At 4.6 miles the path crosses the outlet stream and deposits you at the edge of Big Bear Lake. Surrounded by bare rock with a few stunted stands of western white pine and mountain hemlock, the 28-acre lake is one of the largest in the Trinity Alps. There are great views of Mount Shasta from the basin's eastern edge; in summer little gardens of wildflowers fill the cracks in the granite slabs. Don't be tempted by the first campsite you come to, near the outlet.

Little Bear Lake is just right.

BEAR LAKES

Instead, press on around the southeastern shore of the lake, where you'll find better, more secluded sites on the southwest side.

Little and Wee Bear Lakes are directly to the southeast, on the other side of an unnamed peak (just shy of 7,000 feet) that sits between the two cirques. You can get there one of two ways: If you camp at the far (south) end of Big Bear, hike up to the obvious saddle between the two basins. There's no maintained trail, but the obvious route leads up an open, beautiful slope with great views, wildflowers, and sublime snowmelt pools. Once over the saddle, it's a simple matter to pick your way down to Little Bear and then pond-sized Wee Bear. Alternatively, from the outlet of Big Bear, go around the east side of the peak that separates the two basins and follow cairns on a moderate traverse to the notch that leads to Little and Wee Bear Lakes. There's no established trail, but the 1-mile route is not difficult. For a good day hike, combine the two routes to make a loop. The Little-Wee Bear basin is a great place to visit should you find Big Bear crowded.

Cross this bridge at the start of the Bear Lakes Trail.

MILEAGE AND DIRECTIONS

0.0   Start hiking upstream at Bear Lakes Trailhead.

1.0   Cross the bridge over Bear Creek.

4.6   Arrive at Big Bear Lake.

5.6   Hike off-trail to Little and Wee Bear Lakes. Return the way you came.

11.2   Arrive back at the trailhead.

41 TANGLE BLUE LAKE

Families with young children will appreciate this hike: Relatively short and easy, it leads to a large lake with plenty of diversions, including a beach.

Start: Tangle Blue Lake Trailhead
Type of hike: Day hike or backpack; out-and-back
Distance: 7.6 miles
Hiking time: About 1–3 days
Difficulty: Easy
Elevation gain: 1,100 feet
Best season: Mid-summer through early fall
Canine compatibility: Yes
Nearest town: Weaverville/Trinity Center
Fees and permits: Free wilderness permit required for overnight visitors; free campfire permits required for fires and camp stoves

Schedule: Trails in the Trinity Alps are always open; however, most trailhead access roads are closed or impassable during winter.
Maps: USGS Tangle Blue Lake; USDAFS Trinity Alps Wilderness
Trail contact: Weaverville Ranger Station: (530) 623-2121; www.fs.usda.gov/stnf
Parking and trailhead facilities: Ample parking but no facilities or potable water. The nearest campgrounds are on CA 3 (several along the road toward Coffee Creek).

FINDING THE TRAILHEAD

From Weaverville drive 53 miles north on CA 3 (13.3 miles past Coffee Creek) to the signed left turn (west) onto FR 39N20. The turn is in the middle of a sharp right-hand curve, 0.8 mile after starting uphill toward Scott Mountain Summit. Trailers are not advisable on the narrow road, but passenger cars should be fine. Stay left at the fork at 2 miles, straight at 3 miles. The trailhead is 3.8 miles from the highway. A locked timber company gate marks the start of the trail. GPS: N41 13.677' / W122 42.571'

THE HIKE

If lakes were judged on name alone, Tangle Blue Lake would be my second favorite in the Trinity Alps (Billy-Be-Damned takes first). Local legend attributes the name to a bad hangover. Tangle Blue boasts a beautiful meadow on one side, plush campsites, and plenty of exploring potential. The hike is ideal for families or anyone looking for a gentle route. (**Note:** Cattle sometimes graze in the area. Check with rangers on current conditions.)

From the trailhead parking area, head right (west) on the Grand National Trail (8W23), past the timber company gate and along an old dirt road to a bridge across Tangle Blue Creek. The single-lane bridge spans the creek just upstream from its confluence with Horse Creek. After crossing the bridge stay right as the road climbs westward along the banks of Tangle Blue Creek. The road to the left leads to Horse Creek; a trail marker signals the way if there's any confusion.

Tangle Blue Creek lives up to the allure of its name as much as the lake itself. The stream cascades and tumbles through a rugged canyon, with many clear deep pools and small pour-offs. The moderate grade and wide roadbed make for easy hiking, with a lot

Ambitious hikers can explore the steep terrain above Tangle Blue Lake.

of elbow room for a side-by-side walk with friends. The banks of the creek are lined with dense stands of incense cedar, fir, and pine, with a lush understory of thick ferns.

The trail remains above the creek as it climbs gradually higher. After about 0.5 mile there are dense stands of manzanita on both sides of the trail—anyone who has ever fought through the thick, thorny bushes will appreciate the wide track between them.

Arrive at an old trailhead and forest service gate 1.5 miles from the trailhead (the hike used to be shorter); then walk through a majestic grove of enormous incense cedars 0.25 mile past the gate. Moss on the cedars here is so bright green it seems to glow on a gray

TANGLE BLUE LAKE

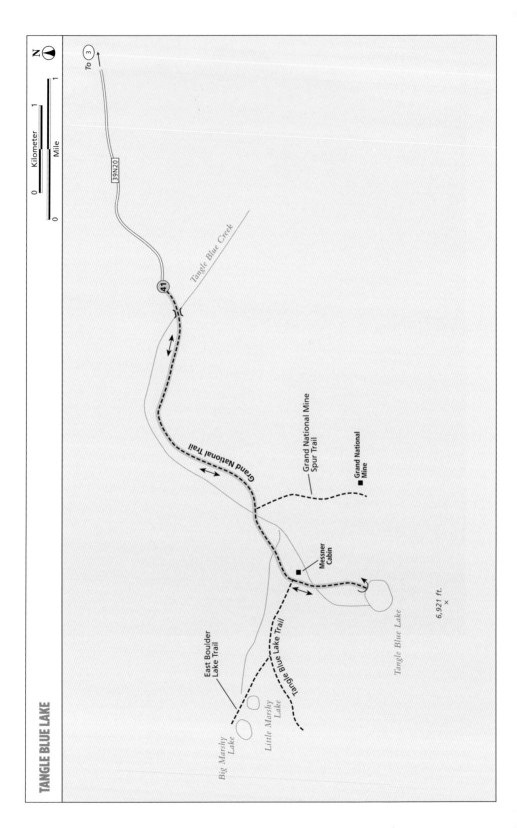

day. Just uphill from the glowing moss (just under 2 miles from the trailhead), arrive at a junction with the spur trail to the historic Grand National Mine. Go left (south) to explore the ruins of the old mine or right (west) to continue toward Tangle Blue Lake. Descend slightly to a creek crossing, which should pose no problems except at the peak of high water. (Purify all water in the Trinity Alps.)

Continue on singletrack trail (not an old jeep road) for the first time since starting the hike. The path continues for all of 0.25 mile and then crosses the outlet from Little Marshy Lake. This creek may actually appear to be two creeks late in the year. After the crossing the trail resumes on an old dirt road.

Hike up the wide, rocky roadbed to a signed trail junction just under 2.7 miles from the trailhead. Tangle Blue Lake is to the left (south) and Marshy Lake is to the right (west). You can also use the right fork to reach the Pacific Crest Trail.

Take the left fork toward Tangle Blue Lake and immediately pass a huge double incense cedar at the head of a meadow. Look up to the left and catch your first glimpse of the granite walls looming over the head of the Tangle Blue basin. Just before the end of the meadow, jog left and cross Tangle Blue Creek for the final time. Pass the remains of the old Messner Cabin site and ascend moderately alongside the creek for the final 0.5 mile to the lake. Little creeklets flow through stands of willow, alder, and fern. Emerge from the willow wonderland at the edge of a large meadow at the north end of Tangle Blue Lake.

Granite peaks tower over the 12-acre lake's southern shore, and you'll find easy walking all the way around the lake's perimeter. Several campsites here are among the few in the Trinity Alps that still have old forest service stoves in place. One of the biggest group sites in the Alps is also located here (across the outlet stream). Together with the easy hike, this makes Tangle Blue popular with youth groups and others with large numbers.

Cattails, unusual in the Alps, thrive here on the east and north shores. There's also a nice white-sand beach—usually submerged until late summer—with accompanying meadow at the southwest shore. Small groups will find good camping here. The unnamed 6,921-foot peak above Tangle Blue Lake makes a fine scramble, but use caution on loose rock. An unmaintained use trail leads up the lake's inlet. The slightly higher (by a few hundred feet) peak on the east side of the lake also offers good scrambling potential.

MILES AND DIRECTIONS

- **0.0** Start at the Tangle Blue Trailhead and almost immediately cross a bridge over Tangle Blue Creek.
- **1.7** Stay right at the Grand National Mine spur trail junction.
- **2.7** Stay left at the Tangle Blue Lake Trail junction.
- **3.8** Reach Tangle Blue Lake. Return the way you came.
- **7.6** Arrive back at the trailhead.

OPTIONS

The East Boulder Lake Trail leads to Marshy Lakes and then connects with the Pacific Crest Trail, just 3 miles away. From there you can access a number of destinations along the Scott Mountains divide.

42 LOG LAKE

No need to hike far or tackle tough terrain to find a scenic lake with total solitude. This off-trail route leads to a quiet lakeside campsite you'll likely have to yourself.

Start: Tangle Blue Trailhead
Type of hike: Day hike or backpack; out-and-back
Distance: 5.6 miles
Hiking time: About 1–2 days
Difficulty: Moderate; it's short, but requires route-finding skills.
Elevation gain: 1,458 feet
Best season: Midsummer through early fall
Canine compatibility: Yes
Nearest town: Weaverville/Trinity Center
Fees and permits: Free wilderness permit required for overnight visitors; free campfire permits required for fires and camp stoves
Schedule: Trails in the Trinity Alps are always open; however, most trailhead access roads are closed or impassable during winter.
Maps: USGS Tangle Blue Lake; USDAFS Trinity Alps Wilderness
Trail contact: Weaverville Ranger Station: (530) 623-2121; www.fs.usda .gov/stnf
Parking and trailhead facilities: Ample parking but no facilities or potable water. The nearest campgrounds are on CA 3 (several along the road toward Coffee Creek).

The hike to Log Lake is short, but off-trail navigation keeps the crowds away.

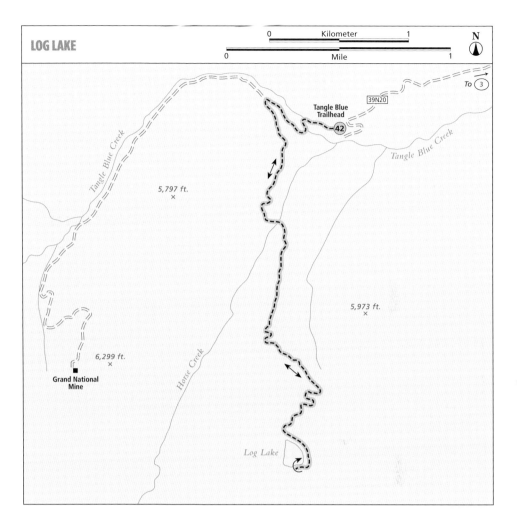

0   Kilometer   1

0   Mile   1

N

To 3

39N20

Tangle Blue
Trailhead

42

Tangle Blue Creek

Tangle Blue Creek

5,797 ft.
×

5,973 ft.
×

6,299 ft.
×

Grand National
Mine

Horse Creek

Log Lake

FINDING THE TRAILHEAD

From Weaverville drive 53 miles north on CA 3 (13.3 miles past Coffee Creek) to the signed left turn (west) onto FR 39N20. The turn is in the middle of a sharp right-hand curve, 0.8 mile after starting uphill toward Scott Mountain Summit. Trailers are not advisable on the narrow road, but passenger cars should be fine. Stay left at the fork at 2 miles, straight at 3 miles. The trailhead is 3.8 miles from the highway. A locked timber company gate marks the start of the trail. GPS: N41 13.677' / W122 42.571'

THE HIKE

Though Log Lake is not far from popular Tangle Blue Lake, it gets only a tiny fraction of the visitors—and not for lack of beauty. Leon Nelson, a local Trinity Alps expert, says little-known Log Lake is one of his all-time favorites thanks to splendid scenery, a short but sporty off-trail hike, and near-guaranteed solitude. The following directions were supplied by Nelson.

From the Tangle Blue Trailhead, cross the bridge over Tangle Blue Creek and take the dirt road to the left. Easy walking on this logging road leads to a landing (where trucks are loaded) at 1.2 miles. This is where the off-trail hiking starts. From here it's a short, easy walk downhill (southeast) to Horse Creek and its junction with an unnamed creeklet. Horse Creek can usually be crossed by July, but don't attempt this hike early in the season.

Once across the stream, you contour south up the drainage through open forest on numerous animal trails. Stay on the hillside, not the ridgetop, and continue climbing to a large willow patch, which can be marshy in early season. At the end of the left side of the willows, climb the first of four boulder chutes that lead up to the basin. Ascending the chutes allows you to avoid hiking through dense brush.

After climbing the last chute, head for a large white rock, which makes a good place for a rest break. From here you climb southwest, ascending through brush to the ridgetop, where you can see Log Lake for the first time. From the ridge, bushwhack through dense brush (so gnarly, Nelson recommends a handheld pruner) to Log's outlet stream. Once at the lake, it's an easy hike to the left along the shoreline to an excellent campsite on the south shore, with space for several tents and a great view of the rocky cirque. You'll also find what Nelson says is the finest campfire ring around, with a 10-foot rear wall of granite that reflects welcoming warmth. Retrace your route to the trailhead.

MILEAGE AND DIRECTIONS

0.0 Start at the Tangle Blue Trailhead.

1.2 Reach the obvious logging road landing and start the off-trail route.

1.3 Cross Horse Creek.

1.9 Ascend the first of four boulder chutes.

2.8 Reach Log Lake. Return the way you came.

5.6 Arrive back at the trailhead.

HIKES FROM FOREST HIGHWAY 93 (CALLAHAN–CECILVILLE ROAD)

Don't hurry through Grizzly Meadow on the way to Grizzly Lake (Hike 52).

43 MILL CREEK AND WASHBASIN LAKES

When you've seen a lot of the "name-brand" Trinities and are ready to discover the forgotten fringes, head to this low-traffic corner of the wilderness. This short hike leads to a small lake with an optional off-trail trek to Washbasin Lake. Expect big views of Scott Valley.

Start: Mill Creek Trailhead
Type of hike: Day hike or backpack; out-and-back
Distance: 8.2 miles
Hiking time: About 1–3 days
Difficulty: Easy to Mill Creek; moderate to Washbasin Lake
Elevation gain: 1,000 feet (Mill Creek); 1,800 feet (Washbasin Lake)
Best season: Midsummer through early fall
Canine compatibility: Yes
Nearest town: Callahan
Fees and permits: Free wilderness permit required for overnight visitors; free campfire permits required for fires and camp stoves

Schedule: Trails in the Trinity Alps are always open; however, most trailhead access roads are closed or impassable during winter.
Maps: USGS Billys Peak and Callahan; USDAFS Trinity Alps Wilderness
Trail contact: Weaverville Ranger Station: (530) 623-2121; www.fs.usda .gov/stnf
Parking and trailhead facilities: Ample parking but no water or other facilities. The nearest forest service campgrounds are Scott Mountain, Hidden Horse, and Trail Creek.

FINDING THE TRAILHEAD

From Callahan (on CA 3, approximately 65 miles north of Weaverville), drive west on South Fork Road to the junction with FR 40N17 and FR 40N16. (You can also take South Fork Road from FH 93 to reach the same junction.) Turn left (southeast) onto FR 40N16 and proceed 4.5 miles to the trailhead at road's end. (Note: Expect very rough going for the last 100 yards.) GPS: N41 15.925' / W122 45.980'

THE HIKE

Mill Creek Lake is a pretty little backcountry pond that seems to go unnoticed—and unvisited—by most Trinity Alps hikers. The 3-acre lake is neatly hidden in a cleft gouged into a granite cirque 3 miles up the Little Mill Trail. You won't miss the lake if you approach from below, but hikers coming over the ridge from East Boulder Lake may mistake an unnamed pond high in the Little Mill Creek drainage for the lake itself and never actually descend far enough to see Mill Creek Lake. Even more rarely seen is Washbasin Lake, a larger body of water located one drainage to the east. No trail leads to Washbasin; it remains well off the beaten track and has no campsites worth mentioning.

A high subalpine meadow, just under the crest of the Scott Mountains, hangs over the cirque. Snowmelt ponds, wildflowers, views of Scott Valley, and fascinating old mine relics make the upper basin a wonderful place to spend a day or two exploring. Though Little Mill is quite close to the popular East Boulder basin, it gets far fewer visitors.

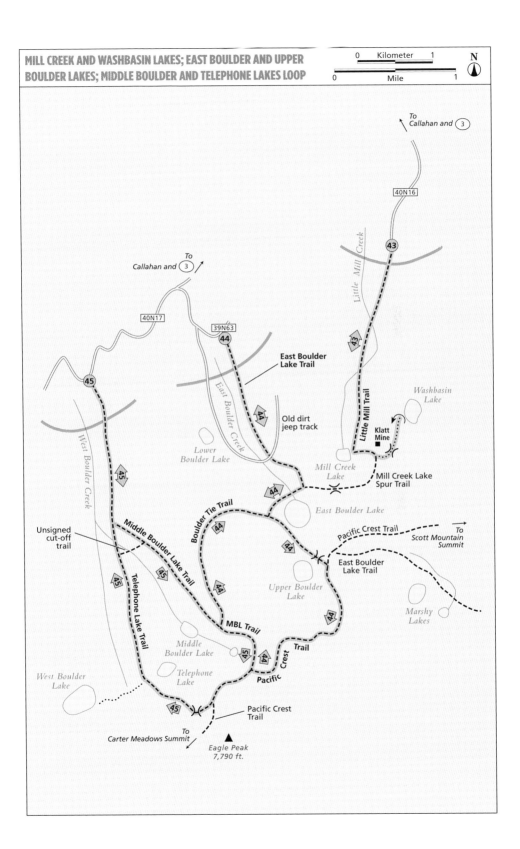

Washbasin Lake has no inlet or outlet stream.

Start hiking south from the trailhead on a wide track in the shade of a dense white fir forest. The Little Mill Trail (8W01) follows the course of Little Mill Creek 3 miles to the lake, passing in and out of forest cover and through several meadows on the way. The meadows here (at least in the lower drainage), like the others on the north side of the Scott Mountains, have been heavily grazed by cattle. Watch your step and purify all water.

After less than 0.5 mile, the old jeep track peters out and the rest of the hike is on a trail. After crossing from the west to the east side of Little Mill Creek, ascend through a series of meadows with alder thickets lining the stream. Cow paths can make the trail somewhat confusing, but cairns generally lead the way. (Don't get confused at an unmarked fork just over 1 mile in; both branches meet again farther upcanyon.)

Good views of the granite headwall above Mill Creek Lake appear as you climb higher. The ascent is extremely easygoing for most of the way but steepens considerably after the third meadow. Switchbacks lead up the east side of the drainage, and before you know it, the trail pops out on a grassy bench just under 3 miles from the trailhead. Rock-lined Mill Creek Lake is just over the granite dike directly ahead. If you're not comfortable with off-trail hiking, this is a good place to turn around.

To reach Washbasin Lake and the trail to East Boulder Lake, head east from Mill Creek Lake and pick up the Little Mill Trail, which climbs the steep, grassy east wall of the basin. The trail passes within 50 yards of a tailings pile from the old Klatt Mine. The historic site, complete with old ore cart, is worth a look. On the north side of the mine, the trail continues switchbacking east up the slope to a wide, grassy bench with more mining relics. Here the trail forks south and north.

Go right (south) along the bench to reach East Boulder Lake. The trail skirts the basin's upper meadows and a pond and then bends around to the west and drops over the ridge to East Boulder Lake (1 mile away).

To follow the off-trail route to Washbasin Lake, turn left (north) and shoot for the saddle on the ridge to the northeast. The trail soon disappears in a maze of old, faint paths, but the route is easy to pick out in the open, nearly treeless terrain. Just angle up to the low gap, 0.5 mile away, and you soon hit the crest of the ridge above Washbasin. From here it's an easy descent through a sparse forest of foxtail and lodgepole pine to the edge of the lake, 0.3 mile east of the ridge. Cairns lead through the forest, but you can't miss it if you walk east from the crest.

Washbasin Lake, as its name implies, sits in a deep, rocky bowl. Red meta-igneous rocks and royal-blue water lend a dash of color to the rugged cirque. The 10-acre lake is very clear, its shoreline very rocky, and its number of visitors very low. Enjoy; then retrace your steps.

MILEAGE AND DIRECTIONS

- 0.0 Start at the Mill Creek Trailhead.
- 3.0 Reach Mill Creek Lake. (**Option:** Turn around here for an easy 6 -mile hike.)
- 3.3 Pass the Klatt Mine; continue climbing.
- 4.1 Reach Washbasin Lake. Return the way you came.
- 8.2 Arrive back at the trailhead.

OPTIONS

Take the spur trail over the ridge to East Boulder Lake. The large lake makes a nice contrast to Little Mill Creek Lake.

44 EAST BOULDER AND UPPER BOULDER LAKES

Unlike some of the deep, rocky cirques found elsewhere in the Trinity Alps, East Boulder Lake and its smaller siblings sit in the middle of a sprawling basin with open meadows and commanding views.

(See map on page 209.)
Start: East Boulder Trailhead
Type of hike: Day hike or overnight; out-and-back (with optional loop)
Distance: 10.0 miles, including side trips
Hiking time: 1–3 days
Difficulty: Easy to moderate with side trips; easy without side trips
Elevation gain: 1,600 feet (800 feet to East Boulder Lake)
Best season: Midsummer through early fall
Canine compatibility: Yes
Nearest town: Callahan
Fees and permits: Free wilderness permit required for overnight

visitors; free campfire permits required for fires and camp stoves
Schedule: Trails in the Trinity Alps are always open; however, most trailhead access roads are closed or impassable during winter.
Maps: USGS Billys Peak; USDAFS Trinity Alps Wilderness
Trail contact: Weaverville Ranger Station: (530) 623-2121; www.fs.usda .gov/stnf
Parking and trailhead facilities: Ample parking but no water or other facilities. The nearest forest service campgrounds are Scott Mountain, Hidden Horse, and Trail Creek.

FINDING THE TRAILHEAD

From Callahan (on CA 3, approximately 65 miles north of Weaverville), drive west on South Fork Road to the junction with FR 40N17 and FR 40N16. (You can also take South Fork Road from FH 93 to reach the same junction.) Go straight (southwest) at the signed junction and follow unpaved FR 40N17 past McKeen Divide. Continue 5 miles to the signed turn for the East Boulder Trailhead. Turn left (east) onto FR 39N63 and follow signs to the trailhead at road's end (9 miles from Callahan). GPS: N41 15.150' / W122 47.669'

THE HIKE

How many Boulder lakes can one wilderness have? This group of Boulders (which includes East, Upper, Middle, West, and Lower) is not to be confused with Big and Little Boulder (near Coffee Creek) or Boulder Creek Lakes (off Canyon Creek). Now that that's cleared up, this particular set of Boulder Lakes (East and Upper) occupies one of the most distinctive cirques in this corner of the Trinity Alps. (**Note:** Lower Boulder is just a pond surrounded by dense forest and many dead trees.)

The wide and open East Boulder basin is dominated by steep headwalls of red peridotite rock, crystal-clear water, and sprawling meadows as smooth and flat as a putting green. A few stands of stunted trees, including white firs and several pine species (lodgepole, western white, etc.), provide shade on a hot day. The basin also harbors a surprising amount of sage, which looks decidedly out of place up here in a subalpine environment. (Cows probably brought sage seeds up from their winter home in Scott Valley.) East

Boulder makes a great base camp for exploring the area. (Stay on the north shore or in the meadow, alongside the pristine creek that bisects the basin.)

A list of the basin's attributes would not differ remarkably from a description of Middle Boulder, one drainage to the west, but the rocks, meadows, peaks, trees, and lakes of the East Boulder basin seem to have been assembled with an artist's touch. Everything is in perfect proportion, everything in its place. Upper Boulder Lake and its two companion ponds, perched on a terrace at the head of the basin, are a delightful surprise hidden just under the crest of the Scott Mountains.

One downside to this hike is the fact that, as with other destinations on the north side of the Scott Mountains, you may encounter cows here during the summer and early fall. The other drawback (which may actually be a plus, depending on your point of view) is that the road comes within 2 easy miles of the lake. Come out of season or midweek if you want solitude. Water is plentiful (treat everything you drink).

From the trailhead the path climbs south along the course of East Boulder Creek on the east side of the stream. (An old dirt track, closed to vehicles, runs along the west side of the creek.) The initial climb is in the shade of mixed fir, pine, and a few incense cedars, ascending gradually through forest intermixed with grassy glades. The trail passes through private property, so please be respectful.

This collection of Boulder Lakes is set in a wide, open basin that's unique in the Trinity Alps.

At 1.6 miles from the trailhead, the path crosses an old road and starts climbing more steeply toward the basin above. Just below the lake, East Boulder Creek cascades down a picturesque waterfall surrounded by colorful gardens of summer wildflowers. The trail ascends a series of moderate switchbacks up the east side of this headwall. At the top the basin is laid out at your feet. The 32-acre lake is one of the biggest in the wilderness.

Two trails branch off from the north side of East Boulder Lake. To the east lies a spur trail that hops over the ridge to Mill Creek Lake. The unnamed path starts on the hillside at the northeast corner of East Boulder, ascends a series of well-defined switchbacks to the ridgeline, and then plunges down into the Mill Creek drainage. The lake is about 1.5 miles away. Don't mistake the pond at the head of Mill Creek for the lake, which is hidden in a granite slot below.

The other trail junction lies on the west side of East Boulder Lake. If the sign has fallen down, look for a path heading west through the shoreline grass. This is the Boulder Tie Trail, which leads around the shoulder of the ridge to the west and over to Middle Boulder Lake. This is the way you return if you follow the hike in the direction described. (It makes no difference which direction you hike the loop.)

To continue to Upper Boulder Lake, follow the East Boulder Lake Trail south and climb the low dike to the terrace in the upper basin. Here you find three teardrop ponds with emerald shores, a few stunted shade trees, and a commanding view of Scott Valley and points north (but no campsites). Steep walls of red rock lend a fortresslike effect to the upper basin. Be sure to fill water bottles before leaving Upper Boulder, as tributaries along the next 3 miles aren't dependable.

Beyond the uppermost pond, the trail ascends steep switchbacks to reach the jagged crest of the Scott Mountains. Here you're treated to a bird's-eye view of the inner Trinity Alps, the granite peaks above Bear Lakes, and a view of Mount Shasta.

Once over the divide, descend a few hundred yards to a junction with the Pacific Crest Trail. A left turn (east) leads along the PCT to Scott Mountain Summit; going straight (south), you continue on the East Boulder Lake Trail, also called the Marshy Lakes Trail on this side of the divide. Marshy Lakes Trail descends 1.5 miles to Big and Little Marshy Lakes. Big and Little Marshy Lakes are a pretty pair of lakes you can see in the drainage below. The trail down is a straightforward descent, steep at first and then turning into an idyllic stroll through meadows and along a stream.

To continue the loop, turn right (west) onto the PCT and follow it 2.5 miles along the crest to the Middle Boulder Lake Trail. With constant views and nearly level walking for most of the way, this section of the PCT offers great rewards for the effort.

At the signed Middle Boulder Lake Trail junction, turn right (north) and descend on steep switchbacks into the basin below. Like the East Boulder basin, Middle Boulder also has two ponds nestled onto a green terrace, high above the larger lake below. Tent sites are at both ends of the upper lake; choose the north one if you crave seclusion. What's the best thing about Middle Boulder? Local hiker and angler Leon Nelson says, "It arguably has more trout in it than any other lake in the Alps." (**Warning:** It also vies for most mosquitoes at certain times of summer.)

After passing the ponds, but before descending all the way to Middle Boulder Lake, look for the Boulder Tie Trail veering off to the right (north). The little-used, unsigned path may be hard to see; it's a faint line that traverses the hillside on a nearly level contour. The trail becomes more distinct as you proceed north, bending around the shoulder of the ridge and heading back toward East Boulder Lake. The trail starts on an open, exposed slope of short grasses and brush but soon becomes more forested as you make your way around the ridge. Arrive back at the western edge of East Boulder Lake. Return to the trailhead the way you came.

MILEAGE AND DIRECTIONS

0.0   Start at the East Boulder Lake Trailhead.

2.0   Reach East Boulder Lake.

2.1   Pass the Mill Creek Lake spur trail.

2.2   Pass the Boulder Tie Trail.

2.6   Arrive at Upper Boulder Lake; continue climbing to the divide.

3.1   Reach the Pacific Crest Trail; turn right.

5.6   Turn right onto the Middle Boulder Trail.

6.3   Reach the Boulder Tie Trail; go right.

8.0   Arrive back at East Boulder Lake; turn left and retrace your steps to the trailhead.

10.0 Arrive back at the trailhead.

OPTIONS

Extend your hike west along the Pacific Crest Trail for up to 12 more miles. You can also climb to the summit of 7,790-foot Eagle Peak on an off-trail walk-up located west of the PCT–Middle Boulder Lake Trail junction. For an easier side trip, take the Mill Creek Lake spur trail (at the north end of East Boulder Lake) and explore the secluded basin east of East Boulder Lake.

45 MIDDLE BOULDER AND TELEPHONE LAKES LOOP

This short loop tours forests and open ridges, with plenty of private lakeside camping and great views.

(See map on page 209.)
Start: Middle Boulder Lake Trailhead
Type of hike: Day hike or backpack; lollipop
Distance: 9.2 miles
Hiking time: About 1–3 days
Difficulty: Moderate
Elevation gain: 2,400 feet
Best season: Midsummer through early fall
Canine compatibility: Yes
Nearest town: Callahan
Fees and permits: Free wilderness permit required for overnight visitors; free campfire permits required for fires and camp stoves

Schedule: Trails in the Trinity Alps are always open; however, most trailhead access roads are closed or impassable during winter.
Maps: USGS Billys Peak; USDAFS Trinity Alps Wilderness
Trail contact: Weaverville Ranger Station: (530) 623-2121; www.fs.usda .gov/stnf
Parking and trailhead facilities: Horse corral and room for a few cars, but no other facilities. Scott Mountain and Trail Creek Campgrounds are nearby.

FINDING THE TRAILHEAD

From Callahan (on CA 3, approximately 65 miles north of Weaverville), drive west on South Fork Road to the junction with FR 40N17 and FR 40N16. (You can also take South Fork Road from FH 93 to reach the same junction.) Go straight at the signed junction and follow unpaved FR 40N17 past McKeen Divide. Continue 5.5 miles to the signed trailhead at a turnout next to West Boulder Creek (6 miles from Callahan). GPS: N41 14.805' / W122 48.974'

THE HIKE

If you're determined to see all of the Boulder Lakes in the Trinity Alps (one map lists seven), you'll pass this way eventually. Your time won't be wasted. Like most of the trails on the north side of the Scott Mountains, this route serves up a gentle hike along meadow-lined creeks, past forest-fringed lakes, and along the Pacific Crest Trail. The only drawback is sharing the lovely scenery with cows—or at least the results of cows passing through.

The trail starts with a moderate ascent as it climbs south along the course of West Boulder Creek. Climb on switchbacks through the shade of mixed fir and pine forest; then level out and contour gently uphill, parallel to and above the creek. Small tributaries cross the trail frequently, but they may dry up in late season (the main creek is never far away). Be sure to treat water from all sources.

After skirting the edge of a meadow, enter a stand of mature incense cedars and start climbing farther above the creek. At 1.6 miles from the trailhead, arrive at a junction. Middle Boulder Lake Trail is to the left (southeast); West Boulder Lake, Telephone Lake, and Eagle Creek Trail are all to the right (southwest). The loop is described here in a

Middle Boulder Lake's meadow-and-forest basin is quiet compared to Trinity's more dramatic granite cirques.

clockwise direction (returning via Telephone Lake), though you could just as easily do it the other way.

The 1.5 miles from the junction to Middle Boulder Lake is a pleasant stroll along the forested canyon bottom, following Middle Boulder's outlet stream as the drainage rises gently toward the forested upper basin. Pass in and out of streamside meadows along the way (plenty of camping opportunities in the forest fringes), and cross an open, grassy glade just before arriving at Middle Boulder's northeast corner. The shallow lake is backed by a rocky headwall to the south, where the terrain suddenly steepens to reach the crest of the Scott Mountains, and by red fir and pines on the north. To the east an open, verdant basin slopes upward to the divide between Middle Boulder and East Boulder Lakes. Two more little pools are perched on a bench 800 feet higher, just below the crest.

The trail (marked by cairns where the meadow engulfs it) leads southeast toward the obvious gap on the ridgeline. Halfway up is the not-so-obvious junction with the spur trail over to East Boulder Lake. If you have extra time, you can use this route to make a loop through the East Boulder drainage by combining the spur trail, the East Boulder Lake Trail, and the PCT.

To continue on the Middle Boulder–Telephone Loop, climb steeply to the junction with the PCT atop the divide, 4.3 miles from the trailhead. The views get better and better with every step as you climb out of the basin and onto the open ridgeline. Once you gain the divide, you can see the heart of the Trinity Alps to the southwest and, back the way you came, the sprawling Scott Valley. The PCT also has the best view of Mount Shasta you'll ever see without climbing a peak.

Turn right (west) on the PCT and hike 0.6 mile through forest cover to the junction with the Telephone Lake Trail on the edge of a small meadow. The junction is at the base of Eagle Peak, a 7,790-foot summit that makes for a nice off-trail ascent. To reach Telephone Lake, turn right (north) and climb 0.3 mile to recross the divide. Then it's all downhill as the trail switchbacks north, crosses a hanging meadow, and then plunges down to the edge of little Telephone Lake. The lake's rocky shore is fringed by dense stands of red fir, hemlock, and pine, and a small granite peak hangs above the southern edge. There's no permanent inlet or outlet, so the water level in the lake fluctuates dramatically each summer. There's also no camping of consequence.

West Boulder Lake (the last of the Boulders) is just under 2 miles due west of Telephone Lake. No trail leads to it, but enough people have made the cross-country trek that a line of cairns (sometimes) helps point the way. (**Note:** If West Boulder is your goal, the route from Mavis Lake via the PCT is better. West Boulder's claim to fame is its white-sand beach, huge rainbow trout, seclusion, and two widely separated campsites, one on each end of the lake.)

Finish the loop by following the trail north from Telephone Lake. The path descends gradually through forest cover, with good views across the alder-thick meadows of West Boulder Creek. Arrive at the junction with the Middle Boulder Trail 1.8 miles from Telephone Lake. Just before the signed junction, you might see a faint trail leading east. It's an unmaintained cutoff that leads over to the Middle Boulder Trail; don't take it unless you plan to do the loop again. From the junction, retrace your footsteps to the trailhead.

MILEAGE AND DIRECTIONS

0.0   Start at the Middle Boulder Lake Trailhead.

1.6   Arrive at the Middle Boulder Lake and Telephone Lake Trail junction; bear left and stay on the Middle Boulder Lake Trail.

3.5   Arrive at Middle Boulder Lake.

3.8   Pass the Boulder Tie Trail; continue climbing.

4.3   Reach the Pacific Crest Trail; turn right.

4.9   Turn right on the Telephone Lake Trail.

5.8   Reach Telephone Lake.

7.6   Turn left at the Middle Boulder Lake and Telephone Lake Trail junction and retrace your steps to the trailhead.

9.2   Arrive back at the trailhead.

OPTIONS

Eagle Peak, located near the Telephone Lake–PCT junction, makes for a great summit detour without straying far. You can also make a nice little loop connecting the Wolford Cabin Trail and PCT for a day hike that takes in great scenery and a historic cabin.

46 FOX CREEK AND MAVIS LAKES

Explore four small lakes in this quiet corner of the Trinity Alps. The forested basin isn't as dramatic as Trinity's granite heart, but the solitude can't be beat. **Note:** The 2020 Fox Fire burned more than 2,000 acres adjacent to the north side of Fox Creek Lake.

Start: Fox Creek Ridge Trailhead
Type of hike: Day hike or backpack; out-and-back
Distance: 8.0 miles
Hiking time: About 1–3 days
Difficulty: Easy
Elevation gain: 1,200 feet
Best season: Midsummer through early fall
Canine compatibility: Yes
Nearest town: Callahan
Fees and permits: Free wilderness permit required for overnight visitors; free campfire permits required for fires and camp stoves

Schedule: Trails in the Trinity Alps are always open; however, most trailhead access roads are closed or impassable during winter.
Maps: USGS Billys Peak; USDAFS Trinity Alps Wilderness
Trail contact: Weaverville Ranger Station: (530) 623-2121; www.fs.usda.gov/stnf
Parking and trailhead facilities: Ample parking in a wide turnout where the road rounds the point of a ridge; no camping or water. The nearest forest service campgrounds are Scott Mountain and Trail Creek (on CA 3 and FH 93, respectively).

FINDING THE TRAILHEAD

From Callahan (on CA 3, approximately 65 miles north of Weaverville), take South Fork Road on the south side of town. Head west through a small residential neighborhood as the road becomes FR 40N17. Follow this unpaved road past McKeen Divide and continue 7.5 miles to the signed Fox Creek Ridge Trailhead. You pass turns for Mill Creek Lake (FR 40N16) and East Boulder Lake (FR 39N63) on the way. GPS: N41 14.953' / W122 50.056'

THE HIKE

The Fox Creek Ridge Trail is the shortest and easiest way to reach Mavis and Fox Creek Lakes, two small lakes in a forested basin on the north side of the Scott Mountain divide (the basin can also be accessed via the Pacific Crest Trail). Each lake has a companion pond, reachable by relatively easy off-trail routes that add to the exploring opportunities. (**Note:** Check current conditions before heading out; a 2020 wildfire burned on the north side of Fox Creek Lake.)

Unlike the other trails on this side of the Scott Mountain divide, which tend to follow canyon bottoms, the Fox Creek Ridge Trail does just what the name implies—follows the spine of a ridge. Because of this, the forested route has far less cow sign than most other hikes on this side of the divide.

The trail starts across the road from the parking area. The path heads south, beginning with a steep, exposed ascent on a rocky backbone of manzanita-covered ridge. Fortunately this attention–grabbing climb is extremely short. You soon reach a shady, mixed-conifer forest, where you continue climbing more gradually along the ridgeline. Look for mature incense cedars and an impressive stand of white firs.

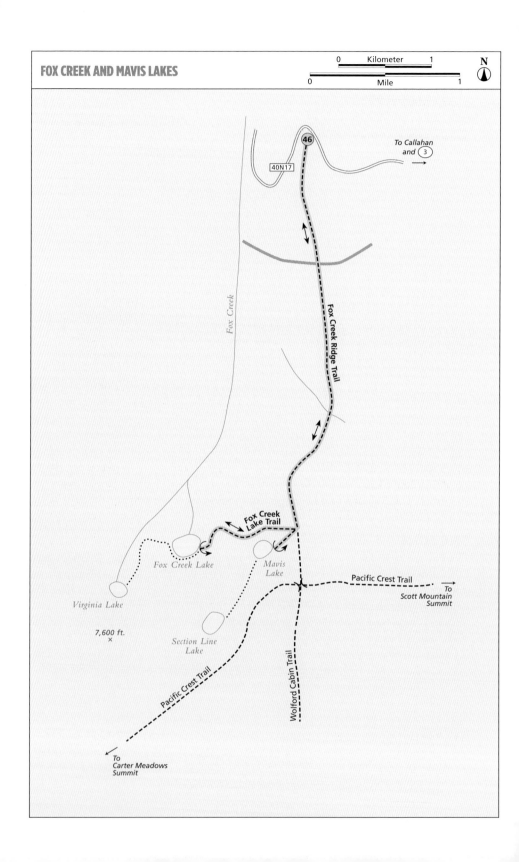

A mile from the trailhead, cross a forested flat where late starters could make a camp (there's water in a nearby creek). Pass another small tributary 1 mile later, after an alder-lined meadow, and then continue the pleasant forest walk to an unmarked trail junction 3 miles from the trailhead. The left fork climbs up to the Pacific Crest Trail, atop the divide; the right fork is the Fox Creek Lake Trail to Mavis and Fox Creek Lakes.

Turn right (west) and follow the level, rocky tread as it bends around into the basin. Another unmarked junction appears after 200 yards (a sign may be on the ground). In any case, Mavis Lake is to the left (south) and Fox Creek Lake is to the right (west).

The path to Mavis climbs over a granite moraine and arrives at the edge of the 3.5-acre lake after skirting a little pond on Mavis's northeast side. Mavis is small and shallow, but it's set in a pretty little bowl surrounded by a dense forest of red fir and hemlock. Horsepackers choose to camp on the east side of the lake at the outlet. The best site for backpackers is across the lake on the west side. Anglers will find good fishing here as well.

Section Line Lake is 1 mile to the south (and slightly west). No trail leads to Section Line, but you should have no problem following cairns to the lake. (**Note:** There's no good fishing or camping.) You can also reach West Boulder from here by continuing up to the PCT, heading east for a short distance, and then leaving the trail at a sharp right-turn and dropping down to West Boulder.

To reach Fox Creek Lake, continue west from the junction and follow the rocky trail as it winds around a spur ridge and drops down into the Fox Creek basin. Arrive at the lake 1 mile from the last junction, 4 miles from the trailhead.

At 9 acres, Fox Creek Lake is by far the largest in this four-lake basin. It boasts grassy fringes, lily pad–lined shores, and spacious campsites. The rocky west shore is best for trout fishing (no lily pads), and the forested edges on the north and east have numerous campsites.

Though no maintained trail leads from here to Virginia Lake, an obvious use trail (look for cairns) has been established. Pick it up at the northwest corner of the lake and follow it over a rocky ridge to the southwest. On the other side of the dike is the outlet creek flowing from Virginia Lake. Stay on the east side of the creek and follow it 0.75 mile to the lake.

Virginia Lake's clear water is cupped in a rocky cirque just beneath the crest of the Scott Mountains. The inviting spot is punctuated by an idyllic meadow near the outlet, one spartan campsite—and almost guaranteed solitude.

MILEAGE AND DIRECTIONS

0.0   Start at the Fox Creek Ridge Trailhead.

3.0   Stay right at the spur trail to Pacific Crest Trail.

3.2   Reach Mavis Lake. Retrace your steps to the Fox Creek Ridge Trail.

4.0   Reach Fox Creek Lake. Return the way you came.

8.0   Arrive back at the trailhead.

OPTIONS

The Pacific Crest Trail is right next door (less than 1 mile from the junction before Mavis Lake). You can follow it to a number of other lakes along the Scott Mountain divide. At the PCT junction another trail leads down to Wolford Cabin and destinations on the south side of the divide.

47 PACIFIC CREST TRAIL

The Pacific Crest Trail (PCT) hugs the spine of the Scott Mountain divide, serving up endless views and access to a string of lakes. This is a great route for hikers who want to poke into several of the rarely visited drainages below the divide.

Start: Carter Meadows Summit
Type of hike: Backpack; out-and back or shuttle
Distance: 24.0 miles out and back at recommended turnaround; 18.9 miles for shuttle
Hiking time: About 3–6 days
Difficulty: Moderate
Elevation gain: 1,600 feet
Best season: Midsummer through early fall
Canine compatibility: Yes
Nearest town: Callahan
Fees and permits: Free wilderness permit required for overnight visitors; free campfire permits required for fires and camp stoves
Schedule: Trails in the Trinity Alps are always open; however, most trailhead access roads are closed or impassable during winter.
Maps: USGS Deadman Peak, Billys Peak, Tangle Blue Lake, and Scott Mountains; USDAFS Trinity Alps Wilderness
Trail contact: Weaverville Ranger Station: (530) 623-2121; www.fs.usda .gov/stnf
Parking and trailhead facilities: Ample parking at both trailheads. No water or other facilities are available at Carter Meadows Summit. Hidden Horse Campground (a forest service site with toilets and water) is located 1 mile away in Carter Meadows. A forest service campground is located next to the Scott Mountain Trailhead (no water).

FINDING THE TRAILHEAD

From the junction of CA 3 and FH 93, just north of Callahan, go west on FH 93 toward Cecilville. Proceed 12 miles to the signed Carter Meadows Summit–PCT Trailhead on the left (south) side of the highway (GPS: N41 13.203' / W122 53.949'). If you pass the entrance to Carter Meadows, you've gone too far. For car shuttles, the other trailhead is at Scott Mountain Summit, 55 miles north of Weaverville on CA 3. The signed PCT Trailhead is on the west side of the highway. To get a head start, you can drive to the edge of the wilderness area boundary by taking the dirt road that leads right (northwest) from the Scott Mountain Trailhead. Follow the road 2.5 miles to a locked gate, and park. This is Marshy Lakes Road (described at the end of this chapter). This road provides access to a youth camp and private property at the Marshy Lakes. Take care to avoid blocking the road or gate.

THE HIKE

The Pacific Crest Trail runs for more than 2,600 miles from Mexico to the Canadian border. Only 18.9 of those miles cross the Trinity Alps Wilderness, but what a stretch it is. The PCT slices across the wilderness along the spine of the Scott Mountains, passing within a stone's throw of more than a dozen lakes, serving up one stunning view after another, and traversing some of the least-crowded areas of the Alps. Most Trinity Alps hikers stick to the better-known routes in the inner Alps, or the lakes north of the PCT, which leaves an uncrowded trail for those willing to seek it out.

The PCT lies between the Scott Mountain summit on the east end and Carter Meadows Summit on the west. It makes for an easy through-hike if you can arrange a car

The Pacific Crest Trail cuts across the Trinity Alps Wilderness on its way from Mexico to Canada.

shuttle or an excellent out-and-back trip, with numerous opportunities for side trips along the way. And since it's built to PCT specifications (no more than a 5 percent grade), the trail delivers incredible scenery without exacting an exorbitant price in sweat and sore legs.

This description starts from Carter Meadows Summit. It's a longer drive, but I like going this direction because you hike toward Mount Shasta on the way out. And if you're hiking out and back (instead of arranging a car shuttle), walking this direction allows you the option of shortening the route by several miles without missing anything noteworthy.

At the Carter Meadows Summit Trailhead, there's a three-way junction. To the right (west) a spur trail descends 0.2 mile to Carter Meadows proper (more parking and a toilet); the path in the middle heads uphill (south) to Hidden Lake. To the left (southeast) the PCT immediately crosses the wilderness boundary and starts a moderate descent on a shady, well-maintained path.

Follow the PCT downhill through mixed conifers, with good views across the South Fork Lakes basin. The trail crosses several small creeks on the gentle descent and passes a number of fern and alder thickets. After 1.4 miles arrive at the junction with the South Fork Lakes Trail. The trail to the left (north) drops to the South Fork Trailhead, while the path to the right (south) climbs very steeply to South Fork Lakes in less than 1 mile.

The PCT continues straight (east), climbing moderately out of the drainage and around a spur ridge. Look for good views across the basin and along the divide above you. An impressive, unnamed peak hangs over the head of the drainage behind you, on the crest of the Scott Mountains. In the next drainage, 2.8 miles from the trailhead, climb gently south to the junction with the Noland Gulch Trail (it drops down to a little-used trailhead). The PCT continues climbing toward the crest on a wide track. The first pass is a false summit, with the real thing a few hundred yards farther along. From the pass, get an unobstructed view of the granite heart of the Trinity Alps, directly to the southwest.

From the top of the divide, the PCT heads east along the ridgeline, while the East Fork Saloon Creek Trail plunges south to connect with Saloon Creek and eventually the North Fork Coffee Creek Trail. From here you can take advantage of a seldom-used loop connecting Saloon Creek with South Fork Lakes and then returning to the trailhead via the PCT. An unmaintained and unnamed trace of a trail heads west along the ridge and soon peters out.

To continue on the PCT, head east and follow the easy grade through shady fir forests, fern-covered hillsides, and countless vistas of Sawtooth Mountain and other peaks. Take advantage of water crossings to refill your bottles, as creeks are less frequent along the next few miles of the PCT. From the Saloon Creek junction to the Fox Creek–Wolford Cabin junction, you traverse 3 miles of PCT bliss, with great views on both sides of the divide. Just before the Fox Creek–Wolford Cabin junction, a cairn marks a little-used cross-country route to Section Line Lake, which is immediately below the divide to the north. At the Fox Creek–Wolford Cabin junction, 6.1 miles from the trailhead, you can make excursions on both sides of the divide. To the north lie Mavis and Fox Creek Lakes; to the south are historic Wolford Cabin and connections to a network of trails on the north side of Coffee Creek.

The PCT continues east, contouring around the south side of the crest. Less than 1 mile from the Fox Creek junction, the trail skirts the top of a drainage that drops steeply away on the north side of the divide. No trail leads down the hill, but West Boulder Lake is tucked away in the canyon below. West Boulder visitors reach the lake via cross-country routes from either the PCT, just before the junction with the Fox Creek Ridge Trail (the better option), or Telephone Lake.

A moderate ascent leads around the prow of a ridge, alternating between stunted tree cover and wide-open views of the wild terrain spread out below, and soon you arrive at the next trail junction, just over 2 miles from the last one. A sign points the way right (south) to the Bloody Run and Eagle Creek Trails. Just downhill from the PCT is a three-way junction with routes leading south, east, and west. The PCT continues its level contour to the left (northeast), bending around the base of Eagle Peak.

Shortly after the Bloody Run–Eagle Creek junction, pass an old miner's camp decorated with an antique wheelbarrow; a nearby spring flows through a metal pipe (purify all water to be safe). Another 0.5 mile of parklike walking brings you to the junction with the Telephone Lake Trail. Telephone Lake, on the north side of the divide, lies less than 1 mile away to the left (northwest). An easy ramble along the crest quickly brings you to the junction with the Middle Boulder Lake Trail, 0.5 mile farther along. From this ridgetop junction you can see Middle Boulder Lake and two companion ponds nestled in the basin below.

The next 2.5 miles are one of the prettiest sections of trail in the whole Trinity Alps Wilderness. The rocky tread winds around the south side of a spur ridge, commanding one endless view after another, with pyramid-shaped Mount Shasta dominating the skyline ahead. Wildflower gardens grow in grassy pockets below the trail where water seeps through the rocks, nourishing little explosions of colorful blooms.

PACIFIC CREST TRAIL

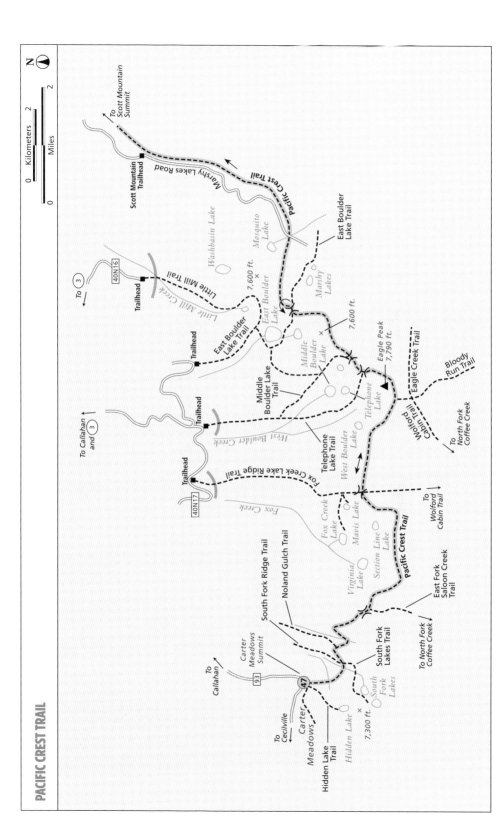

At the East Boulder Lake junction, 12 miles from the trailhead, you again have the option of exploring drainages on both sides of the divide. East Boulder is in an open, grassy basin on the north side of the crest, with several companion ponds that make for an idyllic setting. Below you to the south lies little Marshy Lakes basin, with lush meadows, two small lakes (with marshy shorelines), and great views of nearby granite crags. Both destinations are just 1 mile away from the PCT.

If you haven't dropped off a car or arranged a ride at the Scott Mountain end of the trail, 6.9 miles farther east, you may want to consider turning around here. The rest of the route is less spectacular than the section you've just hiked, and there are fewer opportunities for camping and exploring. The trail parallels a dirt road part of the way and passes an area used as a children's summer camp.

To continue to Scott Mountain, follow the PCT east on a gentle contour around the head of the basin; then descend through mixed forest to a crossing of Marshy Lakes Road (just after crossing the outlet from Mosquito Lake). This dirt road, closed to the public, is used by the camp and other owners of private inholdings. A spur road, located a few hundred yards east of the PCT crossing, leads uphill to the camp and Mosquito Lake.

From the Marshy Lakes Road crossing, you have two options. The PCT continues east, parallel to and slightly below the road for nearly 2 miles. At that point the road and trail almost touch again at a pass atop the divide; then the trail veers away into the forest and traverses the last 3.5 miles to the Scott Mountain Summit Trailhead. Alternatively, the road leads an easy 1.5 miles to a locked gate, where you can leave a car shuttle. The road and trail are both good options from here.

MILEAGE AND DIRECTIONS

0.0 Start at the Carter Meadows Summit Trailhead.

1.4 Reach the South Fork Lakes Trail junction.

2.8 Reach the Noland Gulch Trail junction.

3.1 Reach the Scott Mountain crest–East Fork Saloon Creek Trail junction.

6.1 Reach the Mavis Lake–Wolford Cabin Trail junction.

8.3 Reach the Eagle Creek–Bloody Run Trail junction.

9.0 Reach the Telephone Lake Trail junction.

9.5 Reach Middle Boulder Lake Trail junction.

12.0 Reach East Boulder–Marshy Lakes Trail junction. (This is your turnaround point for the out-and-back hike.)

13.8 Cross Marshy Lakes Road.

15.7 Reach the Scott Mountain crest.

18.9 Arrive at the Scott Mountain Summit Trailhead.

OPTIONS

The PCT passes many trail junctions with options for short and long itineraries. Get out the map and use your imagination. The best peak ascent en route is Eagle Peak (7,790 feet). For a good historic side trip, take the Wolford Cabin Trail and visit several old cabin sites in the North Fork Coffee Creek drainage.

48 SOUTH FORK LAKES

This short but steep hike leads to a secluded cirque with two lakes and plenty of off-trail opportunities. Choose this when you want an easy-access base camp with lots of exploring potential in a private corner of the wilderness.

Start: Carter Meadows Summit–PCT Trailhead
Type of hike: Day hike or overnight; out-and-back
Distance: 5.0 miles (optional 10.0-mile side trip)
Hiking time: About 1–3 days
Difficulty: Moderate
Elevation gain: 900 feet
Best season: Midsummer through early fall
Canine compatibility: Yes
Nearest town: Callahan
Fees and permits: Free wilderness permit required for overnight visitors; free campfire permits required for fires and camp stoves
Schedule: Trails in the Trinity Alps are always open; however, most trailhead access roads are closed or impassable during winter.
Maps: USGS Deadman Peak; USDAFS Trinity Alps Wilderness
Trail contact: Weaverville Ranger Station: (530) 623-2121; www.fs.usda .gov/stnf
Parking and trailhead facilities: Ample parking, though you may have to resort to Carter Meadows on particularly crowded weekends (a short spur trail links the two parking areas). No water or other facilities at Carter Meadows Summit—except for a paved helipad! Hidden Horse Campground, a forest service site with toilets and water, is located 1 mile away in Carter Meadows.

FINDING THE TRAILHEAD

From the junction of CA 3 and FH 93 just north of Callahan, go west on FH 93 toward Cecilville. Proceed 12 miles to the signed Carter Meadows Summit–PCT Trailhead on the left (south) side of the highway. If you pass the entrance to Carter Meadows, you've gone too far. GPS: N41 13.203' / W122 53.949'

THE HIKE

Despite the short distance to South Fork Lakes, an extremely steep section of trail makes it feel as though you're really going somewhere. And thanks to the beauty of the large, rugged basin, you really are. The cirque serves up an equal mix of shady woods; grass-fringed shoreline; and rocky cliffs. Good views of the South Fork Scott River drainage can be seen from the east side of the lower lake.

At the Carter Meadows Summit Trailhead, there's a three-way junction. To the right (west) a spur trail descends 0.2 mile to Carter Meadows proper (more parking and a toilet); the path in the middle heads uphill (south) to Hidden Lake. To the left (southeast) the Pacific Crest Trail immediately crosses the wilderness boundary and starts a moderate descent on a shady, well-maintained path.

Follow the PCT downhill through mixed conifers, with good views across the South Fork Lakes basin between the branches. The trail crosses several small creeks on the gentle descent and passes a number of fern and alder thickets. The path fords South Fork Scott River in the lush canyon bottom where alders, ferns, and willows create a mini-garden with a tropical feel.

SOUTH FORK LAKES; HIDDEN LAKE

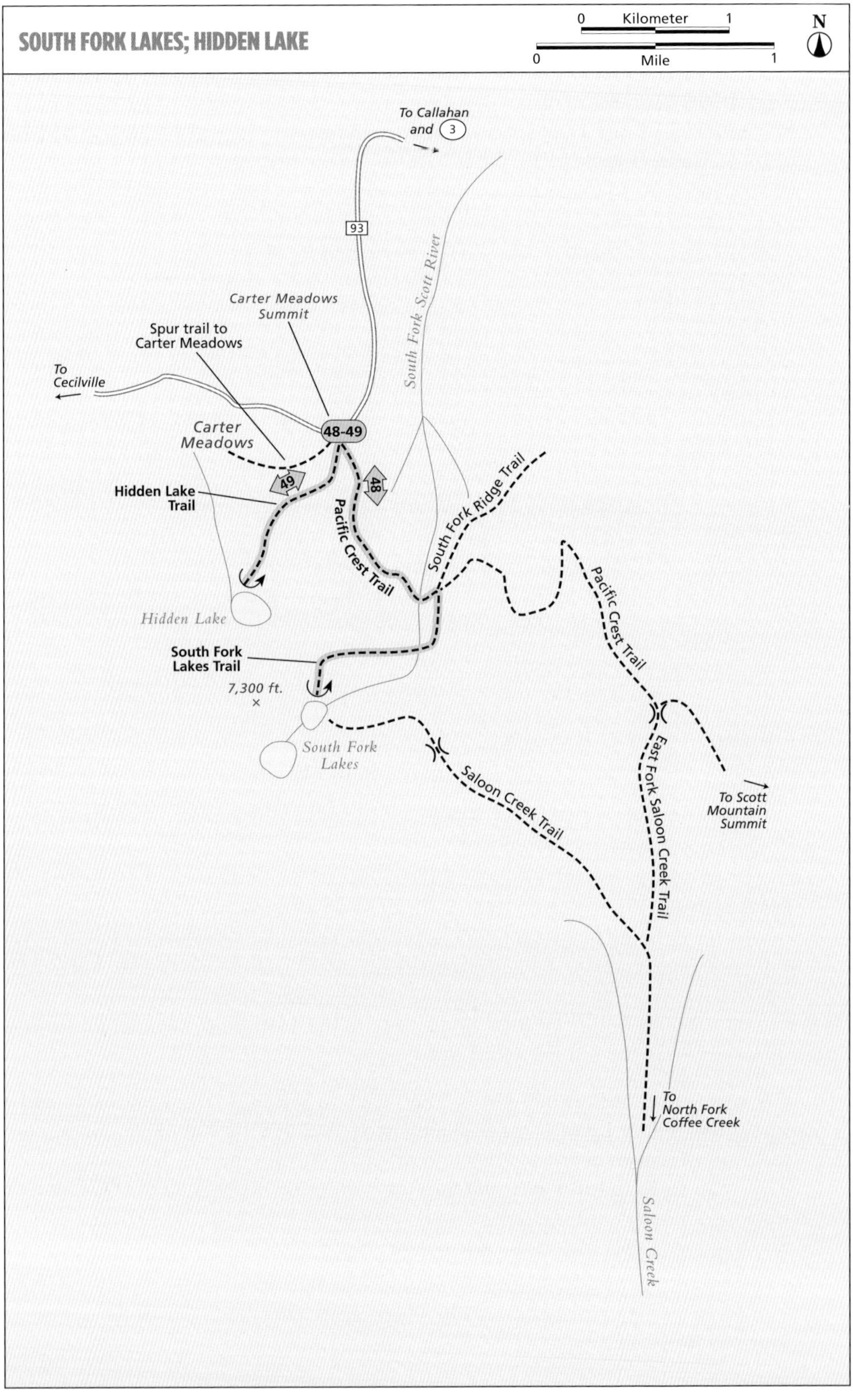

0 Kilometer 1
0 Mile 1
N
To Callahan and 3
93
South Fork Scott River
Carter Meadows Summit
Spur trail to Carter Meadows
To Cecilville
Carter Meadows
48-49
49
48
Hidden Lake Trail
Pacific Crest Trail
South Fork Ridge Trail
Hidden Lake
South Fork Lakes Trail
7,300 ft.
South Fork Lakes
Saloon Creek Trail
Pacific Crest Trail
East Fork Saloon Creek Trail
To Scott Mountain Summit
To North Fork Coffee Creek
Saloon Creek

After crossing the South Fork, ascend to the junction with the South Fork Lakes Trail, 1.4 miles from the trailhead. The junction has not been signed in recent years, but the well-used trail should be obvious. Turn right (south) to reach South Fork Lakes. A left (north) turn leads downhill to the South Fork Trailhead (Carter Meadows Summit is a better starting point). The PCT continues straight (east).

Soon after turning onto the South Fork Lakes Trail, you learn why the forest service warns equestrians to use extreme caution on this route: It's short but very steep. A moderate ascent leads to the bottom of a wide, grassy valley that holds the main stem of South Fork Lakes' outlet stream. A quick look around, however, reveals this is not the cirque that holds South Fork Lakes. The cirque you're after lies another 800 feet above you, atop that vertical headwall to the west. The trail winds through a stand of fir and then climbs the steep canyon wall in a series of switchbacks. The grueling ascent is balanced by good views and summer wildflowers fed by a number of little creeklets and seeps that make it seem as if the mountain itself is leaking.

Once you reach the top, it's a short walk across near-level terrain to the lower of the two South Fork Lakes. The upper lake is just 0.25 mile southwest of the lower lake. (A use trail leads along the west side of the lower lake and then follows the inlet stream to the upper one.) A thick forest of pine and fir separates the two bodies of water. The lakes are 4 and 6 acres, respectively, and have remarkably different settings. Horsepackers prefer the lower lake. Backpackers prefer the upper lake. Both have campsites.

The 7,794-foot peak to the south of Upper South Fork Lake is an easy off-trail summit with a great view. Return the way you came or see the optional side trip below.

MILES AND DIRECTIONS

- 0.0 Start at Carter Meadows Summit–PCT Trailhead.
- 1.4 Turn right at the South Fork Lakes trail junction.
- 2.5 Reach South Fork Lakes. Return the way you came.
- 5.0 Arrive back at the trailhead.

OPTIONS

Buck Lake: This little pond is but a speck on the map, but it's a worthwhile detour for hikers who crave solitude. To get there, simply head south 1 mile from South Fork Lakes, over the ridge and down to Buck Lake. You'll find a single small campsite here, as befits the solitary setting. In early season the outlet stream creates a waterfall.

Another option: You can make a longer loop (add 10 miles) by taking the Saloon Creek and East Fork Saloon Creek Trails back to the PCT. From the south side of Lower South Fork Lake, find the Saloon Creek Trail (9W01) and head southeast, over the Scott Mountain divide and down to the junction with the East Fork Saloon Creek Trail (9W03). Turn left (north) and follow it back to a junction with the PCT atop the divide. Turn left (northwest) and return to the trailhead. Longer options are possible on the PCT and North Fork Coffee Creek.

49 HIDDEN LAKE

Short on time or taking small kids? Or just want an easy hike so you can bring plenty of luxe camping gear? Target this little lake on the north side of the Scott Mountain divide. The quality of the scenery for the effort is astounding.

(See map on page 228.)
Start: Carter Meadows Summit–PCT Trailhead
Type of hike: Day hike or overnight; out-and-back
Distance: 2.0 miles
Hiking time: A few hours to 2 days
Difficulty: Easy
Elevation gain: 500 feet
Best season: Midsummer through early fall
Canine compatibility: Yes
Nearest town: Callahan
Fees and permits: Free wilderness permit required for overnight visitors; free campfire permits required for fires and camp stoves
Schedule: Trails in the Trinity Alps are always open; however, most trailhead access roads are closed or impassable during winter.
Maps: USGS Deadman Peak; USDAFS Trinity Alps Wilderness
Trail contact: Weaverville Ranger Station: (530) 623-2121; www.fs.usda.gov/stnf
Parking and trailhead facilities: Ample parking is available, though you may have to resort to Carter Meadows on particularly crowded weekends (a short spur trail links the two parking areas). No water or other facilities are available at Carter Meadows Summit. Hidden Horse Campground, a forest service site with toilets and water, is located 1 mile away in Carter Meadows.

FINDING THE TRAILHEAD

From the junction of CA 3 and FH 93 just north of Callahan, go west on FH 93 toward Cecilville. Proceed 12 miles to the signed Carter Meadows Summit–PCT Trailhead on the left (south) side of the highway. If you pass the entrance to Carter Meadows, you've gone too far. GPS: N41 13.203' / W122 53.949'

THE HIKE

With a name like Hidden Lake, you might expect this to be a difficult hike into a remote basin. Don't come here if that's what you're after. Hidden Lake is actually one of the most accessible, easy-to-reach bodies of water in the Trinity Alps. It's a pretty little 3-acre lake in a rugged cirque gouged into the north side of the Scott Mountains—a good destination for a short day hike (when a leisurely picnic is the priority), or an overnight trip for families with small children.

The Hidden Lake Trail starts at Carter Meadows Summit, heading south up a ridge that splits two other trails. To the left (southeast) the Pacific Crest Trail starts its 18.9-mile run through the Trinity Alps Wilderness; a spur trail to Carter Meadows veers right (southwest).

Ascend moderately up the rocky ridgeline through red fir and mountain hemlock. Soon emerge into open, brushy terrain with good views over the South Fork Scott River and the wild country along the divide. Once over the crest of the ridge, the trail again winds through forest cover and abruptly ends at the edge of Hidden Lake, 1 mile from the trailhead.

Low-lying clouds make the forest moody and intimate.

The clear water serves up good swimming, fishing, and simple afternoon daydreaming—not necessarily in that order. An impressive cliff rises from the lake's south side, and summer wildflowers sprinkle the nearby hills. There's plenty of shady elbow room to wile away an afternoon. Retrace your route to the trailhead.

MILEAGE AND DIRECTIONS

0.0 Start at the Carter Meadows Summit–PCT Trailhead.

1.0 Reach Hidden Lake. Return the way you came.

2.0 Arrive back at the trailhead.

50 TRAIL GULCH– LONG GULCH LOOP

Find great swimming, fishing, and ridgetop views at these easy-access lakes. Do the whole loop for the most satisfying route, or just go to one lake for a quick trip.

Start: Trail Gulch Lake Trailhead
Type of hike: Day hike or backpack; loop
Distance: 9.0 miles
Hiking time: About 1–3 days
Difficulty: Moderate
Elevation gain: 1,950 feet
Best season: Midsummer through early fall
Canine compatibility: Yes
Nearest town: Callahan
Fees and permits: Free wilderness permit required for overnight visitors; free campfire permits required for fires and camp stoves
Schedule: Trails in the Trinity Alps are always open; however, most trailhead access roads are closed or impassable during winter.
Maps: USGS Deadman Peak; USDAFS Trinity Alps Wilderness
Trail contact: Weaverville Ranger Station: (530) 623-2121; www.fs.usda.gov/stnf
Parking and trailhead facilities: Parking at both trailheads; no facilities. Hidden Horse Campground, a forest service site with toilets and water, is located 1 mile away in Carter Meadows; Trail Creek Campground is 5 miles west, where FR 39N08 rejoins FH 93.

FINDING THE TRAILHEAD

From the junction of CA 3 and FH 93 just north of Callahan, go west on FH 93 toward Cecilville. Proceed 12.5 miles to the signed Carter Meadows access road (FR 39N08), on the left (south) side of the highway. Proceed 2.5 miles to the signed trailhead for Trail Gulch Lake on the left (GPS: N41 12.999' / W122 55.677'). Long Gulch Trailhead is 0.8 mile farther (GPS: N41 12.968' / W122 55.255').

THE HIKE

This short loop makes a great day hike or an easy overnight. The two lakes en route, Trail Gulch and Long Gulch, are deep, blue, and tucked into nearly identical deep-set granite cirques. They aren't quite as spectacular as the Trinity Alps' more famous lakes, such as Caribou and Sapphire, but they're a lot easier to reach and get a mere fraction of the visitors.

There's some confusion over the names of these lakes. Decades ago, mapmakers reversed the names of Trail Gulch and Long Gulch Lakes, causing considerable consternation among old-timers who remembered the lakes' correct names. But once a mistake is committed to paper, it's difficult to change. The USDA Forest Service wilderness map shows the names correctly, and at last report, trail signs agreed with the map, which places Long Gulch to the west, Trail Gulch to the east. The confusion has not been totally laid to rest, however; the USGS quad still shows the lakes in reverse. Just to be clear, this text refers to the lakes as they appear on the Forest Service wilderness map.

To do the loop, park at the Trail Gulch Trailhead and start hiking south on the Trail Gulch Trail (9W15). Doing the loop in reverse is equally good.

Long Gulch Lake offers one of the best reward-to-effort ratios in the Trinity Alps.

The trail climbs steadily along the outlet creek. First on the west bank, then on the east, you follow the little stream through mixed fir and mountain hemlock, alder thickets, and meadow grass. This drainage and Long Gulch show the effects of cattle grazing. Be sure to purify all water and carry plenty to drink on the ridgetop trail between lakes; no water is available above the lakes.

After 2 easy miles with a couple of steep sections, arrive at the spur trail that leads to Trail Gulch Lake. Turn right (southwest) to reach the lake in just under 0.5 mile. The campsites are all snuggled close together on the northeast side of the lake. Horsepackers generally overnight at Long Gulch Lake.

To continue the loop, go straight and make a steep, switchbacking ascent to the ridgeline above. On top of the ridge, at nearly 7,000 feet, get a bird's-eye view of the lake and a sea of peaks in every direction. The Marble Mountains dominate the horizon to the north.

A three-way trail junction is just a few yards down the other side of the ridge. The North Fork Coffee Creek and Steveale Creek Trails head downhill to the south. Until the 1990s, you had to hike down to Steveale Creek and then all the way back up to do this loop. Now you can take a path that cuts across the top of the drainage. Turn right (west) on this signed trail and stroll through open forest to the saddle above Long Gulch Lake. There you find the old trail from Steveale Creek coming up from the southeast. (The new trail is shown on the forest service wilderness map but not the USGS quad.)

Look down on Long Gulch Lake on the way from Trail Gulch.

Find spacious camping at Long Gulch Lake.

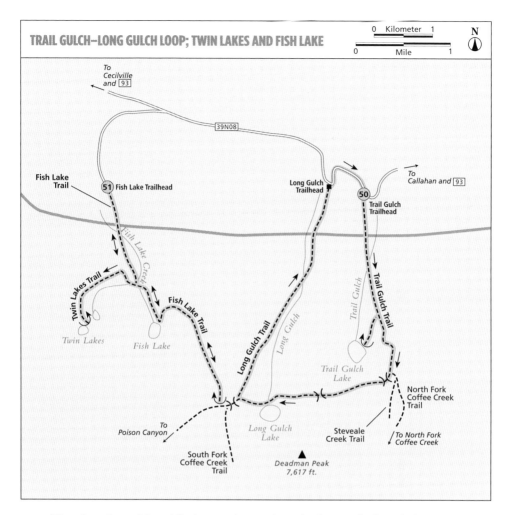

The view from this saddle is even better than the last, with the whole Long Gulch basin laid out beneath your feet. Deadman Peak towers to 7,617 feet directly south along the ridgeline. Next, head over the side and plunge downhill on a welcome set of switchbacks.

At the bottom the trail crosses the outlet creek near a large (treeless) campsite and then meanders along the forested north shore of Long Gulch Lake. On a hot day the island out in the middle of the blue water demands a visit. The lake is a favorite of horsepackers. They usually overnight on the northeast shore, leaving the best campsite on the lake for backpackers to find, out of sight from the main trail on the westernmost tip of the lake.

On the west side of the lake, follow the trail 0.3 mile west over level, rocky terrain to a junction with the Long Gulch Trail (9W14). A left turn (southwest) leads up to the ridgeline and a three-way trail junction, where the South Fork Coffee Creek Trail heads south.

The route back to the trailhead lies to the right (north), down the Long Gulch Trail. The next 3 miles are much like the approach up the Trail Gulch drainage—a gently descending path through forest and cow-trampled meadow and a crossing from the west to east bank of the stream before arriving at the trailhead. Trail Gulch Trailhead lies 0.8 mile to the east along FR 39N08.

MILEAGE AND DIRECTIONS

0.0   Start at the Trail Gulch Lake Trailhead.

2.0   Pass the Trail Gulch Trail junction.

2.5   Reach Trail Gulch Lake.

3.0   Stay right at the Steveale Creek–North Fork Coffee Creek junction.

4.6   Arrive at Long Gulch Lake.

4.8   Take the Long Gulch Trail.

8.2   Reach the Long Gulch Trailhead. Turn right onto FR 39N08.

9.0   Arrive back at the Trail Gulch Lake Trailhead.

OPTIONS

This hike can be extended on both the South Fork Coffee Creek and North Fork Coffee Creek Trails. Schlomberg Cabin, a historic site at the head of the North Fork Coffee Creek drainage, is an easy side trip.

51 TWIN LAKES AND FISH LAKE

Seen most of what the Trinity Alps have to offer? You should make a journey to this rarely visited corner of the wilderness. The short hike leads to a tranquil pond that stretches the definition of lake.

(See map on page 235.)
Start: Fish Lake Trailhead
Type of hike: Day hike or overnight; out-and-back
Distance: 3.8 miles
Hiking time: A few hours to 2 days
Difficulty: Easy
Elevation gain: 900 feet (Fish Lake); 1,300 feet (Twin Lakes)
Best season: Midsummer through early fall
Canine compatibility: Yes
Nearest town: Callahan
Fees and permits: Free wilderness permit required for overnight

visitors; free campfire permits required for fires and camp stoves
Schedule: Trails in the Trinity Alps are always open; however, most trailhead access roads are closed or impassable during winter.
Maps: USGS Deadman Peak; USDAFS Trinity Alps Wilderness
Trail contact: Weaverville Ranger Station: (530) 623-2121; www.fs.usda.gov/stnf
Parking and trailhead facilities: Ample parking; no water or other facilities. Trail Creek Campground, a forest service site with toilets and water, is the closest developed site.

FINDING THE TRAILHEAD

From the junction of CA 3 and FH 93 just north of Callahan, go west on FH 93 toward Cecilville. Proceed 17 miles to the signed turn for Trail Creek Campground–FR 39N08. Turn left (south) and proceed 1 mile on FR 39N08 to the signed turn (right) for Fish Lake Trailhead. Continue 2 miles on this dirt road to the trailhead. GPS: N41 12.949' / W122 58.414'

THE HIKE

Twin Lakes and Fish Lake are shallow little ponds that sit in an isolated drainage northwest of Deadman Peak. Neither big nor deep nor very well known, the lakes don't attract much attention, which makes them eminently suitable for a quiet overnight if you're looking to avoid the more popular destinations nearby. Like the other drainages on the north side of the Scott Mountain divide, however, this one is subject to cattle grazing.

Fish Lake is still a nice place to visit in the early season. (Cows usually don't arrive until after the Fourth of July.) The 3-acre pond is in a gentle setting of meadows and shady forest glades, the whole tucked into a glacial basin under the 7,500-foot crest of the Scott Mountains. The lake's name is no lie: Fishing for brook trout is usually good.

The trail climbs south from the parking area, paralleling Fish Lake Creek on a 1.9-mile, 900-foot climb to the lake. The route virtually follows the course of the creek the entire way, crossing the stream twice en route. Ascend through forest, eventually crossing a number of grassy benches before reaching the lake. The open grassland offers good views across the headwaters of the South Fork Salmon River.

Just over midway, at 1.2 miles, arrive at a junction with the Twin Lakes Trail. A right (west) turn here leads 0.7 mile to Twin Lakes—a pair of small ponds. To reach Fish Lake, continue south at the junction and climb moderately to the sheltered basin. Return the way you came.

MILEAGE AND DIRECTIONS

0.0 Start at the Fish Lake Trailhead.

1.2 Stay right (west) at the Twin Lakes–Fish Lake Trail junction. (**Option:** Turn left to visit Fish Lake.)

1.9 Reach Twin Lakes. (**Option:** Reach Fish Lake if you turned left at the junction.) Return the way you came.

3.8 Arrive back at the trailhead.

OPTIONS

The Fish Lake Trail continues southeast from the lake, ascending to a three-way trail junction atop the divide below Deadman Peak. The Long Gulch Trail descends to Long Gulch Lake and offers a possible loop if you return to the trailhead on FR 39N08. The South Fork Coffee Creek Trail continues south to Coffee Creek Road. The Poison Trail (more commonly known as the Taylor Creek Trail) heads west along the crest and then down to Taylor Creek and the little-used Poison Trailhead—not to be confused with Poison Canyon along North Fork Swift Creek.

52 CHINA SPRING TRAIL TO GRIZZLY LAKE

This is the quickest route to Grizzly Lake—hence the quickest way to heaven. Grizzly's amazing setting—with a gorgeous waterfall back-dropped by granite cirque—will wow any hiker. Expect company during the summer.

Start: China Spring Trailhead
Type of hike: Backpack; out-and-back
Distance: 13.4 miles
Hiking time: About 2–5 days
Difficulty: Strenuous
Elevation gain: 5,400 feet
Best season: Midsummer through early fall
Canine compatibility: Yes, except for last steep scramble to Grizzly Lake
Nearest town: Callahan
Fees and permits: Free wilderness permit required for overnight visitors; free campfire permits required for fires and camp stoves
Schedule: Trails in the Trinity Alps are always open; however, most trailhead access roads are closed or impassable during winter.
Maps: USGS Thompson Peak; USDAFS Trinity Alps Wilderness
Trail contact: Weaverville Ranger Station: (530) 623-2121; www.fs.usda.gov/stnf
Parking and trailhead facilities: Roadside parking but no facilities or water. The closest camping is at East Fork Campground.

FINDING THE TRAILHEAD

From Cecilville (30 miles west of Callahan on FH 93), drive 3 miles east on FH 93 to the signed turn for East Fork Campground–Petersburg Ranger Station (CR 003). Turn right (south) and drive 5 miles, past the ranger station, to a signed fork just after the road becomes unpaved (and just after crossing a bridge over the South Fork Salmon River). Take the right fork, signed China Spring Trailhead, and follow FR 37N07 the rest of the way to the trailhead. FR 37N07 winds uphill for just under 6 miles to the signed trailhead on the right. GPS: N41 4.458' / W123 5.124'

THE HIKE

If Grizzly Lake is your idea of heaven, then the China Spring Trail is where you want to be on Judgment Day. This steep 6.7-mile hike will get you there much faster than any other route. Grizzly Lake, perched on a castle-like granite shelf at 7,100 feet, crowned by Thompson Peak and a glacieret, guarded by a cliff-like approach and a waterfall pouring off its ramparts, and buffered by a sublime meadow at its base, is heaven on earth for anyone who appreciates mountain scenery. The downside? Expect company.

In the past, part of Grizzly's appeal was the long, glorious hike along the North Fork Trinity River to get there. The 18.5-mile route (one-way) kept traffic to a minimum. For anyone with the time and inclination, the North Fork (Hike 1) route is still a great way to go. It's hands down a prettier hike, and definitely one of my favorite trails.

For hikers with a limited amount of time, however, China Spring is the trail of choice. Driving time is a little longer (unless you're coming from Oregon), but you can dive into Grizzly's icy water just hours after you leave the trailhead.

The final approach to Grizzly Lake climbs a steep, rocky slope.

From the trailhead the China Spring Trail (11W08) contours south, across China Creek, to begin a steep, waterless ascent to the Salmon River divide. The forest of Douglas fir and ponderosa pine gives way to red fir as you climb. On the way up, the stiff climb is somewhat compensated for by the ever-increasing views across the Salmon River drainage. It takes just over 1 mile and a considerable amount of sweat to gain 1,600 feet and the top of the divide. On the other side, descend 1.3 miles, through mature Douglas fir and pine, to the junction with the North Fork Trail (12W01).

You can find cold, clear, and much appreciated water in a stream just west of the junction, down the North Fork Trail. To continue to Grizzly, turn left on the North Fork Trail, which climbs southeast more than 2,000 feet over the next 4.2 miles, most of it in one final steep scramble at the end. The path parallels the ever-steepening Grizzly Creek drainage toward its source at the head of the canyon. Several small waterfalls, lush gardens of ferns and berries, and welcome vistas up and down the drainage soon appear. At the top of a rocky outcropping you're treated to your first glimpse of the cirque above Grizzly Lake, with Thompson Peak and its snowfields towering over the basin.

After several more tantalizing glimpses of the high country, the path crosses a series of emerald meadows and deposits you in the heart of Grizzly Meadows amid stands of red and white fir, summer wildflowers galore, granite-lined glades, and the crash of Grizzly Falls. The lake is hidden above the sheer cliff ahead, up where the falls pour from the sky. There's a way up there, but even the forest service hesitates to call it a trail.

The agency calls it the Grizzly Scramble, which means that a route exists, but you'll need your hands free to scramble up it. From the meadow, cairns lead up the left (east) side of the boulder field. Before the base of the falls, the route veers left (east) and climbs a loose talus slope up the side of the canyon. Pick your way up through the rock band (that's the scramble part); then traverse upward and back to the southwest to reach lake level, 0.5 mile and 800 feet above the canyon floor. You should arrive at the shore near the top of the waterfall. There are campsites scattered around the shore, on both sides of the outlet stream, but they are close to the lake; for more privacy and to reduce impact on the lake, it's better to overnight along Grizzly Creek, in the meadow below the lake. Bonus: Enjoy a great view of the waterfall, and the lower campsites also eliminate the need to carry a heavy pack up the Grizzly Scramble.

Scramble above Grizzly Lake for great views and to summit Thompson Peak.

Grizzly Lake is cold and inviting.

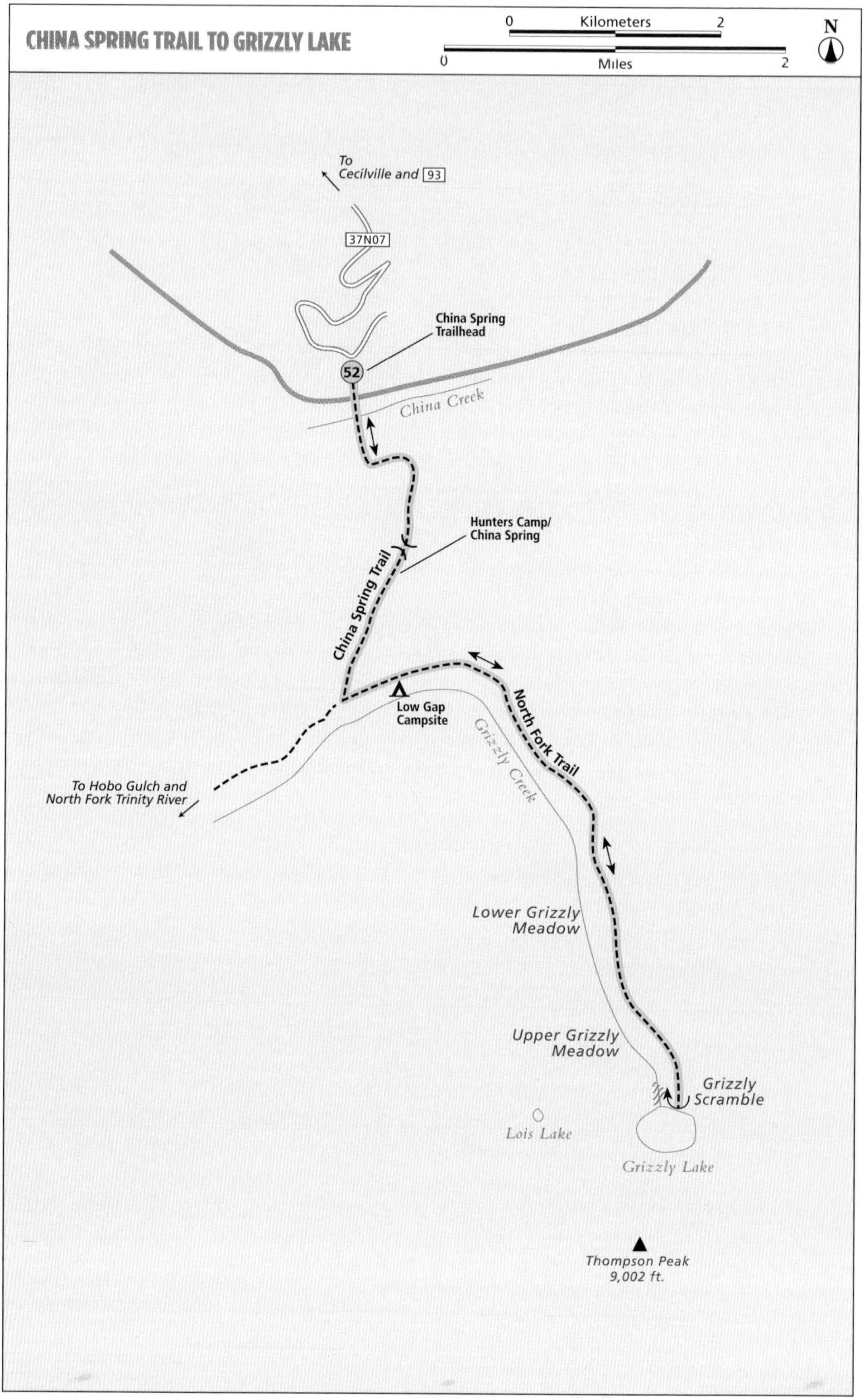
CHINA SPRING TRAIL TO GRIZZLY LAKE
0
Kilometers
2
0
Miles
2
N
To
Cecilville and 93
37N07
China Spring
Trailhead
52
China Creek
Hunters Camp/
China Spring
China Spring Trail
Low Gap
Campsite
North Fork Trail
Grizzly Creek
To Hobo Gulch and
North Fork Trinity River
Lower Grizzly
Meadow
Upper Grizzly
Meadow
Grizzly
Scramble
Lois Lake
Grizzly Lake
Thompson Peak
9,002 ft.

Find good camping and great views in Grizzly Meadow.

Icy water fed by Grizzly Glacier, a glacieret (a fast-melting remnant of the last period of glaciation, about 10,000 years ago) on Thompson Peak, fills the 42-acre lake. Swimming is excellent if you can bear the temperature; on most summer days, sun baked granite slabs are in abundance if you can't. A sparse scattering of stunted fir and mountain hemlock grows in the rocky basin, but mostly it's just rock and snow and water. Gray and massive Thompson Peak, the highest summit in the Trinity Alps at 9,002 feet, looms over it all. Experienced peak baggers will have no problem finding a line to the summit; the obvious ridgeline approach is on the west side. That's also the best route to take for a day hike to high and lonely Lois Lake. When on the ridgetop, turn right instead of left and take a short hike to where you can view the lake. Small and barren (no trees), Lois is good for bragging rights, but not much else.

MILEAGE AND DIRECTIONS

0.0 Start at the China Springs Trailhead.

1.2 Reach Hunters Camp/China Spring.

2.5 Turn left at the North Fork Trail junction.

2.9 Pass Low Gap Campsite.

6.0 Arrive at Upper Grizzly Meadows.

6.7 Reach Grizzly Lake. Return the way you came.

13.4 Arrive back at the trailhead.

OPTIONS

Experienced navigators can make several off-trail hikes from Grizzly Lake. Besides Thompson Peak, other destinations in the area include Lois, Little South Fork, and Mirror Lakes. Use the map and good judgment. Trail options include the North Fork, Bobs Farm, and Rattlesnake Creek.

APPENDIX A:
CONTACT INFORMATION

WILDERNESS PERMITS

All overnight visitors to the Trinity Alps Wilderness must obtain a wilderness permit before entering the backcountry. Permits are free and are available without reservation. Simply stop by one of the ranger stations on the way to the trailhead (see contact information below) and pick one up. If you arrive after hours, you can fill out a permit form at self-registration boxes located outside the stations. Self-registration kiosks are also available at various locations, such as Coffee Creek Fire Station, but they're not always stocked with permits so it's best to call and check if you plan to use one of them. Campfire/stove permits are also required and are available where you get your wilderness permit. Always check to see if any special fire hazards or restrictions are in effect.

FOR MORE INFORMATION:

Shasta-Trinity National Forest Headquarters
(530) 226-2500

Hayfork Ranger Station
(530) 628-5227

McCloud Ranger Station
(530) 964-2184

Weaverville Ranger Station
(530) 623-2121

Harrison Gulch Ranger Station (Platina)
(530) 352-4211

Trinity County Chamber of Commerce
trinitycounty.com

USGS Map Distribution
(888) ASK-USGS (275-8747)
usgs.gov

APPENDIX B: ZERO IMPACT

Going into a wild area is like visiting a famous museum. You obviously do not want to leave your mark on an art treasure in a museum. If everybody going through the museum left one little mark, that piece of art would be quickly destroyed—and of what value is a big building full of trashed art? The same goes for pristine wildlands. If we all left just one little mark on the landscape, the backcountry would soon be spoiled.

A wilderness can accommodate human use as long as everybody behaves responsibly. But a few thoughtless or uninformed visitors can ruin it for everybody who follows. All backcountry users have a responsibility to know and follow the rules of zero-impact camping. Enjoy the wild but leave no trace of your visit.

THREE FALCON PRINCIPLES OF ZERO IMPACT

Leave with everything you brought in.

Leave no sign of your visit.

Leave the landscape as you found it.

Pack it in/pack it out. Most of us know better than to litter—in or out of the backcountry. Be sure you leave nothing, regardless of how small it is, along the trail or at your campsite. You should pack out everything, including orange peels, flip-tops, cigarette butts, and gum wrappers. Also pick up any trash others leave behind.

Stay on the main trail. Avoid cutting switchbacks and walking on trailside vegetation. Don't pick up "souvenirs" such as rocks, antlers, or wildflowers. The next person wants to see them too, and collecting such souvenirs violates many regulations.

Avoid making loud noises on the trail (unless you are in bear country) or in camp. Be courteous. Remember: Sound travels easily in the backcountry, especially across water.

Bury your waste. Carry a lightweight trowel to bury human waste 6 to 8 inches deep and at least 300 feet from any water source. Pack out used toilet paper.

Go without a campfire. Carry a stove for cooking and a flashlight, candle lantern, or headlamp for light. For emergencies, learn how to build a no-trace fire.

Camp in obviously used sites when available. Otherwise, camp and cook on durable surfaces such as bedrock, sand, gravel bars, or bare ground.

APPENDIX C: MAKE IT A SAFE TRIP

As a leader of wilderness trips for youth, I always told my students to be prepared. For starters, this means carrying survival and first-aid materials, proper clothing, a compass, and a topographic map—and knowing how to use them. Many hikers these days also choose to carry a cell phone (reception is possible at high vantage points in the Trinity Alps, often where you can see Mount Shasta) and/or emergency communication devices that use satellites to enable rescue signals or contact with friends and family (available for rent or purchase).

Perhaps the second-best piece of safety advice is to tell somebody where you're going and when you plan to return. Pilots must file flight plans before every trip, and anybody venturing into the backcountry should do the same. File your "flight plan" with a friend or relative before taking off, and make sure they know who to call if you don't return as scheduled.

Close behind your flight plan and being prepared with proper knowledge and equipment is physical conditioning. Being fit not only makes wilderness travel more fun but also makes it safer. Here are a few more tips, and keep reading for more detailed advice on avoiding special hazards like lightning, hypothermia, river fords, and wild animals:

- Check the weather forecast. Be careful not to get caught at high altitude by a bad storm or along a stream in a flash flood. Watch cloud formations closely so that you don't get stranded on a ridgeline during a lightning storm. Avoid traveling during prolonged periods of cold weather.

- Avoid traveling alone in the wilderness if you're not sufficiently experienced, and keep your party together.

- Study basic survival and first aid before leaving home.

- Before you leave for the trailhead, find out as much as you can about the route, especially any potential hazards.

- Don't exhaust yourself or other members of your party by traveling too far or too fast. Let the slowest person set the pace.

- Don't wait until you're confused to look at your maps. Follow them as you go along—from the moment you start moving up the trail—so that you have a continual fix on your location.

- If you get lost, don't panic. Sit down and relax for a few minutes while you carefully check your topo map and take a compass reading. Confidently plan your next move. It's often smart to retrace your steps until you find familiar ground, even if it might lengthen your trip. Lots of people get temporarily lost in the wilderness and survive—usually by calmly and rationally dealing with the situation.

- Stay clear of all wild animals.
  - Take a first-aid kit that includes, at a minimum, the following items: sewing needle, aspirin, antibacterial ointment, antiseptic swabs, butterfly bandages, adhesive tape, adhesive strips, gauze pads, triangular bandages, codeine tablets, an inflatable splint, moleskin or Second Skin for blisters, 3-inch gauze, CPR shield, rubber gloves, and lightweight, waterproof first-aid instructions.
  - Take a survival kit that includes, at a minimum, the following items: compass, whistle, matches in a waterproof container, lighter, candle, signal mirror, flashlight, fire starter, aluminum foil, water purification tablets, space blanket, and flare.
  - Don't forget that the best defense against unexpected hazards is knowledge. Get the Falcon/Backpacker guide *Outdoor Survival: Skills to Survive and Stay Alive*.

LIGHTNING: YOU MIGHT NEVER KNOW WHAT HIT YOU

Mountains are prone to sudden thunderstorms. If you get caught in a lightning storm, take special precautions. Remember:

- Lightning can travel far ahead of the storm, so be sure to take cover before the storm hits.
- Don't try to make it back to your vehicle (unless the trailhead is very close). Instead, seek shelter. Lightning storms usually don't last long, and from a safe vantage point, you might enjoy the sights and sounds.
- Be especially careful not to get caught on a mountaintop or exposed ridge; under large, solitary trees; in the open; or near standing water.
- Seek shelter in a low-lying area, ideally in a dense stand of small, uniformly sized trees.
- Stay away from anything that might attract lightning, such as metal tent poles, graphite fishing rods, or metal pack frames.
- Crouch with both feet firmly on the ground.
- If you have a pack (without a metal frame) or a sleeping pad with you, put your feet on it for extra insulation against shock.
- Don't walk or huddle together. Instead, stay 50 feet apart; if somebody gets hit by lightning, others in your party can give first aid.
- If you're in a tent, stay in your sleeping bag with your feet on your sleeping pad.

HYPOTHERMIA: THE SILENT KILLER

Be aware of hypothermia—a condition in which the body's internal temperature drops below normal. It can lead to mental and physical collapse, even death.

Hypothermia is caused by exposure to cold and is aggravated by wetness, wind, and exhaustion. The moment you begin to lose heat faster than your body produces it, you're suffering from exposure. Your body starts involuntary exercise, such as shivering, to stay warm; it makes involuntary adjustments to preserve normal temperature in vital organs, restricting blood flow in the extremities. Both responses drain your energy reserves. The only way to stop the drain is to reduce the degree of exposure.

With full-blown hypothermia, as energy reserves are exhausted, cooled blood reaches the brain, depriving you of good judgment and reasoning power. You won't be aware that this is happening. You lose control of your hands; your internal temperature slides downward. Without treatment, this slide leads to stupor, collapse, and death.

To defend against hypothermia, stay dry. When clothes get wet, they lose about 90 percent of their insulating value. Wool and some synthetics lose relatively less heat; cotton, down, and some synthetics lose more. Choose rain clothes that cover the head, neck, body, and legs and provide good protection against wind-driven rain. Most hypothermia cases develop in air temperatures between 30°F and 50°F, but hypothermia can develop in warmer temperatures.

If your party is exposed to wind, cold, and wet, think hypothermia. Watch yourself and others for uncontrollable fits of shivering; vague, slow, slurred speech; memory lapses; incoherence; immobile or fumbling hands; frequent stumbling or a lurching gait; drowsiness (to sleep is to die); apparent exhaustion; and inability to get up after a rest. When a member of your party has hypothermia, he or she may deny any problem. Believe the symptoms, not the victim. Even mild symptoms demand treatment, as follows:

- Get the victim out of the wind and rain.

- Strip off all wet clothes.

- If the victim is only mildly impaired, give him or her warm drinks and food if they can eat. Then get the victim into warm clothes and a warm sleeping bag. Place well-wrapped water bottles filled with heated water close to the victim.

- If the victim is badly impaired, attempt to keep him or her awake. Put the victim in a sleeping bag with a person who is warm—both naked. If you have a double bag, put two warm people in with the victim.

FORDING RIVERS

Early summer hiking in the Trinity Alps may involve crossing streams swollen with runoff. When done correctly and carefully, crossing a big river can be safe, but you must know your limits.

The most important advice is to be smart. There are cases where you simply should turn back. Even if only one member of your party (such as a child) might not be able to follow larger, stronger members, you might not want to try a risky ford. Never be embarrassed by being cautious.

When you get to the ford, carefully assess the situation. Don't automatically cross at the point where the trail comes to the stream and head on a straight line for the other side. A mountain river can change every spring during high runoff, so a ford that was safe last year might be too deep this year. Study upstream and downstream and look for a place where the stream widens and the water is not over waist deep (if the current is slow) on the shortest member of your party. If the current is fast, don't attempt to cross anything over knee-deep. The tail end of an island is usually a good place, as is a long riffle. The inside of a meander sometimes makes a safe ford, but in other cases a long shallow section can be followed by a short deep section next to the outside of the bend where the current picks up speed and carves out a deep channel.

Before starting any serious ford, make sure your matches, camera, billfold, clothes, sleeping bag, and other items you must keep dry are in watertight bags.

Most streams in the Trinity Alps are cold, so have dry clothes ready when you get to the other side to minimize the risk of hypothermia—especially on a cold, rainy day.

Minimize the amount of time you spend in the water, but don't rush across. Instead, go slowly and deliberately, taking one step at a time, being careful to get each foot securely planted before lifting the other foot. Take a 45-degree angle instead of going straight across, following a riffle line if possible.

Don't try to ford with bare feet. Wear hiking boots without the socks, sneakers, or tightly strapped sandals.

Stay sideways to the current; turning upstream or downstream increases the current's force against your body.

In some cases, two or three people can cross together, locking forearms with the strongest person on the upstream side.

If you have a choice, ford in the early morning, when the stream isn't as deep. In the mountains, the cool overnight temperatures slow snowmelt and reduce the water flow into the rivers.

On small streams a sturdy walking stick used on the upstream side for balance helps prevent a fall, but in a major river with a fast current, a walking stick offers little help.

Unbuckle the belt and loosen the straps on your pack. If you fall or get washed downstream, a waterlogged pack can anchor you to the bottom, so you must be able to easily release your pack.

If you're 6'4" and a strong swimmer, you might feel secure crossing a big river. if you have children or smaller hikers in your party, the strongest person can cross first and string a line across the river to aid those who follow. But remember, the crossing must be safe for the smallest among your party. Ask yourself: What will happen if someone slips and falls?

Be prepared for the worst. You might underestimate the depth of the channel or strength of the current, especially after a thunderstorm when a muddy river hides its true depth. In these cases, whether you like it or not, you might end up swimming. If this happens, don't panic. Do not try to swim directly across; instead, pick a long angle and gradually cross to the other side, taking as much as 100 yards or more to finally get across. If your pack starts to drag you down, get out of it immediately, even if you have to abandon it. If you lose control and get washed downstream, go feet first so that you don't hit your head on rocks or logs.

Finally, be sure to report any dangerous ford to a ranger as soon as you finish your trip.

BE MOUNTAIN LION ALERT

You're sure to see plenty of deer in the Trinity Alps Wilderness, which means mountain lions probably aren't far away. Cougars feed on deer, and the remote backcountry of Northern California constitutes some of the best cougar habitat in the West. Though many people consider themselves lucky indeed to see a mountain lion in the wild, the big cats—nature's perfect predators—are potentially dangerous. Attacks on humans are extremely rare, but it's wise to educate yourself before heading into mountain lion habitat.

To stay as safe as possible when hiking in mountain lion country, follow this advice:

- Travel with a companion or a group. There's safety in numbers.
- Don't let small children wander away by themselves.
- Don't let pets run unleashed.

- Avoid hiking at dawn and dusk, when mountain lions are most active.
- Know how to behave if you encounter a mountain lion.

What to do if you encounter a mountain lion. In the majority of mountain lion encounters, these animals exhibit avoidance, indifference, or curiosity that never results in human injury, but it is natural to be alarmed if you have an encounter of any kind. Try to keep your cool and consider the following:

- **Recognize threatening mountain lion behavior.** A few cues may help you gauge the risk of attack. If a mountain lion is more than 50 yards away and directs its attention to you, it may be only curious. This situation represents only a slight risk for adults but a more serious risk to unaccompanied children. At this point you should move away while keeping the animal in your peripheral vision. Look for rocks, sticks, or something to use as a weapon—just in case. If a mountain lion is crouched and staring at you from less than 50 yards away, it may be gauging the chances of a successful attack. If this behavior continues, your risk may be high.

- **Do not approach a mountain lion.** Instead give the animal the opportunity to move on. Slowly back away but maintain eye contact if close. Mountain lions are not known to attack humans to defend young or a kill, but they have been reported to "charge" in rare instances when they want to stay in the area. It's best to choose another route.

- **Do not run from a mountain lion.** Running may stimulate a predatory response.

- **Make noise.** If you encounter a mountain lion, be vocal and talk or yell loudly and regularly. Try not to panic. Shout also to make others in the area aware of the situation.

- **Maintain eye contact.** Eye contact shows the lion you are aware of its presence. However, if the mountain lion's behavior is not threatening (for example, it's grooming or periodically looking away), maintain visual contact through your peripheral vision and move away.

- **Make yourself appear larger than you are.** Raise your arms above your head and make steady waving motions. Raise your jacket or another object above your head. Do not bend over, as this will make you appear smaller and more "prey-like."

- **If you are with small children, pick them up.** Maintaining eye contact with the lion, bring the children close to you without bending over. If you are with other children or adults, band together.

- **Defend yourself.** If attacked, fight back. Try to remain standing. Do not feign death. Pick up a branch or rock; pull out a knife, pepper spray, or other deterrent device. Everything is a potential weapon, and individuals have fended off mountain lions with rocks, tree limbs, and even cameras.

BE BEAR AWARE

The first step of any hike in bear country is an attitude adjustment. Being prepared for bears means having the right information as well as the right equipment. The black bears in the Trinity Alps rarely approach humans, but they may pose a danger if you handle